Steven Primrose-Smith was born in Darwen, near Blackburn, in 1970. He has a BA in English Language and Philosophy, a BSc in Mathematics and an MA in Philosophy. His first book, *No Place Like Home, Thank God*, an Amazon International bestseller, described his three-year, 22,000-mile bicycle ride around Europe during which he ate various unsavoury items including a brain, a handful of maggots and a marmot. He followed this with more bestsellers, *Route Britannia*, about his 5,000-mile bicycle ride through every county in Britain, and a comic novel, *George Pearly is a Miserable Old Sod*, about the most hated man on the Costa del Sol. *Biking Broken Europe* is his eighth book.

BIKING BROKEN EUROPE

6,000 Miles through an Unstable Continent

Steven Primrose-Smith

First published in 2019 by Rosebery Publications
1 Perwick Rise, Port St Mary, Isle of Man

ISBN-13: 9781795754132

Names have been changed where appropriate.

Photographs and maps related to this book can be found at *primrose-smith.com*.

Table of Contents

Chapter 1: Plasticised Fields Forever

Andalusia, Eastern Andalusia and Murcia

Was this really such a good idea? On a windless, steel grey morning I'm the only person cycling across the crumbling 870-metre-long Enguri Bridge. Cars aren't allowed here. Everyone else is on foot, trudging in the opposite direction, mostly old and crocodile-skinned, hauling huge plastic bags-for-life. And these bags *are* their lives, stuffed full of whatever they can scrape together to sell at market on the other side of the bridge. That is, if they want to eat today.

I've been looking forward to this crossing. I'm travelling from the safety of a sovereign UN-recognized nation, Georgia, with its British Embassy to rescue me from trouble should I land in it, to an unrecognised, breakaway *de facto* state, a frozen conflict held in a wobbly, Russian-backed headlock, a place both the UK Foreign Office and the US Department of State tell you not to visit. The governmental warnings are clear. If something bad happens to me, I'm on my own. The US web page goes even further:

"Entering the occupied territories will likely result in your arrest, imprisonment and/or a fine."

I'm no hero, nor reckless idiot. I've done my research, and this statement is, to be blunt, total bollocks. Ahead of me I can see bleary-eyed Russian soldiers with machine guns, military roadblocks and razor wire-topped fences. It's at times like these you really hope your fact-finding was thorough. But if not?

Welcome to Abkhazia!

*

A very long way from Abkhazia, I begin in Spain's Andalusia, a place that has something in common with that damaged corner of Georgia, as well as with dozens of other regions I'll visit on this adventure: There's a movement for its independence.

A while back, I cycled a huge 22,000 miles through every country in mainland Europe (*No Place Like Home, Thank God*). As though it were some sort of culinary and cultural video game, I figured I'd "completed" the continent. But at the end of 2017 the Catalan independence referendum suggested a brand new nation might be born, kicking and screaming and being hit in the head by baton-wielding Spanish psycho-cops. In reality it didn't happen, or at least it hasn't happened at the time of writing, but it got me thinking. How many other places in Europe wished to splinter off, brand-new wannabe countries I hadn't yet visited? The answer was freakin' gazillions.

These regions were varied. Many already had something approaching a national identity, their own history, cuisine and traditions. Some had been independent in the past and longed for a return to a supposed golden age. A few had actually claimed independence but had remained unrecognised by the international community. And one or two, if we're being totally honest, were just a few people dicking about.

I compiled a list of wannabe nations. It's important to note the varying credibility of these movements. No one doubts the sincerity of Scotland, or at least a large percentage of those who live there, in wanting to go it alone, but I might provoke a smirk if I mention Cornwall doing the same. It didn't matter. Lack of credibility wasn't an issue for me. As long as there was a movement of some kind, it could go on my list. Three geriatrics sitting in a pub with a map and a marker pen would be enough to qualify.

So I had my list. Many of the places on it I'd accidentally seen on previous rides. I didn't need to revisit those. These included, amongst others, the Basque Country, Northern Cyprus, the Åland Islands, Brittany, the two competing factions within Bosnia as well as absolutely everywhere in Britain. And I mean *everywhere*.

Of the locations that remained, I found a way to cobble most of them into a near-uninterrupted route of independence-hungry regions stretching from Andalusia all the way to the Caucasus on the opposite shore of the Black Sea. On only a couple of occasions would I visit somewhere I'd seen before. Even better, some of these areas are untouched by tourists, but that doesn't make them any less fascinating. In fact, if you've even heard of many of them, you're probably Kevin from *Eggheads*.

This is not a political book. I'll provide as little historical and governmental background for each independence movement as I can get away with. In any case, politics is a turn-off, unless you're a youthful Jeremy Corbyn meeting the lust-crazed eyes of a nubile Diane Abbott, in which case it's utterly stomach-churning.

This also isn't a fair book. It doesn't attempt to treat each independence movement equally. We'll breeze through the earlier ones and linger over the latter. Western Europe's rules and regulations are no match for Eastern Europe's madness and machine guns. Inconsequential independence endeavours will make way for those soaked in blood.

Now, it's entirely possible you could get halfway through these pages and find yourself asking, "Are *all* these movements going to be this half-arsed?", and I think you'd be totally justified. But bear with me. The tales become darker the farther east I travel. In many ways, this book is like *The Sound of Music*. Remember how that started? Dancing nuns and singing kids and flibbertigibbets? And then, out of nowhere, the Nazis turn up and it all gets a bit deathy? Well, I can't promise any nuns, nor any musical tweens, and I don't even know what a flibbertigibbet is, but we do set out with some degree of frivolity, bumbling along happily for a while. And then, out of nowhere, around eastern Slovakia, the Russians turn up, and that deathy bit kicks in. And they stick around and become steadily more deathy with each passing page. It's a musical waiting to happen, I tells ya.

And finally, before I set off, there's something I need to make clear. Some independence movements are highly contentious, especially within the nation from which a region wants to secede, as in the case of Catalonia and Spain. Please don't assume just because I visit a place I'm endorsing its bid for freedom, but, conversely, don't assume I take the side of the host country. Don't write to call me a monster and tell me off for seeing somewhere. I can go where I like. You're not the boss of me.

*

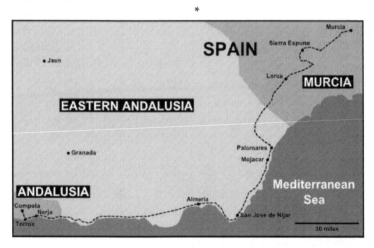

It was Day One, a stunning sunny morning in early April after the wettest winter southern Spain had seen for years. My farewell tapas run had been replaced by a tapas swim.

In the days before I set off, I'd been keeping an eye on the weather, desperate for a dry start, but it'd looked like I'd get the opposite. Then, on the very morning that mattered, the sun came out. The Weather Gods smiled benevolently upon me.

"Give him a week or two of sunshine," they said. "And then let's drown the bugger."

First days are usually nice. Your legs might be untested, but they're also fresh and eager for the road. And after the bike's thorough pre-ride service you can forget about technical worries. Without a care in my empty head I sang to myself as I freewheeled the glorious three miles down the steep hill from Cómpeta, a white-washed mountain village, and then, just as the road rose and I had to pedal for the first time, I discovered my gears didn't work. Fantastic.

I spent a few minutes cursing the local bike shop and then remembered I'd bungeed a walking pole tightly to my top tube, the very place the gear cable ran. I untied the pole, released the constricted wire and had effected this tour's first roadside repair. Don't be impressed. That's as technical as I get.

I continued downhill to Torrox Costa, a resort popular with German tourists and also home to a house Generalissimo Franco gifted to Eva Braun. I'm not suggesting for a second there's a link between those two facts.

It's hard to discover what sort of appetite there is for independence in Andalusia. However, at least one person *definitely* wants it, and that's Pedro Ignacio Altamirano, president of the Andalusian National Assembly and "poet, playwright and Spanish painter", although when reported by a local news site, they put these attributes in scare quotes as I did, suggesting he's actually none of those things.

Altamirano announced that, on December 4th 2017, he would declare independence for Andalusia, one containing all its traditional bits but also neighbouring Murcia, the Portuguese Algarve and lumps of Morocco, whether they liked the idea or not. On the big day he hoped to entice 400,000 people on to the streets to seal the claim for independence. In reality, everyone just went to work as normal and later asked "Altamirano who?"

The readers' comments on the news article were particularly scathing, calling into question Altamirano's mental health, although at least a couple of folk were on board and so the idea isn't entirely dead. Still, according to political analyst Maximiliano Herrera, whose website I'll refer to throughout this book as the Wannabe Bible, Andalusia's chances are very low indeed. Rest easy, Portugal and Morocco, you won't be invaded any time soon.

Up the road from Torrox Costa is Nerja, once my home for five years. Sitting in the tiny, well-hidden square of Plaza Andalucia is a bust of Blas Infante, a man described as the father of Andalusian nationalism. So low-key is this little corner of Nerja I'd never seen nor heard of it, despite being literally two hundred metres from where I'd lived. That's how big a deal Andalusian independence is.

It was time for breakfast. There was a bakery near the square. They had something called a *torrija*. I'm a sucker for food I've never tried before, but what kind of thing was it?

"*¿Dulce?*" I asked, pointing at the pastry, a lazy way to ask if it's sweet.

"*¿Doce?*" the shop assistant replied, misunderstanding my clumsy Spanish and verifying that I did indeed want twelve of them.

It was just as well I stuck with one. A torrija is a white-bread custard sandwich dipped in egg, deep-fried and then drowned in syrup. For a Spanish speciality it was exceedingly Scottish. It tasted alright but it was a good hour before the mild nausea passed.

I continued along the coast road eastwards, the beautiful azure Mediterranean sparkling on my right and the snow-topped Sierra Nevada flexing its muscles to my left. Between the two, however, wasn't always so handsome. The plastic greenhouses that would reach their nadir around Almeria had already begun to litter the landscape. If you had to guess the region's primary agricultural crop by sight only, you'd probably say it was polythene.

I thought I was being clever by starting my cycle tour in this easterly direction. After all, inland and north are massive mountains, and the coast westwards has suicidal main roads. East would be gently undulating and quiet. I knew this from experience, but it was knowledge gained on a much better bicycle, the light one I've used for touring in the past, rather than this heavy mountain bike. And I'd also been a lot younger, trimmer and fitter. In reality, today came in at around seventy miles and well over two thousand metres of ascent. I reached this evening's campsite completely shattered, having also endured a few hours of uncomfortable knee pain. This wasn't the start I'd been hoping for.

At least I could now relax in my tent, I thought. But, as it turned out, I couldn't. I'd focussed all my pre-ride energies on my route rather than my gear. For the sole reason that it was close to hand, I was using an old one-man tent, one I'd bought at least twenty years earlier and had used about twice. Unfortunately, I'd forgotten how small it was, approximately the size of a coffin. Its only entrance was at one end, meaning I had to go in feet first employing an awkward arse-shuffle technique or climb in head first and then carry out a near impossible twist that strained the fabric. I couldn't even nearly sit up in it. To make matters worse, when I now set it up I realised all the waterproofing was peeling off, giving it the appearance of a tent suffering from terrible eczema. Still, an inability to deflect water wasn't an issue for tonight. The

Weather Gods continued to smile upon me, biding their time.

*

"What's the next wannabe country you're going to visit?" I can hear you screaming impatiently. Well, if we're being strict, I was already there and had been since I crossed into the Andalusian province of Granada yesterday. If you thought, quite rightly, that Andalusia's independence claim was sickly, this next one is positively cadaverous.

While the Andalusian movement wants to shake itself free of the shackles of Madrid, the *Eastern* Andalusian movement wants to end the tyranny of Seville, Andalusia's capital. The Platform for Eastern Andalusia claims the provinces of Granada, Jaén and Almería are routinely ignored by the rest of Andalusia, which may well be true, but this independence movement is also ignored by absolutely everybody and so I won't mention it again.

I was still in Andalusia. For the next couple of days the coast road became wilder and less populated but with ever increasing plastic. I'd always wanted to see this south-east corner of Spain, the location of Europe's only desert and the lonely, rugged Cabo de Gata. But first, on a very hot morning, I had to cross Almería, nearly 200,000 people living in this continent's driest city. On average, each year sees just twenty-six days of rain. My home town, Blackburn, has that much most weekends.

Examine this region using Google Earth and, among the dusty yellow and brown rocks, suddenly there's a vast area of bright white, the tightly-packed sea of plastic greenhouses responsible for much of the year-round fruit on British plates. Perhaps John Lennon was being prophetic when he visited Almería in 1966 and wrote *Strawberry Fields Forever*.

I freed myself of the city's chaos via a cycle path. At its end, in the same yellow paint used to mark the trail, was a large penis. I suppose workmen need to grab their fun where

14

they can.

Although the official Tabernas Desert is a little farther north of here, the terrain approaching Cabo de Gata is desolate, with endless low, spiky shrubs, stones and not much else. These volcanic rock formations, a mostly empty Natural Park of nearly two hundred square miles, have attracted desperate African migrants to its lonely beaches, where the chances of going unnoticed are high but the likelihood of surviving the sea's mountainous waves are low. It's a stunningly gorgeous part of the world. Its luminosity feels like a television screen with the brightness cranked up to eleven.

Avoiding the main loop around the park, I opted for the rougher track along the coast, officially one of the most beautiful roads in Spain. There was nowhere for this route to go but up and over these ragged hills. On such a hot afternoon it was a sweaty climb. I was wetter than the front row at a Michael Bublé concert.

In a move that might placate both of cycling's warring factions over helmet use, let me make two seemingly contradictory statements. 1) I hate wearing a helmet. 2) On this ride I'm wearing an ugly orange-pink helmet. Y'see, I'd hurriedly purchased a travel insurance policy, and only later did I read its get-out clause that they wouldn't pay up unless I'd taken "every measure" to protect myself. There was no way they'd cough up a bean if I didn't wear a lid, and one that was as visible as possible. Taking the policy's get-out to its logical conclusion, I should also have worn a Kevlar vest beneath a suit of armour and filled the insides with feathers.

The reason I mention this here is because there's one particularly unpleasant aspect of a helmet that, not normally wearing one, I didn't know about. The band of foam protecting my forehead from its hard shell was absorbent. After an hour of high temperature wheezing and gasping, I was suddenly atop a huge hill, gazing down to the rough coast's cliffs and its lonesome lighthouse. I sat on a wall, feeling the breeze on my face, my feet brushing the undergrowth, the air heavy with the scent of wild thyme. I squeezed my helmet against my forehead and about a pint of sweat pissed out of it. It looked and felt like I'd tipped out my brains.

For the first time on this trip I was thankful for choosing a mountain bike. The ascent had been hard work, but on the steep downhill the tarmac gave way to gravel. As the descent flattened and I reached sea level, a beach appeared on my right, quite a famous one. Monsul Beach, with its huge, toad-like rock sitting centrally on the shoreline, was the location for the unlikely scene in *Indiana Jones and the Last Crusade* when Sean Connery uses his brolly to scare a flock of seagulls into the propellers of an attacking Nazi plane. If Churchill had thought of that, the war would've been won by 1940.

Closer to civilisation now, I passed a lone windmill and a field of white goats, munching on wild herbs. The sea shone silver behind them, crashing waves on to the coastline's green-brown hills. An occasional carload of beachgoers cruised slowly by, crunching gravel beneath their tyres. This corner of the Iberian peninsula is known for its savage weather. For the first time in my life I was blown along the track by a tailwind so strong I accelerated without pedalling.

I reached my destination. San José de Nijar, a town of a thousand inhabitants, was reminiscent of a Greek island village, cube-shaped, whitewashed houses, some topped with sky blue domes. San José hosted one of Spain's typically rubbish campsites, concrete-hard and expensive. With the amount they charged you'd think they could afford to employ someone who'd graduated primary school. But no, the young woman on reception needed a calculator to add six and eight together. Twice.

I turned north-eastwards, a direction I'd travel for most of the next seven weeks, all the way to Strasbourg in the upper third of France. The route continued its desolate theme. The occasional vivid scarlet poppy couldn't alleviate the grimness of the dying prickly pear cacti, shrivelled and covered in chalky dust, each one a victim of the insect-borne White Cactus Plague that's ravaging the warmer provinces of Spain. It was a sad sight.

For forty miles I passed through infrequent and forgettably bleak settlements, but the land still expected me to scale endless hills to do so. A sign told me it was sixteen miles to Mojácar, today's destination. The coast road turned inland and climbed into the air importantly, as though it had a meeting with some local deity on a distant cliff-top. The gradients defeated me and my painful knee. I got off and pushed, but it was still hard work. I wasn't sure I could manage sixteen miles of this. I stopped for a breather and took a second to empty my brains on to the tarmac.

From high up in the sky I looked down on the pale ribbon of road snaking up the seaside mountain I'd already climbed. Andalusia, and Spain as a whole, refuses to give you an easy ride, but sometimes there are surprises. Mojácar appeared six miles earlier than suggested and all was forgiven, especially incorrect road signs.

Despite being two notches more touristic than Nerja, Mojácar has an inviting seafront. It hit the news the previous summer when a bunch of holidaymakers yanked a baby dolphin out of the sea in order to take Flipper-flavoured selfies. There were photos showing some kids inadvertently covering its blowhole, which I suppose is better than using it as somewhere to hold your ice cream cone, but in the end the poor thing still died.

Enough talk of death. Don't let this tale reflect badly on

Mojácar. I had a tasty Chinese meal there, served to me by a very friendly lady who simply refused to believe I could be a cyclist. Did I mention I'd put on a lot of weight?

*

Not far out of Mojácar, I entered the town of Playas de Vera, which claims to be the largest nudist resort in the world. It includes a mile and a half of beach and twelve housing estates containing thousands of homes. Given previous experience with naturist sites, I was grateful the weather had taken a chilly turn resulting in a distinct lack of morbidly obese pensioners flopping their bits all over the place.

A couple of miles down the road was a nuclear attack of sorts, and you'd probably want to be wearing clothes if that happened. Back in 1966, two American planes collided in the sky here. To make matters worse, one of the aircraft shed its load of four nuclear bombs, three of which fell on the small town of Palomares. They detonated upon impact but without setting off an explosion. One square mile was contaminated with plutonium. Even today, fifty years on, radiation levels are higher than they should be. Maybe I'd go back and have a second look at that nudey beach, keeping an eye out for three-breasted women and men with seven penises.

It was time to enter another potential country, one the Wannabe Bible suggests is less likely to appear than Andalusia, probably because there isn't even a political party campaigning for its independence. Welcome to Murcia!

Hang on, you might be thinking. I knew Spain had that Catalonia thing going on, and obviously the Basques caused a bit of grief for a while, but now you're telling me that Andalusia *and* Murcia want out too? Just how much of the country wants to go it alone?

Some bits of Spain are absolutely serious about their independence, but there's an awful lot of other movements too. In fact, by land mass, 64% of Spain has groups that would choose to splinter. You might think 64% is high, but other European countries have a similarly fractured score. Germany has 33% and France 51%. But these three are small fry when compared to the giants of wobbly Eurolands.

In third place is Belgium with a score of 100%. Basically, the country has movements that'd split it into two halves, hence the reason for a seemingly maximum mark. And yet it's only third. How could somewhere score *higher* than 100%?

The answer is that some countries have independence movements containing smaller independence movements within them. This is the case in Britain and why it scores 109%. You probably know about the Scottish, Welsh and Northern Irish independence groups, but it wasn't until I researched this trip I discovered there's an *English* independence faction too. Yes, the English Democrats believe England should leave the United Kingdom and become an independent country. It wouldn't be a very united kingdom if none of its three remaining pieces shared a land border.

England plus Scotland plus Wales plus Northern Ireland only makes 100%, but there are also movements for Orkney and for Shetland to become independent. Less credibly, there's a Cornish independence push and a more recent one for Yorkshire. Yes, the pasties and puddings want out. Well, about six people who live in those places do.

Speaking of Yorkshire, it even has a football team signed up to CONIFA, the Confederation of Independent Football Associations, an organisation that runs a mini-World Cup for non-recognized pseudo-countries like the ones I'm visiting. It must be a difficult competition to put together, especially when the venue is a war zone your players are specifically warned against entering.

The tournament in 2016 was hosted by Abkhazia, that Russian-backed frozen conflict I mentioned right at the start, and four of the qualifying teams, including the Isle of Man's, withdrew citing security concerns. It isn't easy to organise even when the venue is a less scary country like Hungary. In 2015, both Abkhazia and South Ossetia had to bail because Hungarian authorities refused to grant their players any visas. Maybe this is why Yorkshire wants independence, so they can bar entry to London and Manchester clubs whenever Leeds United has a home game.

And so if the United Kingdom is in position number two, who's first? I'll tell you when we get there.

Despite moving northwards, Murcia felt just as desert-like as Almería. This area receives an average of 365 mm of rain a year, but it doesn't come down at a steady one millimetre per day. No, on occasion, half the amount can fall in a single twenty-four hour period, and when it does it's often on to hard, dry land from which it rolls away into the sea rather than being absorbed. Plastic greenhouses and polytunnels still dotted the landscape and the only visible workers came from somewhere a lot farther south than Spain. It felt like cycling through Africa.

After another twenty miles I landed in Lorca. Sharing its name with Spain's most famous poet had given me the impression this town of 92,000 people might be a pretty sort of place. It isn't. There's a castle up on a hill, but it becomes less interesting the closer you get to it. The only memorable thing from my short visit here was a snack bar called Chemo Fried Chicken. Nothing shifts buckets of breaded poultry like the sexiness of cancer.

*

I woke up to a blue sky and cycled on a flat road with a much appreciated tailwind. I passed through the town of La Hoya, home to a football team with the ugliest kit in the world. Since Murcia tags itself "the vegetable garden of Spain", someone thought it a good idea to design a kit that looked like broccoli. Let's hope they don't play like vegetables.

I was heading to the forests of the Sierra Espuña. I knew there was a supposedly haunted sanatorium at an altitude of around 700 metres and so figured I wouldn't have much farther than that to climb. What I didn't know was the road would first take me up to 1,200 metres before I reached my target. The pass wound close to the highest peak in this national park, the Morrón de Espuña, a tall, limestone outcrop, not dissimilar to the hill in *Close Encounters of the Third Kind* that attracted all those aliens. It's an impressive sight, even without extraterrestrials.

Soon after, buried in the woods, I located the sanatorium. Due to an increase in leprosy, construction on this four-storey, sand-coloured building began in 1913, but it wasn't finished until 1934. The healthier patients had to complete it themselves after – compulsory leprosy joke warning! – the original contractors threw in their hands.

Over its useful lifetime, hundreds of people lived and died here. Without modern drugs, some of their deaths would have been truly agonizing. By the early 1950s, medicine had pretty much eradicated the sanatorium's purpose and instead it was given a short-lived resurrection as a creepy orphanage. The doors finally closed in 1962. It's been abandoned ever since and is only of interest to ghost hunters, even more so after a film crew descended upon it and apparently recorded a spook poking its head out of one of the upstairs windows. By "apparently" I mean "obviously utterly fraudulently".

Online reports said the building was rarely visited and so I planned to sleep inside and then, purely for my own amusement, make wailing noises if anyone else turned up. But once I was through the security fence – it wasn't difficult as it'd already been bent out of shape – it was clear it was more popular than expected. A small group was going in ahead of me. In any case, sleeping inside would have been

21

extremely uncomfortable. The floor was inch-deep in rubble and broken glass. Doors had been wrenched off their hinges. Where the roof had caved in, tiles hung by mere threads, ready to brain an unfortunate below. It wasn't all ugliness. At times, bright sunlight filtered attractively through the mangled ceiling. It felt about as spooky as a busy shopping mall on a Saturday afternoon.

I kept looking around. By now I thought the other party had left the building. On my way down the rickety stairs I almost bumped into a young woman.

"Sorry," I said, although oddly she didn't acknowledge my apology.

"Is someone there?" called out a male voice in Spanish from the floor below, presumably to his girlfriend.

"No. No-one," she replied while looking right at me. Or maybe it was right *through* me. Perhaps I was the ghost!

Deciding against a night of picking shards of glass out of my back, I camped in the woods across the road from the sanatorium. Throughout the evening I could hear kids inside the building, running around and screaming. Either that or they were long-dead leprous orphan spirits, but, y'know, I doubt it.

*

Stopped for breakfast in a nearby town the next morning, with my bike leaning against the café wall, I noticed my back tyre was a little under-inflated. After a closer look, I found a bigger problem. Bloody hell! I'm usually months into a ride before spokes start pinging off. I'd only been cycling a week.

It wasn't far to the city of Murcia, capital of this wannabe country. I located a bicycle shop run by a friendly bloke called Juan, and that wasn't just because he gave me a glass of his delicious home-brew porter while he worked on my bike.

"It hadn't tasted so good when I made it at first," he said. "And so I left it in the bottle for two years."

That's more willpower than I could've mustered, but it'd done the trick.

Juan was also a tourer. He'd cycled in Mongolia and even ridden from Minsk to Istanbul on a Brompton, those tiny-wheeled but well-made folding bicycles. His absolute favourite place to bike was Iran. He'd been impressed by the local hospitality.

"I was invited to breakfast, lunch and dinner every day. I had to refuse sometimes just to get a bit of personal space."

Juan was lucky. Being single and without kids, he could close up the shop and take off whenever he wanted to. His marital status had confused the Iranians.

"They always asked me if I was gay."

He finished replacing the spoke and tapped the wheel rim.

"That won't last long," he prophesied, accurately as it turned out.

Murcia is unlikely to be considered one of Spain's great cities, but it's a pleasant place to waste a day or two. There's an impressively ornate cathedral, as well as a giant plastic sardine emerging from the River Segura that runs through the city. After much searching, I located the bullfighting museum, basically a few rooms at the back of a bar, full of the stuffed heads of famous bulls, camp sparkly matador outfits and lots of photos, but there weren't enough humans getting gored for my liking.

I was halfway through Spain, and it still had three more wannabe nations to offer, but before I got to the next one, Jesus was about to save my life.

Chapter 2: Attack of the Pensioner Pornographers

Valencia, Catalonia and Val d'Aran

I'd received an invitation. Renata had seen my route on a Facebook cycling group and suggested I swing by the house she was currently looking after in Elche. She's Hungarian and a recent convert to long-distance biking. She'd been backpacking around Southeast Asia when, because it seemed like a cheap and adventurous way to continue travelling, she bought a bike in Singapore, pointed it towards Hungary and cycled 12,000 miles home.

Today I set off late, knowing it was only thirty miles to Renata's place. It was another beautiful day with, defying all odds, another delicious tailwind. Three miles out from the centre of Murcia, I could see a rocky mound up ahead, 150 metres tall. There was some sort of statue on top. The mound eventually grew into a small mountain, and I recognized that bloke on top. It was our good old friend Jeezipoos with his holy arms outstretched, like Rio's Christ the Redeemer in miniature but still impressive enough. As I passed the rock, I turned my head leftwards to get a closer look, my mouth slightly agape at its beauty, and a wasp the size of a sparrow thumped me in the right cheek. Had I not been distracted by the Lord, the stripey bastard would've gone straight down my gullet, stinging me repeatedly and causing my throat to swell until I choked to an agonizing death. My life had been saved! So Jesus, thanks for that, but what exactly was the point of those wasps in the first place?

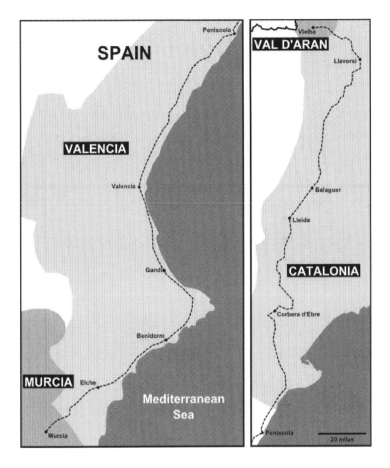

Not long afterwards, I passed a sign telling me I was entering the wannabe country of Valencia. Now, unlike the other places I've visited so far, Valencia really does have an independence movement but one that could perhaps be better coordinated. For example, there are seven nationalist political parties and yet only one of them seems to have an online presence, a sort of 1830s approach to internet marketing.

In October 2017, shortly after the Catalan referendum,

locals took to the streets in support of Valencian independence and immediately found themselves in trouble. Far-right fascists attacked them with batons. What the hell were those thugs doing? Didn't they know that was the job of the Spanish police?

I kept moving forward through a changing landscape. While the road stayed flat, rugged mini-mountains appeared on my left, and the right-hand side became an endless plateau of palm trees. Did you know the palm branch was a symbol of triumph in pre-Christian times? This was ironic because I was about to feel distinctly untriumphant.

Six miles from Elche, in the small town of Crevillent, my back tyre suddenly exploded. I whipped out a spare tube and also my bicycle pump, but since the last time I'd used it, whenever that was, it'd decided to retire itself from active duty. The reason for the puncture was a long tear in the tyre's side wall and so that'd need replacing too. I looked at the time. It was five past two. This being Spain – sorry, this being the independent nation of Valencia – any local bike shop would have just closed for lunch and wouldn't reopen until at least five o'clock. While the mechanic got stuck into his three-hour paella, I was stuck in Crevillent.

I properly took in my surroundings for the first time. I was on the car park of a restaurant, but what was that over there, not twenty metres away? This was incredible. It was the entrance to a campsite. Spain has dozens of camping grounds scattered along its coastline, but inland they are as rare as gay Premier League footballers (i.e., they exist but locating them is next to impossible). This was too much of a gift to pass up. Renata agreed to wait another day. I'd stay here tonight and sort the bike in the morning. Assuming the mechanic had finished his lunch by then.

*

With a new back tyre of dubious quality, I cycled out of

Crevillent and, twenty minutes later, arrived in Elche. I found the fourth-floor apartment Renata was looking after. She greeted me with a big welcoming smile. It was a bit of a struggle to get my bike up all the stairs, but Renata, a woman who clearly packed a lot of power into her diminutive frame, carried my bags. She was stronger than a Scotch bonnet.

We sat and chatted about her travels. Having worked in Britain, Renata spoke flawless English, but her mother hadn't been too happy about her choice of country. After all, Britain and Hungary had been on opposing sides in both World Wars.

"How can you allow yourself to set a foot on that land?" she'd said to her.

Renata had done her huge bike ride on a budget of five dollars a day. This involved a lot of wild camping and crashing at temples. As a result of her trip, Renata had become something of a media sensation in Hungary, being badgered by the press. The opportunity to escape to Spain came at the perfect time.

"Hungarian women don't do this sort of thing," she said.

She'd had her fair share of adventure, good and bad, including being hassled relentlessly by the Burmese authorities, but the women she met in India didn't make her feel too great about her choices.

"I was told what I was doing was disrespectful, because I should've been at home looking after my children."

"You have kids?" I asked.

"No. But they thought I should have. Instead of doing this."

And despite what Murcian bike shop owner Juan had said about Iran, Renata's memories were much more negative.

"A lot of women experience serious sexual harassment over there," she said. "I was nearly raped."

Luckily, she managed to fight off her attacker and get

27

away, but it made her wary of all men in the rest of the country. As well as thinking rape was acceptable, Iranian men also had a complete misunderstanding of pornography.

"I was seriously asked if all women in the West are like porn stars," Renata said, "y'know, sleeping with their sons, or their plumbers, or the pizza boy."

That'd be hilarious if it wasn't so horrifying to think an Iranian bloke might actually believe it and then act as though it were true when he met a Westerner. If the Koran is indeed the repository of all knowledge, where are the verses about internet porn?

Before her travels Renata had also worked in Norway as a physiotherapist.

"I can work anywhere I like," she said. "But I don't know what to do. I'm finding it difficult to settle back into normal life."

"You've made yourself too big for the world," I replied. "But that'll pass."

It's common after a huge bike ride. Once home, everyday life, the one 99% of people live, with jobs and kids and Netflix, seems mundane by comparison. Your feet are still itchy. But unless you're going to move around forever, you have to reintegrate, and you'll almost certainly have to earn some money if you don't want to starve to death. For a lot of people it's a weird and unsettling few months. Don't let this stop you though. Go on, buy a bike! But it's probably best to avoid Iran if you're female.

*

I liked Renata. She was smart, fun and a lot braver than me. I hope in return for a free place to sleep I'd provided a useful ear. She asked me to stay another day, but I was already behind schedule and so, after breakfast, I continued on my way. I felt sad leaving her, friendless in a Spanish town and without any of the local language, but she was tough, and it was only for a few weeks. She'd be fine.

I generally try to avoid touristy places. They're usually expensive and unpleasantly busy. But there was one such place on this coast I'd never seen and something about it made me think it'd be an amusing detour. I was on my way to Benidorm, the uber-resort, and like Uber it's popular, cheap but you can't guarantee you won't get assaulted.

For the most part, today's fifty mile ride was uneventful. I passed along the coast road through a forgettable Alicante. Then came lots of hills and even more traffic, but I finally arrived at a campsite in Benidorm, twenty quid for a pitch I could only penetrate with the help of a friendly German's hammer.

I walked the twenty-odd minutes to the centre of town and immediately wished I hadn't. I was following two completely wasted English blokes in their thirties. You know how young fellas wear their jeans low, exposing the tops of their underpants? Well, one of these lads was wearing his Levis *so* low the waistband sat comfortably beneath the cheeks of his arse. The worst bit, though, was he wasn't wearing any underwear. Just like The Waterboys, I saw the whole of the moon. Classy.

Farther down the road, we came to a six foot tall garden wall and the two fellas clambered over it – you can imagine how picturesque that was – inducing a little old Spanish lady to utter a "madre mia!" and cross herself theatrically.

Every bar had whooping hen dos or fwoarrring stag dos, competing for who could be the horniest. There was also a lot of play-fighting and, when this got too boring, some actual fighting. A high percentage of people were falling-down drunk, and this was only about half six on an April evening. Imagine what it's like at three in the morning in August. I bet this is what Gomorrah was like.

I found a quiet restaurant and watched as processions of

arseholed revellers passed the window on each other's backs, screaming like babies. I felt I was viewing a video of a dystopian future where climate change had turned all the rainwater into vodka.

Benidorm must have been stunning once, with its golden sandy beach, an attractive island not too far out in a deep blue sea, and a range of rugged mountains in the hinterland. Unfortunately, now it's hideous. Many of the twelve million tower blocks look Soviet Russian and everything else is a tatty Nag's Head or a British Bulldog pub. Despite all this Englishness, it wasn't enough for one online reviewer from Blackburn. She complained there were too many Spanish here. Yes, how dare they live in their own country?

*

I continued winding my way up Valencia's coast. By the time I reached Gandia at the end of Day Thirteen, through windswept tunnels and past teams of roadside prostitutes, I'd cycled five hundred miles and already climbed the equivalent of an Everest. The daily distance was unremarkable, but the heavy bike was turning this into a chore. I was beginning to despise the iron lump. It would have been easier getting around Europe on a lathe.

The next morning the sky was a brilliant blue. I biked right by the sea on a promenade cycle path. After what felt like no time at all, I arrived in Valencia.

It's always nice when a town has a drink or snack for which it's famous, and even better when it has one of each. Best of all is when that snack also has a stupid name. Valencia scores highly in this department. Its drink is *horchata*, made from tigernuts, whatever the hell they are, and is like a thin, nutty milkshake, full of vitamins. It's traditionally served with a pastry accompaniment, *fartons*, frosted cakey fingers you dip into the drink. They taste a lot better than they sound.

Snack devoured, I was now hoping to complete a mission that had eluded both the Knights Templar and Monty Python. I was on a quest to find the Holy Grail. After all the hype, it was surprisingly easy to locate.

I entered Valencia Cathedral and wasted a pleasant hour wandering around the various chapels and looking at the museum. There were bits of old books and tons of relics, including the leathery mummified arm of Saint Vincent, which had been taken on a pilgrimage to the Holy Land by the Bishop of Valencia in 1104 for good luck. It didn't bring him much. He died in Italy, but the arm found its way back home. Not of its own volition, obviously.

Saving the best room till last, I entered the tiny incense-scented chapel containing the Holy Grail. Yes, it's just there, casually sitting around in its display case, and has been all along. Indiana Jones could have saved himself a ton of hassle if he'd known.

Different legends are attached to the Holy Grail and what it was used for. In some of them the cup collected blood from the stomach wound inflicted on Jesus while nailed to the cross. This one though merely claims to be the one used by Jesus at the Last Supper. The original cup is only the top part of what we see today, having been pimped up in the intervening years with dozens of gemstones, just as Jesus would have wanted.

Legend has it the Holy Grail has many special powers including, for those who drink from it, eternal youth. I wondered if they'd unlock the case and let me have a swig from it. Maybe it'd cure my sodding knee.

*

I was on my way to Peñiscola, a town that sounds like the worst idea Pepsi ever had.

I'd expected today's route to be quiet, as it ran beside a motorway. However, because the motorway was a toll road very few drivers and not a single trucker would touch it. I could see it in the near distance, three lanes in both directions almost totally empty. Mine, however, had a huge lorry pass me approximately every two seconds. I wish I'd been cycling on the motorway.

The route took me close to Castellón airport, an extremely costly project that was inaugurated in 2011 and then sat unused for five years because it couldn't get a licence to operate. In 2015, a plane did finally arrive at the "ghost airport", as it became known. It was one of RyanAir's. Presumably the airline was marketing it as Paris South.

I eventually reached Peñiscola with shattered nerves. This place is a member of an organisation called *Asociación de los pueblos más bonitos de España,* or the Most Beautiful Villages in Spain. It's based on a similar French concept and, like there, is used to drive more and more tourists to villages that already have too many, rather than directing them elsewhere to places that could do with the publicity.

There's no question Peñiscola is a pretty spot, built high on a rocky promontory sticking out into the Med, barely connected to the mainland. A thirteenth century castle sits on top and the whole town is surrounded by well-preserved walls. It has the nickname "The City in the Sea", although calling it a city is a massive exaggeration. It's also known as "The Gibraltar of Valencia", which, as you'll understand if you've ever been to Gibraltar, is hardly a compliment. The old bit is truly lovely – this was one of the reasons it was chosen as a location for *Game of Thrones* – but the larger resort that surrounds it is as unmemorable as the name of that specky guy who works in Accounts.

I arrived on a relatively quiet day tourist-wise, but there were still plenty of us around. Like most places that have stopped functioning as real towns to concentrate on their daily incomers, almost every shop in its steep, white-washed streets sold snacks or trinkets. It must be difficult to live here without transport, having to survive on a diet of ice cream and castanets.

*

Today I'd planned another wild camp. You might have thought that after my £1-a-day adventure (*Hungry for Miles*), where we wild-camped almost every night, I'd be comfortable with it by now, but I'm not. It's just sometimes there are things to see that have no affordable accommodation anywhere nearby and sticking a tent in a field is the only option.

I rode along the coast for a bit, careful not to stop on the way in the small town of Benircarlo for refreshments. A couple of years ago, Andres Lorente ordered a glass of wine in a café there and was mistakenly served dishwasher detergent. He died soon afterwards. It says something about the quality of Spanish vino that he got to the bottom of the glass before he realised he was drinking bleach.

I cycled onwards through Alcanar. It was in this town one of the terrorists from the cell involved in the 2017 Barcelona attack accidentally blew himself up, along with his entire house and an imam said to be the brains behind the plot, so that day wasn't all bad news.

By coming here I'd left Valencia. I was now in Catalonia. And you don't need me to tell you how serious the Catalans are about converting their autonomous region into a fully fledged country. People here are prepared to bleed for it, especially when the Spanish police turn up.

I continued beside a wide, mud-coloured river, climbing high. Dusty terraces tried to tease food from the orange sandy soil. The watercourse waved goodbye to the road and the narrow track became steeper, with ten-metre-tall, olive-topped cliffs on either side, turning what had earlier been an airy riverside ride into something more claustrophobic. It was also damn hot. My brains leaked copiously from my helmet.

Nearly eighty miles from Peñiscola I arrived in Corbera d'Ebre. This was a ghost village, one abandoned after being bombed in the 1930s during the Spanish Civil War, a fossilized remainder of why it's not a good idea to set upon your own countryfolk. I'd figured a ghost town would be a quiet place to camp. I hadn't thought of the possibility it might be attached to a newer rebuild of the village, housing people rather than memories.

I had a nosey through the wreckage, walking down sandy lanes beside half-buildings and smashed homes, trying to imagine a happier occasion when children chased dogs chasing chickens through the dust before being called in for dinner. The crumbling church still stood tall. Everything felt so ancient, trapped in another time, but the people bombed here would have been the same age as my grandparents, except that mine made it into their seventies and this lot didn't.

If I wanted somewhere to sleep I'd have to move on. Two miles down the road a track disappeared into a field and over a hill. I went to investigate. Within seconds I was well-hidden from the traffic, tucked away behind some olive trees and out of sight of any property. This would do. As I curled up inside my minuscule tent, I considered the irony that this wild camp was the most comfortable ground I'd slept on in the last two weeks.

*

Rather than battle my way through Barcelona's traffic – I'd once lived there for six months and didn't need to experience it on this trip – I headed towards the Pyrenees, the natural barrier holding back the rest of Europe, something Nigel Farage can only dream of.

The route took me through Lleida, a town that hadn't improved since the last time I'd seen it. I counted the flags hanging from apartment balconies, approximately ten Catalan banners for every Spanish one. Did this reflect the true percentage of who wanted out of Spain? Or do most people only campaign when trying to change the status quo? In any case, independence was a real, in-your-face thing here, in a way it hadn't been in Spain's other wannabes on this ride. It's just a shame the thing in their face is sometimes a police baton.

Sixteen miles farther, in Balaguer, a place of overwhelming support for the Catalan cause, no Spanish flags flew at all. On referendum day, the locals had a premonition of the police brutality that'd be unleashed. They organised a festival in the main square, purely to make it difficult for the authorities to enter the village and disrupt the ballot. Fearing even this wouldn't be enough, they used tractors to block roads into town.

As I cycled out of this Catalan stronghold, a man sold piles of *calçots* at the side of the tarmac. This is a traditional Catalan vegetable, like a large, less bulbous and milder spring onion. They're grilled over a hot fire and dipped into a sauce made with tomatoes and nuts. Without any means to cook them myself, I left them unsampled. Why no cooking? Y'see, to save a little weight on my heavy bike I'd foolishly decided to travel without a stove. Without resorting to unhealthy takeaways or expensive restaurants I'd condemned myself to several months of cold food. Some people swear by a raw food diet. I'd started to swear *at* it.

I could now feel the foothills of the Pyrenees approaching. In the Serra del Montsec I cycled in an amazing gorge that climbed through a couple of tunnels and passed a dam with water exploding powerfully down the valley. And then came a sight I found hard to believe was real. With the evening setting in, the scene was lit like a Renaissance landscape. In the distance, behind a large lake, a huge chalk cliff had been turned to gold in the low sunlight. I stood and stared at it, mouth wide, for several minutes. I must have looked a right spoon.

The hills climbed for miles and miles and were wearing me down. After a thousand metres straight up I spotted a campsite and stopped. In its outside bar I tried to imbibe a beer as well as the impressive mountain views, but I was distracted. Three female members of the owner's family were also sitting on the terrace and taking great pleasure in squeezing each other's spots. It's amazing how teenage, acne-bursting squeals can affect the beauty of a place.

Later, female pus now drained, I sat on the terrace alone and for the sake of my sanity had the site owner cook me something warming. He rustled up some seafood noodles with *aioli*, which were delicious, especially with a chilled glass of white wine and the rugged views for company. Some moments of travel offer utter contentment and this was one, although perhaps I'd have felt differently if I were still sharing the terrace with a bunch of girls with their zits out.

*

The climbing continued for the whole day, but at least the scenery compensated and the overcast sky kept me cool. Architecture in the Pyrenees is different to the rest of Spain. Gone were the white-washed houses. Here, local stone was used and it was a darker rock. Things felt medieval.

Somewhere near Llavorsi it started to rain, my first of the trip so far. I got lucky when, a couple of minutes later, I stumbled upon a campsite. But not *that* lucky.

"We're closed," said the owner, when I finally found him.

"Ah."

"Yes, we've no water. Where's your next destination?"

"Vielha."

It's basically on the other side of the Pyrenees, over a 2,100 metre pass. He looked doubtful.

"Not in this weather," he said. He thought for a second. "You can use the water in one of our chalets if you like."

I didn't trust my tent in this rain, not with its vanishing water-proofing, and so I also erected a tarp I was carrying. The tiny porch of the tent was left uncovered, and I was right to be suspicious. The water poured inside as though the fabric were made of newspaper. I was dry for now, but I needed a more permanent solution. I lay in my tent watching the rain and fell asleep as soon as it got dark, just after eight. Rock 'n' roll, baby! Sixty-five miles and 2,200 metres of ascent on a shit bike will do that to you. Well, it'll do it to me.

*

Gone were the grey skies. On the day I'd be traversing the spine of the Pyrenees I had a beautiful blue-sky morning. The air had a crystal clarity that made the mountains sparkle. It was like they'd just had a visit from Mr Sheen.

The climb to the top was a steady 9% gradient and, while it was long and hard, I didn't have to push. The views became more and more spectacular as I ascended, the landscape changing from green grass to frost-dusted to snow-covered to metres-deep in ice. It never felt cold, although during the final miles the roadside snow was three or four metres high. This was proper mountain cycling. A couple of serious racers in Lycra came in the opposite direction. One of them looked at me toiling up the hill with my heavy bags, said "Wow!" and gave me a thumbs-up and a big grin.

After five hours of climbing I reached the Port de la Bonaigua pass at 2,072 metres above sea level, knowing today's hard work was over. I crossed into my final wannabe country within Spain's borders, and it was an odd one.

Val d'Aran, about the size of Merseyside, sits in the far north-west corner of Catalonia and yet there isn't much Catalan feeling here at all. In fact, the region recently held its own referendum in which the locals decided that if Catalonia became independent of Spain, Val d'Aran would become independent of Catalonia. These people aren't messing about. The Unity of Aran, an Aranese nationalist organisation, is currently the most popular local political party.

I screamed down the other side of the mountain into a stunningly handsome valley. The architecture was different again to the black stone buildings I'd seen on the way here. The houses were witchy and Romanian-looking, with orange-brown stone and tall, steep, black roofs, designed for deflecting falling snow on to the heads of anyone walking by. The majority of people around here, it seemed, lived in the attic.

Vielha, the capital of Val d'Aran despite having only 5,000 inhabitants, looked perfectly clean and alpine. Snow-capped mountains ringed the town. It deserves to be much better known, although I suppose the difficulty in getting here will always keep visitor numbers low. Considering it's in Spain, it's actually on the French side of the Pyrenees.

I'd brought a little tripod in an attempt to get action photos of myself, something you're usually denied when you travel alone. This involved lying at the side of the road, lining up the camera with where I hoped to be, and hitting the multi-shot ten-second self-timer before sprinting back to my bike and setting off. After a whirlwind of clicks I'd return to the camera to find ten images, each with a different section of my body missing. It was a lot of work for minimal reward. And it caused some well-meaning people to be concerned. With the bicycle on its side and me on the floor messing with my Canon, a fellow cyclist came past and asked me how badly hurt I was. Sheepishly, I had to explain I hadn't actually fallen off.

To complicate matters here, this valley speaks its own tongue. I chatted to the woman on the campsite's reception desk.

"So what language do we use now? Spanish, French or..."

"Aranese?" we both said at the same time.

I was keen to learn more.

"OK, how do you say 'thank you' in Aranese?"

"*Gracias*."

"Ah, like Spanish then. And 'hello'."

"*Ola*."

In Spanish that'd be "*hola*", but they don't pronounce initial aitches. If you're going to have your own language, at least make it different.

I set up my tent and immediately had a visitor, a pensioner from south London who, within minutes, had shown me his penis.

"You speak English?" he started.

"Yep, I *am* English."

He clocked my accent.

"Ah, some of your lot are comin' here in a camper in a second."

By "your lot" he meant northerners. We're apparently a breed apart and can only communicate with other northerners, and only then if it's on the subject of whippets.

"What're you doin' here anyway?" he asked.

I told him, fighting the urge to include an "Ee by gum" in my answer. My ride impressed him so much he wanted a photo of me. But then he flicked through his phone's picture gallery.

"Look at that," he said, handing me his mobile.

The image showed him standing bollock-naked, trousers around his ankles, in a snowy field. I wasn't sure how to respond to that. Anything complimentary would've sounded creepy and, besides, would've been entirely undeserved. It looked very cold after all. You can't expect to wow anyone with the poundage of your manhood in sub-zero temperatures. Mercifully, he wandered off before he could show me any photos of him and the missus going for it.

I was now at the end of Spain, and after just over three weeks, nearly a thousand miles and two Everests of climbing I'd seen six wannabe countries. And tomorrow I'd roll into another one, hopefully one with fewer naked pensioners.

Chapter 3: French Dejection

Occitania

The hoped-for freewheeling scream down the other side of the Pyrenees didn't happen. A strong headwind did its best to push me back to the Mediterranean. The blue skies of Spain disappeared the instant I hit France and, although I didn't know it yet, they were going to stay disappeared for almost my entire time here. But I'm not here to talk about France. I'd hit another wannabe country, Occitania. Sadly, there was no welcome sign.

Without being too precise, Occitania is the southern third of France, stretching from the central Pyrenees to nearly as far east as Lyon, but its exact dimensions differ depending on which map you see. Sometimes it includes Val d'Aran, other parts of Spain and bits of Italy too.

The Partit de la Nacion Occitana is the political lightweight gunning for its independence, but they're roundly ignored, currently managing fewer than 1% of votes in recent elections. The present extent of the nationalist's ambition is to demand a daily hour of Occitan-language programming on the French equivalent of BBC2. The number of nations worldwide beginning with the letter 'O' is not about to be doubled any time soon.

The flatness of the lighting had a way of stripping even the Pyrenees of their grandeur. The rest of the day involved hopping from one faceless village to another that was identical. Well, I assume it was identical, because I'd already forgotten the previous one.

By four o'clock I'd found a lakeside campsite near the

village of Roquefort-sur-Garonne, whose registration process was the strangest I'd ever encountered.

No one else was camping here, although there was a handful of cars outside the chalets on the edge of the site. The reception was locked. A telephone number was written on its door. The only person about was a ten-year-old girl pedalling a pink bicycle. My plan was to wait. Receptions normally kicked into life late afternoon.

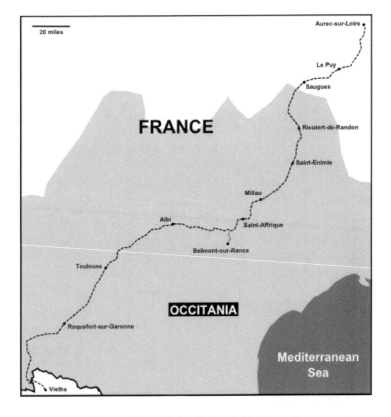

"You need to call," said the little girl in French.

I can usually muddle by in *le francais* when speaking face-to-face because I morph into Marcel Marceau. It becomes less a linguistic exchange and more a piece of interpretive dance. This approach wasn't going to work by phone and so I jabbed the numbers in, waited for a response and simply barked "Camping!", which *is* a real French word, so ner.

Ten minutes later, the warden arrived. He took my details and presented me with a key for the toilet block.

"How much is it?" I asked, fishing out my wallet.

He gave a Gallic shrug. How could he, the warden, not know?

"You don't pay me," he said.

"Then where do I pay?"

"The town hall."

What a wonderfully user-friendly system!

I cycled the mile or so back to the village's central square, assumed the grandest building was the town hall and went inside.

"I need to pay for camping," I told the woman on the desk.

What followed was a twenty minute transaction during which she copied down my passport details, made a couple of phone calls to confirm how much to charge me and finally asked for £4.30. That warden must be a real wrong 'un if he can't be trusted with such sums of hard cash.

On the way back to the campsite I stopped at a supermarket for dinner ingredients. From our £1-a-day trip I had fond memories of France's ubiquitous tins of lentils and sausage, but they were a far less appealing prospect without a stove to warm them. I lay in the porch of a tiny tent, scruffily covered with my tarp to keep off the rain, and ate cold pulses from a can. I'd be lying if I said I didn't feel a bit trampy.

*

I really wasn't getting into this ride. The heavy bike was making it more of a chore than I was used to. I woke up to another grey morning and didn't want to leave the confines of my tent. At least today would be flat, I thought, and prised myself out of my sleeping bag.

I spent the day crawling from village to village, most of them stuffed full of shops, just like English ones aren't. I passed a sign for the *Clinique d'Occitanie*, proving at last I really *had* arrived in my new country, for there was zero other evidence.

I'd made a decision. I'd ditch my useless and leaky coffin-sized tent and find a Decathlon to buy a replacement. Considering how biker- and hiker-friendly their products are, their stores' locations couldn't be more awkward, almost always on the edge of a motorway or a killer dual carriageway. The one ten miles outside of Toulouse, the capital of Occitania, was no exception. Cycling to it was as much fun as a knife fight and twice as dangerous.

On a campsite on the outskirts of Toulouse I pitched my new two-man tent, a Quecha Quickhiker Ultralight, a model I was familiar with because I'd previously used one to death. It felt absolutely massive, like I could've hosted a banquet inside, provided I didn't invite anyone else.

The trip had been reborn, with more room and without the worry of rain pouring in and buggering my electronics. My improved mood didn't wane even when I discovered the campsite's showers were cold. I stood at the water's edge and flicked freezing droplets on to me. I'd have been shit in the army.

*

Today was a rest day. It was also an exploration day, and the target was Toulouse, *La Ville Rose* – the Pink City – so-called because of the town's terracotta stonework rather than any particular LGBT leanings.

Looking at the map, the city centre only seemed a couple of miles away and so I decided to go on foot. It turned out to be well over triple that distance. Some day off!

The town is lovely, with four- and five-storey pink buildings, each with intricate ironwork on its balconies. With its narrow streets it was an easy place to get lost. While perusing the city map I discovered the *Maison de l'Occitanie*, the wannabe nation's Cultural Centre, here in its capital. Obviously I had to pay a visit.

Down a scruffy side street, the whole experience was a bit underwhelming. A couple of middle-aged women sat at a desk, guarding a collection of leaflets. The building also had an exhibition room, but it was entirely empty except for a wall-sized map showing the extent of Occitania. I looked at it for as long as I could, but I wasn't able to stretch this into a Louvre-quality experience.

Occitania has its own language, Occitan, a dialect of which is Aranese, the one we met in Val d'Aran, and it was a booklet about this tongue that was the only thing I could take away from Occitania HQ. The pamphlet was called *Occitan – Qu'es aquò?*, or *What is Occitan?* in Occitan. Presumably if you could read the booklet's title, you already knew what Occitan was. Inside a few phrases were spelled out. I learned *Vòles dançar amb ieu?* ("Do you want to dance with me?") and the logical next step in that conversation, *Ne vòls?* ("Do you want some?"), and then the most useful phrase in any foreign language once you realise you're never going to master it, *Compreni pas!* ("I don't understand.")

Maybe the half-arsed nature of the Cultural Centre summed up Occitania's future chances of becoming an independent nation. The Wannabe Bible puts Occitania's long-term hopes at only 2%. Compare that to Catalonia's 60%.

I needed Wi-Fi. I'd also planned to eat something fresh tonight rather than more cold tinned crap. I fancied tomatoes, but tomatoes aren't any good without salt. Against my better judgement I thought I'd solve both the Wi-Fi and salt issues on the way back to the campsite by visiting McDonald's. And it was there I realised I'm a useless old man.

For a start I couldn't even buy a sodding meal. Since my last soul-destroying appointment with McDonald's in about 1980, humans have been replaced by a touchscreen ordering system, and that it was only in French didn't help. In the end I was hand-held through the selection process by a teenage girl who may as well have finished by saying in a condescending tone, "Now go to the counter, grandad, and fetch your din-dins!"

I carried a truly awful burger and potato-free chips to a table and then realised I couldn't access their Wi-Fi either. To get going, I apparently had to scan a QR code, but I didn't have a QR scanning app, and without Wi-Fi I couldn't get one. So I'd basically paid a fiver for two sachets of salt. I'd have been better off buying a kilo of the stuff and donating my leftovers to a local slug-hating gardener. Still, the tomatoes tasted nice.

*

I spent one full day cycling away from Toulouse over increasingly and annoyingly lumpy terrain and then another one that was quickly aborted in Albi. I located the town's magnificent cathedral and then heard a rumble of thunder. I looked to the sky and a fat raindrop hit me in the eye. Then another one. I pedalled until I found shelter, and I waited. And waited.

I wasn't worried about my panniers getting wet. They were famously watertight Ortliebs, but the hip bag holding all my tech was untested. Its manufacturer had made no waterproof claims and so I had to assume it wasn't. It contained my DSLR camera, which had spent six months refusing to work the last time it got wet. (A group of us got soaked while carrying a fish the forty or so miles on foot across the Sierra Almijara mountains from Cómpeta to Granada. Don't ask.)

I waited for about an hour, but the rain was going nowhere. Until I could find a way to protect my tech bag, another solution was required. In the end I resorted to a budget Ibis and watched the water pour for the rest of the day, a pastime I was going to have to get used to.

*

It was the last day of April. For some reason I'd imagined a fairly flat route today, but not long out of Albi the road started to climb, a slope that continued for a full twenty-one miles. It was never steep, but it was a slog. At least the height provided some impressive vistas, endless green hills rolling to the horizon, densely covered in trees with only the occasional village to break them up. Considering how far south we were, the countryside was remarkably English. Then again, so was the weather.

My back wheel was making a strange rubbing sound. I checked the brakes, but they were fine. I employed my usual tactic of ignoring it and seeing how it developed.

It developed badly. Just the other side of that huge hill, as I was about to enjoy its delicious descent, my back wheel blew up. Upon removing the tyre and inner tube, the reason for the puncture became obvious. As predicted by Juan in Murcia, the rim had split. I gaffer-taped it back together, hoping I could reapply the tyre and hobble to the nearest bike shop. Instead the Fates smiled generously upon me. With my bicycle still upside down at the side of the road, a car pulled up. Inside were Philippe and Bernadette.

The middle-aged French couple were from Bordeaux but here on holiday. Philippe was also a cyclist who'd been helped out by kindly strangers in the past and was repaying the debt. A quick search on my tablet showed the nearest bike shop was a long way away, but they said they'd at least take me to a campsite, the one I'd been planning to reach today, Camping Le Val Fleuri in Belmont-sur-Rance. It was still a good fifteen miles away.

We arrived to be greeted by its friendly Dutch owner, Marjan, and a massive rainstorm. Without the help of Philippe and Bernadette, I'd have been pushing my bicycle through the downpour while simultaneously drowning my camera and the rest of my electronics. I thanked them profusely as they rolled away from the campsite. Never believe anyone who tells you French people aren't great.

"Do you know where the nearest bike shop is?" I asked Marjan.

"There's one in Saint-Affrique," she replied.

"Ah, good. How far's that?"

"Twenty-five kilometres."

If your brain doesn't do metric, that's about fifteen miles.

"Ah."

"But it's not open tomorrow. It's May Day."

This was getting worse. But maybe I could cobble together a repair here in the village.

"Are there any other shops in Belmont?"

"Yes. But they're all closed today."

"Eh?"

"It's Monday."

Many businesses close on both Sunday and Monday, especially in rural France.

"So I can't get any food either."

She smiled.

"There's a travelling pizza van here this evening."

This was the one bright spot in an otherwise stormy sky. I'd got lucky. The van hopped from village to village and was only here every alternate Monday. It was nice to eat warm grub again. Not bringing a stove had been a mistake, psychologically and financially. A fifty-pence packet of noodles and a bit of ropey old sausage was much more satisfying than the five quid it sometimes cost to throw together a ham and cheese baguette.

Was I going to be able to cycle the fifteen miles to Saint-Affrique on my broken wheel or was I in for a very long walk?

*

That today was May Day and everything was closed turned out to be incidental. It rained so hard I'd have been stuck in my tent all day in any case.

I was weighing up my options for tomorrow. The idea of going to the bike shop fully loaded seemed like the worst one. If taping up the rim didn't work and resulted in another puncture, then pushing for fifteen miles with a flat wheel and heavy bags would destroy my new back tyre. On the other hand, cycling to Saint-Affrique unloaded and then returning to the campsite would put me a further day behind schedule.

I amused myself in my rainy prison by reading a book called *How to Live in a Van and Travel*. I compared the author's experiences to my own. He wouldn't have to worry about rain. That said, if he blew a tyre, a lovely French couple couldn't stick his Ford Transit in the boot of their car and take him to safety.

In the afternoon the dampness eased and so I had a look around the village. There was no one about. I walked its cobbled streets alone. The forlorn-looking tourist office told me Occitan was their language despite there being no one inside to speak it. The shops were all closed for the day or, in some cases, for good. One seemingly thriving business was a strange medical store that sold prosthetic limbs, an oddly niche enterprise for such a little village.

"I'm just popping to the shops, François. Do you want anything?"

"Yeah, get me some Jaffa Cakes and a false leg, ta."

I thought I'd grab a closer look at the Gothic church. I could hear its bells clanging mournfully. Nearing the

49

building, I turned a corner and was faced with about three hundred sombrely dressed folk. Clearly, this was a funeral and that of someone who mattered deeply. I figured my bright blue sweatshirt and shorts probably didn't belong here. I returned to my tent.

Around seven I went to the campsite bar although there wasn't really anywhere to sit outside when it was raining. I spoke to Marjan.

"Is it fun running a campsite?" I asked.

She gave a sad smile.

"It used to be."

She'd come to France with a boyfriend a few years earlier and together they'd run a campsite in the south-west of the country. But they broke up and so she moved here. To make friends she joined a local band – Marjan plays trumpet – and fell in love with a fellow musician. He worked with her on this campsite and they had a great time, eventually having two daughters together. Unfortunately, two years ago he died.

"I'm so thankful for my two girls," she said. She gave a brave smile. "It'll be fun again."

I hope so. Marjan was a lovely, kind woman, not least because she also solved my bike problems by offering to drive me to Saint-Affrique in the morning.

"My accountant is there," she said. "I need to go and see him anyway."

As I left the bar under a grey sky, a tiny voice called out to me. It was one of Marjan's little daughters. With an enormous beaming smile, she opened both of her hands to reveal two fat frogs she'd caught. She could keep them with the other animals on the site, a cat, chickens, a goat and a donkey. This place was a little sanctuary. It just needed the sun to shine upon it once again.

*

It was a cold night, my sleeping bag only warm enough if I

wore my thick fleece, leggings and woolly socks. I received a message in the morning from my cousin Vicky, who lives near Monaco, to tell me I wasn't the only one suffering unseasonal weather in France. This had been a terrible spring for the whole country.

There was a carload for the journey to Saint-Affrique, Marjan, her two daughters and the son of a friend. On the way Marjan told me how Belmont-sur-Rance sometimes felt like a cursed village. Despite a population of just one thousand, three teenage kids had been killed in road accidents in the last year alone. There was also a higher than normal incidence of cancer.

But it wasn't all bad news. This summer the Tour de France was heading through the village for the first time ever, and this would bring a lot of visitors to a place whose only accommodation was provided by Marjan.

The drive to Saint-Affrique was stunning. It would've been a great ride in today's sunshine. After twenty minutes we arrived at the bike shop. The owner went to work immediately.

With the bike as good as new, the hill from Saint-Affrique to Millau was done with ease. And the sight of the Millau Viaduct, the tallest bridge in the entire world, was impressive. It carries a four-lane highway the one-and-a-half miles from one side of the Tarn valley to the other, 343 metres in the air. Even looking at it, it's hard to get your head around its size.

The tent was still sodden from the previous twenty-four hours of rain and so I decided to take advantage of the sunshine, stopping early in Millau to dry it, and myself, out. While creating some vitamin D, I thought again about Marjan. Outside the bike shop I'd said goodbye to her. She gave me a big hug and told me to send her a postcard from my final destination. That seemed like a fair deal to me. Good luck, Marjan, and thank you. I hope everything works out for you, the girls and the campsite.

*

The road out of Millau took me through the Gorges du Tarn, beside a river with vertical cliffs, and even the grey skies couldn't spoil the views. The thirty-five miles to Sainte-Enimie, one of France's Beautiful Villages, were uphill all the way, the climb hardly steep in itself, but a strong easterly wind increased the workload. Occasionally I'd turn a bend and be met with a huge sweep of the river, trees on either bank piling up among the cliff faces, or a lonely and ancient beige-stone village on the opposite shore.

Waiting for a red light to change to green outside one of the winding road's miniature tunnels, a pretty brunette beeped her horn and waved so enthusiastically I thought perhaps I knew her, which seemed unlikely given where I was. I was still carrying a few too many pounds. Maybe she'd mistaken me for Gérard Depardieu.

From Sainte-Enimie I climbed steeply out of the Mesozoic gorge. I'd scaled over 2,000 metres today and was really feeling it. Reaching the top, what followed was a equally severe three-mile descent, which was, with a long since departed sun, absolutely freezing. Both of my brakes were clenched so tightly that, with the icy air, my hands suffered a sort of pre-death rigor mortis. At the bottom I had to stop and twist my paws back into some vaguely human shape.

I found a campsite in a village without any restaurants. I crawled into my tent, put on all my clothes and ate a cold, miserable meal. The south of France in May wasn't supposed to be like this. Where could I write for a refund?

*

Today my legs were weary from the outset. The initial route out of the village took me up two hundred metres with no time to warm up, and then I saw what no overloaded cyclist wants to see, a sign to inform me of whether the forthcoming mountain pass was open or not. I put my head down and pedalled, ignoring the pain in my legs. Eventually, I topped out at 1,237 metres. I thought being high was supposed to feel good.

Down the other side, I stopped for a sandwich in Rieutort-de-Randon and ate it sitting inside a bus shelter to protect me from the freezing wind. In front of me was a dilapidated old barn from which hung not one but two signs saying *No Urinating*. Was it the locals fondness for tinkling all over this wooden structure that had reduced it to such a knackered state?

It rained on and off all day, never hard enough to worry about the gear in my tech bag but a quantity sufficient to put a dampener on proceedings. I was getting utterly sick of France's atrocious weather.

Today's endpoint was Saugues, a town that announces itself with monster-sized paw prints painted on the road. These relate to the Beast of Gévauden, an eighteenth century man-eating wolf creature responsible for the deaths of 113 people, often by having their throats ripped out and then at least partially devoured. This story cheered me up a bit. I mean, there's always someone worse off than yourself.

*

It poured down overnight, and this morning I packed the tent away sodden. The rain in Spain falls mainly in France, it seems.

Today's hills weren't as awful as I'd been expecting. Sure, there was a six-hundred metre climb, but there was a rarely seen fiery ball in the sky that illuminated the dense forests through which the mountain road twisted, and the way was dotted with charming villages. The best part was a shallow twelve-mile descent into Le Puy-en-Velay, an attractive town of red-tiled roofs and tall rock pedestals on top of which sat a church or statue.

I left my drying tent and went for a walk. Le Puy was hosting a car boot sale that specialized in items better off thrown away. I'd worked up a thirst and so popped into a nearby café for a *pichet* of cool white wine. Unfortunately, the glass they gave me was approximately the same size as a contact lens.

Sitting behind me was a Moroccan lad. He was disappointed with his car boot purchase, a three-CD collection of Bob Marley classics minus the third CD in the set, the one that contained most of his best stuff. I commiserated with his plight and returned to my wine.

He tapped me on the shoulder. He wanted to explain to me his appreciation of the French female form. After outlining an hour-glass figure with his index fingers, he then gurned in the direction of an eighteen-year-old waif, a very beautiful woman but one who couldn't have been less like an hour-glass if she were a 32A bra hanging off a broomstick.

I'd had enough. I needed hot food and lots of it. The campsite had its own restaurant and I opted for a dish from an upcoming wannabe country, a *pizza Savoyarde*, one covered in the staples of that mountain region, potatoes, onions, lardons and cream. It was the size of the M25 and utterly delicious.

I went to bed with the sky grumbling. I'm not even going to tell you about the next day. I basically whined the whole way. The route was dull, the weather minging and the cold campsite food awful. You don't need to hear all that. I ended up in Aurec-sur-Loire in another thunderstorm.

Why, you might be thinking, didn't I just buy a stove? Unfortunately, I had no room for one, my panniers already full. And it wouldn't only have been a new stove. I'd need to pack fuel, a pan, a plate and food. I was so looking forward to the near future, when I would reach the eastern half of Europe and prices for everything would tumble, allowing me to eat like royalty rather than like an Inuit. Before then, I had the rest of France to see, and another four of its wannabes.

Chapter 4: Depot of Pain

The Sovereign State of Barbe Island, Savoy, Romandie, Franche-Comté and Alsace

I woke early to a grumbling sky that developed into the dangerous grey-blue of a serious thunderstorm. I leapt from bus shelter to bus shelter, dodging the deluge and looking longingly as vans rolled past, their drivers all snug and dry, while I dripped a mixture of sweat and rainwater.

The storm eased and so I left the protection of my latest shelter. Now that I was exposed, the Weather Gods redoubled their efforts and I got another soaking, my rain jacket wrapped around my tech bag instead of me. I reached Firminy and suffered my first old-fashioned puncture, a shard of glass lodging in my tyre. I now also dripped chain oil and road dirt.

Feeling peckish, I stopped for something to eat at a bakery. I love how around these parts a *pâtisserie* is often called a *depot de pain*, sounding like a S & M dungeon but with croissants.

The roads here were in a terrible state. This had been the case since I'd crossed the Pyrenees, but they were particularly bad today. I don't remember conditions like this on previous visits. Whatever France's tax take was being spent on, it wasn't the road network. It's probably all blown on Werther's Originals for Macron's missus.

I made it the seventy miles to a campsite on the edge of Lyon. I had a field to myself, along with – luxury of luxuries – a picnic bench beside an enclosure of assorted animals. I sat in comfort, watching a pigeon trying to shag a hen. A man appeared and threw bread to his chickens. This sparked an aerial war involving sparrows, pigeons and magpies. It was like the Battle of Britain but, y'know, with less bullets and more feathers.

When I originally planned this trip I decided to include a day off in Lyon just because it sounded like an interesting city and not because it was part of any wannabe nation. But then I learned about the Sovereign State of Barbe Island. I was stumbling over independence movements when I wasn't even looking for them.

Barbe Island was a micronation before the term was invented. Unlike tiny, recognized micro*states*, such as Andorra and San Marino, micronations are in many cases eccentric, occasionally well-intentioned land grabs. Perhaps a strategically worthless area was forgotten when borders were redrawn, and someone comes along to claim it for himself. (Historically, it's almost always been a *him*self rather than a *her*self.) He usually adopts an overblown title such as President or Emperor and then swans about dressed like General Pinochet. There's at least one amusing video on YouTube in which several of these "heads of state" meet up and stamp each other's passports, which, as everyone knows, is the primary function of a head of state.

The land possessed by these micronations doesn't even have to be fixed to the ground. One of the few women involved, Carolyn Yagjian, the Grand Marshall of Obsidia, carries around her micronation in a briefcase. It's a lump of volcanic rock that doubles as a portable country.

Barbe Island is also a lump of rock, a third of a mile long, and sits in the River Saône, one of two mighty waterways that meet in Lyon. It's quite a way from the centre of the city and so I cycled there. As I rolled towards it, Lyon felt very chilled and classy in a French sort of way. Tall, expensive-looking buildings lined the wide Saône. Teenage art students sat by the river, sketching statues. I bet in a nearby café young pipe-smokers were discussing existentialism.

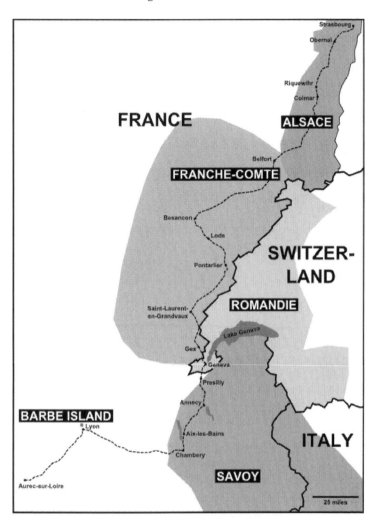

Eventually, I reached the narrow bridge that takes you to the island. You can stay high and simply cross to the opposite bank of the river, or you can do what I did and take a turning to descend to the island itself. Here was a scrubby field surrounded by trees on which a tiny festival was being dismantled. I followed the only road to the other side of this land – it was just a few metres really – and was met by a sign saying non-residents couldn't go any further. It was comfortably the dullest wannabe of my trip so far.

The owner of Barbe Island announced its independence in 1977 and even applied to the United Nations Security Council. All this seemed to be largely ignored by the rest of Lyon and officially it sits in the city's ninth *arrondissement*.

Across the river, I biked into the centre of town, down a cycle path hugging the water, and jumped from one elegant square to another, finally reaching the confluence of the Saône and the Rhône. I then climbed the steep cobbled streets of the old town to see the basilica, sitting high above the red roofs of the city. Lyon really is a dream.

*

Today's target was the wannabe country of Savoy, but more crappy weather caused me to quit early. I raised my mood at a campsite restaurant with a carafe of wine and *tartiflette*, a wonderfully calorific Savoyard dish made with potatoes, cheese, lardons and cream, four ingredients that seem to appear in every recipe from this mountainous region. Unsurprisingly, googling "supermodels from Savoy" returns zero results.

During the next two days, Savoy demonstrated why the local food is so full of fat. Both involved well over a thousand metres of climbing amongst gloriously Alpine scenery. I was burning calories like an uphill skier.

The highlight of the first day was Chambéry, the capital of Savoy, a town reluctant to tell you that you've arrived or where the centre is. It's every bit as lovely as I'd expected it to be, which is to say very lovely indeed. Its quaint streets, lined with cafés and restaurants, looked even prettier now the sun had dared to put in an appearance. Don't worry, it'll disappear again soon enough.

As I rode around the town I came across another cycle tourer, and I thought I had problems with the weight of my bike! He hauled a heavy-duty trailer, twice the length of his bicycle, that carried, amongst other things, a huge, four-paned solar panel, the sort of device that normally lives on the roof of a house. God knows what electronics he needed to juice up, but with enough sunshine he could have powered the Glastonbury Festival. Unfortunately, with the weather France was currently having, he couldn't have charged his phone.

"Hello," I said in English.

He stopped his huge machine.

"Where you go?" he replied in a South American accent.

I told him.

"And you?" I asked.

"Yes. Goodbye!" he said firmly.

"No," I continued, speaking more slowly. "Where are *you* going?"

He smiled.

"Yes. Goodbye."

And then he left. Fair enough.

Chambéry is in a bowl with only one natural exit. Low tree-filled mountains sit to its east and west with proper Alpine snow-capped peaks to the south. The way north wasn't exactly flat either.

I finally reached Aix-les-Bains, on the shore of Lake Bourget. At its campsite I couldn't find the key for my bicycle lock. It doesn't matter, I thought. If someone steals the useless bloody thing, I'll finish this trip in a more comfortable way, like on a train. I later found the key, but the idea of the bike's unplanned disappearance was so appealing I didn't bother to lock it.

The next day took me to an even prettier town, Annecy, sitting on its own lake. Rugged, snow-dusted mountains crowd the opposite shore. This place is a burst of colour, its pastel-shaded houses looking almost edible. To be honest, it would've made a better capital for Savoy than Chambéry. Judging by tourist numbers, a lot of people agreed.

There was another Savoyard speciality I'd wanted to try. Usually served at a family get-together, the chances of finding it in a restaurant were slim. So, after the ride, I cooked it up for my parents. It is called *le farcement*, an unusual mix of potatoes, bacon and prunes. Basically, line a plant-pot-shaped dish with rashers and then fill it to the top with fried onions, lardons, grated potato, prunes and raisins. Bake it in a bain marie for several hours, turn it out on to a plate and – *voilà!* – you have a large fruity, bacony potato cake. It tasted fine to me, but my dad said it would've been better with some custard.

The route from Annecy involved more climbing and, in these Alpine surroundings, the incongruous arrival of roadside prostitutes. I cycled on to a great bridge with fairy tale turrets over a massive gorge and, after several more hills, to the village of Présilly and the strangest campsite of the journey.

Hungry after a long day, I was excited at the site's advertised restaurant and market, but things weren't as they appeared. The market was infrequent and in any case only sold organic vegetables – not much use to a man without a stove – and the restaurant had been converted into a hall, today hosting a mother and toddler event.

There was an air of hippy commune about the whole place. I had to pass an empty yurt to reach my pitch. The site's guests, or in some cases long-term residents, all wore baggy, MC Hammer-style pantaloons and were one meal short of emaciated. De rigueur for the male half of each hollow-cheeked couple was a straggly ponytail. A noticeboard offered various yoga and alternative therapy happenings from visiting practitioners. The unisex bathrooms were covered in supposedly profound but ultimately banal statements written in French, such as "Saying what one thinks doesn't equal thinking what one says", and there was a box of possibly communal knickers by its door. It was a friendly place though with plentiful, free-roaming chickens and a single skinny duck that walked with a limp.

From up here on this hill I could see Geneva, but then I couldn't because thunderclouds rolled in and swamped the mountains. They opened up and it rained tropically for a straight thirty-six hours, trapping me in my plastic den with no food except my emergency rations of pistachios and dried figs.

For good reason, tents weren't a popular choice here. Every other visitor arrived in a van. They came and went, unhindered by the weather, and looked at me with sad eyes. I was being pitied by people whose idea of a tasty meal was tofu.

*

By nine in the morning it'd finally stopped raining and so, feeling light-headed from lack of food, I set off to Geneva. The main road into town was horribly busy but alleviated by bike lanes and sensible Swiss drivers. And then my front wheel started to make a strange clanking sound. Wonderful.

By cycling into this French-speaking part of Switzerland I'd sort of entered another independence-seeking area, Romandie. I say "sort of" because the Wannabe Bible was the only place to know about this and gave it a mere 1% chance of coming to fruition. I couldn't find a single other credible reference to it anywhere on the internet and so I'll say no more.

Having biked in Switzerland before, I knew it was hellishly overpriced and my intention had been to get in and out without spending a penny. My bike had other ideas. On a previous ride, when my bottom bracket had dissolved, the pedals became so unstable it was like cycling on a blancmange. If the same collapse happened to my front wheel, I'd be off. And even wearing the hated helmet there was no guarantee of survival. I had to get it replaced and now.

I did a quick tour of the centre, but Geneva was easily the least impressive Swiss city I'd seen. Down by the lake there's an utterly pointless jet that fires water up to 140 metres into the air. This is apparently the city's most famous landmark. Given how much energy it surely used, it was the perfect metaphor for Geneva: Wet, boring and expensive.

I found a bike shop, a pricey place even my Swiss standards. The bicycles in its window cost over four thousand pounds. I took my pezzy iron beast inside, feeling like Steptoe at a royal wedding. They couldn't sell me a replacement because 26-inch wheels are "old-fashioned and no one uses them any more". Hmm, the internet begs to differ. Instead, he agreed to have a dabble with its bearings to keep me going long enough to find one of those quaint, Victorian bike shops that still sell 26-inchers.

"It's OK for now," he said after the quick fix, "but the...what eez ze word? Eet eez very worn." He stuck out a forefinger and twisted it.

"Axle?"

He shrugged.

"Perhaps," he continued, "eet eez very worn. Old. Like ze whole bike."

He looked down at my machine and flicked one of its brake cables with disdain. The expression on his face told me what he really wanted to say.

"Monsieur, your bike eez, how do you say...a pees of sheeet."

Then he relieved me of £22, a transaction increased by the robbing bastards at Halifax, who also charged me £12 for having the temerity to use my own money abroad.

I cycled out of town on a silent bicycle, passing the CERN building, famous for both the Large Hadron Collider (LHC) and the birthplace of the World Wide Web, ironically the means by which so much fear was disseminated about how the LHC was going to cause a black hole that would kill us all.

Back in France, I stopped at a campsite in Gex and, for the second time in three days, was trapped there for an additional twenty-four hours by apocalyptic weather. Stuck inside my tent, I could feel something unusual on my neck. I appeared to be developing gills.

*

Today, France completed its series of lectures on why I should hate cycle touring.

Once at the top of a seven hundred metre climb and starting to roll down the other side, I began to feel the cold. I stopped to put on a fleece.

"Oh, you need some warmth, do you, softie?" said a Weather God. "Well, how about this then?"

Spots of water began to fall from the sky. I had the cheek to continue and so the volume was turned up. It rained so hard I could see a procession of animals walking up the road, two by two, as if heading somewhere important.

I threw on my bright yellow coat and manufactured a cover for my tech case from a carrier bag, and still it rained harder. Coming to a small hotel, I sheltered beneath the overhang of its roof. A sign outside said I could stay there half-board for £63. It was more than I'd normally pay, but I looked through the window and could see a log fire, flickering toastily inside a plush lounge. I caught my reflection in the glass, hair plastered to my pale forehead and rivulets of water leaking down my miserable face. I turned back to face reality. Black clouds marched overhead. Should I stay here, troughing mood-improving food in comfort, despite having cycled barely ten miles today?

I stood there for half an hour until the rain started to ease. It was an old Weather God ploy. As soon as I was out in the open again, a fresh wave of grief descended. After a thorough drenching, the outbuilding of a second hotel provided shelter. The Weather God sent a dry and inviting white van to drive past gloatingly, the evil sod.

This was no good. I was freezing. It was better to keep moving and risk my arms mutating into pectoral fins. Unfortunately, the road was still going downhill and so no warmth was forthcoming. The tarmac steepened. I squeezed my brakes tightly. Rendered useless by the rain, I barely slowed. By the time I'd reached the bottom I must've worn an inch off the soles of my trainers.

After just thirty miles I arrived at the nondescript townlet of Saint-Laurent-en-Grandvaux, set up my tent and realised that most of the things in my rucksack, the one strapped to the back rack and protected by two rain covers, were damp, including my sleeping bag. I can't tell you how happy this made me.

The brightest point of a dismal day was provided by a brief walk around town in squelchy trainers. There, I saw a car repair shop called *Garage Cretin*. It had all been worth it, he said sarcastically.

The only other positive was that I'd arrived in yet another wannabe country, Franche-Comté. So insignificant was the independence movement in this region that, three months from now, I'd meet a Frenchman from here who told me no such movement existed.

Despite these tiny silver linings, if every day was like today, there wouldn't be any more days.

*

It was my birthday and something miraculous had happened to the weather. A fat, yellow sun shone from a crisp, blue sky and made every scene twice as pretty. And there was an awful lot of prettiness to begin with.

From the dreary main road north out of Pontarlier, I took a smaller, unexpectedly spectacular one. Something of an optical illusion occurred. The tarmac fell for what seemed like hundreds of metres of descent. The landscape indicated we were reaching the valley floor. Then I turned a corner and suddenly I was high in the sky again, looking down on a splendid scene. In front of me, appearing almost close enough to touch, was a tall, round, tree-covered mountain, encircled by a deep river. The whole place felt highly improbable.

The loveliness continued. I kept on falling into the valley and soon passed through Lods, officially one of France's Most Beautiful Villages. Old houses are pushed right up to the banks of a gurgling stream and happily topped by a gleaming white church. A raft of daring ducks had made a nest on the twig-tangled lip of a tiny waterfall.

My only payment for all of today's downhill was a three mile climb near the end of the day, but I eventually arrived in Besançon, the capital of Franche-Comté, and found the hotel I'd booked for a couple of nights. I was putting the misery of the previous week's weather behind me. Birthday fun would be had. And tonight it was going to be in the form of a Chinese and way, way too much wine.

*

During the night my IBIS hotel had turned into a doll's house. This was the only conclusion I could draw when faced with the micro-crockery of their self-service breakfast. Juice glasses were the size of thimbles and cereal bowls like ashtrays. After my seventeenth visit to the buffet to refill my two-pence-sized plate, I calculated I was using more calories in acquiring my food than I was receiving in its consumption.

Rather than die of malnutrition I hit the town. I imagine Besançon's cathedral was grand 'n' everything, but all the scaffolding made it impossible to be sure. This is the location of a famous astronomical clock. Supposedly. I went inside to look at it. Being the only person in such a massive place felt eerie. But could I find the clock? I went back outside, a bit confused.

Three French folk, two women and a map-carrying man, were searching around. One of them pointed to something off to the side of the building. Clearly, they were looking for the clock too. I said hello and followed them around the back of the cathedral. They opened a door that led to a pitch black stone staircase. I went in behind them, one of women lighting the way with her phone. We rounded a corner and came to another door. This was exciting, like one of those rubbish graphic adventures on the Commodore 64. They opened the door and, lo and behold, I found myself back inside the empty cathedral. We never managed to find the clock.

It was a warm day – there was no need for the gods to waste their energy on rain if I wasn't cycling – and after trudging around town for a few hours I'd worked up a thirst, one that was expensively quenched with a ridiculous seven quid beer. France is pricier than it was even a few years ago. It didn't help that one British pound currently had the value of a bag of leaves.

And then I found it, the proof that, despite what that Frenchman would tell me a few months from now, there really *is* an independence movement for the Franche-Comté region. In the centre of town was the organisation's shop-cum-office. Sadly, there was no life inside and the letter M in its sign's "*Mouvement*" had fallen off, but at least there was a

Franche-Comté flag in its window, one I'd seen flown absolutely nowhere in Besançon, nor anywhere else in the region for that matter.

Later I walked by a few stalls, including a couple flogging flags. They had lots of French and EU ones, a Brazilian, even one for the UK, but Franche-Comté was not an option. That made sense. Where's the market for an independence flag when even the local residents don't know there's an independence movement?

*

The ride north out of Besançon slid me along the delightful River Doubs. Little cliffs interrupted the tree-lined cycle path. Men walked dogs, and couples strolled hand-in-hand. Dads took their boys fishing. A teenager on a skateboard was treated to a husky ride as it dragged him along the track. He veered off to the right and fell into some long grass before standing up and looking around sheepishly to see if anyone had seen him. I gave him a little wave.

Facilities were scarce. The first patisserie didn't show itself until three hours later. After surveying the shop's glass cabinet, I pointed to a chocolate muffin. The young woman behind the counter smiled.

"It's cheese," she said in English.

That took me by surprise.

"Is it?" I asked, confused.

"Sorry, I mean chocolate."

After a total of eighty miles, I ended the day in the town of Belfort, right in the middle of a music festival. Groups all wearing the same colour t-shirt walked around, singing like choirs. One song was a seemingly Christian ditty, wailing how they wanted to see the light, although I suppose it might have just been about shopping at B&Q.

*

Another sixty miles the next day took me to Colmar, a

place I'd been looking forward to. Not only that, but I left Franche-Comté and entered my final fully French independence movement, Alsace. Clearly, this one was more popular than Franche-Comté's. It was the first campaign since Catalonia for which I saw supporting graffiti, and multilingual graffiti at that: *"Alsace Libre! Elsass Frei!"* The Wannabe Bible still only gave it a 5% long-term possibility of happening though.

I guess Alsace's independence movement was borne out of the upheaval of being swapped again and again, along with Lorraine farther north, between France and Germany. It was first annexed by Germany in 1871 at the end of the Franco-Prussian War and then reclaimed by France after the First World War. It became German again in 1942 before returning to France a few years later. It'd be entirely understandable if the locals thought of themselves as neither French nor German and would prefer instead to be Alsatians. They'll do anything for a biscuit. Nah, c'mon, I mean *bredele*, this region's traditional Christmas cookie.

Colmar was pretty but a victim of its own success. Photographs depict it as a diminutive Germanic-looking Venice, plentiful canals but with the addition of tidy flowers and multi-coloured half-timbered houses. These pictures must have been taken at six in the morning, because they didn't show the fourteen billion tourists. Thinking about it, they must have been taken at six in the morning during the early 1940s. I can't imagine there were many holidaymakers here then.

I got to the campsite just as a storm exploded overhead. A blackboard in its reception had a hastily chalked up list of suggestions about what there was to do in Colmar if it was raining. Obviously it wasn't only me suffering with the wet stuff.

*

After starting the day with a delicious cheese and lardon-covered pretzel, I cycled out of Colmar, passing its own Statue of Liberty, commemorating its designer's association with the town. Standing plinth-less in the centre of a busy roundabout and at around a third of the height of New York's, it looked distinctly unimpressive, more like a Garden Ornament of Liberty.

Riding over the many small hills in the Alsace wine region, I headed for another of France's Most Beautiful Villages, Riquewihr. It had the same flowers and pastel-coloured half-timbered houses as Colmar, but replaced its canals with cobblestones. Not a single shop in the centre of town offered anything a local might want to buy. The place felt fake, like Disneyland. I made a mental note to stop visiting this sort of thing. Oh, for the sometimes grim but always earthy honesty of farther east rather than the twee, over-commercialized toss of the west!

I looked to the heavens and didn't like what I saw. Knowing Obernai, today's destination, was only fifteen miles away, I stretched myself too far. I raced the storm that was building over the Vosges Mountains and arrived utterly burnt out. The Weather Gods sniggered. While I lay gasping on the ground they folded up their squall and carried it elsewhere.

*

My map told me I was still inside France, but I'd clearly already entered Germany if the attitude to cyclists was any measure. Your average German expects you to use their bike lanes if one has been provided, and they'll happily scream at you if you don't, even if you didn't see it. And sometimes they'll shout at you even if there's no cycle path at all. Today this happened three times in the space of twenty miles.

And then on a busy main road into Strasbourg, another one lacking any sort of bicycle path, a Ford Ka slowed down beside me. The passenger window opened to reveal a robust elderly female driver and her scrawny husband, built like a couple from a saucy seaside postcard. With her eyes firmly on the car ahead, the woman endlessly repeated a monotone mantra, loud enough for me to hear. I could've sworn it was "Knobhead, knobhead, knobhead."

Strasbourg was a surprise. I'd expected some dull, indistinct Euro capital, a place full of dreary offices and pen-pushers, but the centre of town couldn't have been more different. Its Gothic cathedral was possibly the finest structure I'd ever seen. Until 150 years ago, it was the world's tallest building. And with its canals and a size large enough to absorb its visitors with ease, Strasbourg was the place I was expecting Colmar to be. There was also a distinct lack of traffic. I wheeled around the centre for hours, taking in the laid-back groove of this extremely beautiful city, the capital of Alsace.

It had taken me nearly two months, two thousand miles and four Everests of ascent to cycle through Spain and France. Almost all the regions I'd visited were new to me, but so familiar was I with these two lands that sometimes it felt like I was covering old, and usually soggy, ground. But from this point onwards, I would barely spend more than a week in any one country, and the cultures, food and languages, and occasionally even alphabets, would be changing thick and fast.

Goodbye France. Bring on Germany!

Chapter 5: Day Trip to Dachau

Fürstentum Rheinbergen and Bavaria

Leaving Strasbourg, Germany was just on the other side of a large bridge, but before I got there I'd pass over another micronation. Many micronations are created for frivolous reasons but not Fürstentum Rheinbergen. It's an ecological movement. Unlike the others, it doesn't claim any land of its own, not even a volcanic rock in a briefcase. However, it does assert ownership of rather a lot of water, all the liquid in the River Rhine to be exact. Importantly, it lays no claim to the riverbed, which belongs to Germany or France or any of the other four countries through which its 765-mile length runs. If you help to promote the river's ecosystem, you can even become a citizen. Living in the Rhine couldn't be any damper than living in France.

Germany provides a lot of cycling routes, and I figured if they'd bothered to create them, I could at least use them. Unfortunately, in their desperate attempt to keep you from sharing any road with a car, you get sent the long way around. After five hours I'd travelled only twenty miles as the crow flies.

The bike path from Oppenau wanted to take me over an unnecessary mountain. The cars with their mighty engines didn't have to go up the huge slope. With only my legs for power, why should I? I joined the main road instead and risked being called a knobhead again.

But whatever my route, Germany was going to present me with a mountain to climb. At 600 metres above sea level, after snaking uphill through the dense Black Forest, surely I was near the top. But then into my nose drifted the smell every heavily-loaded tourer dreads, that of burning brakes accompanying each car coming downwards. This acrid odour told me there was more hill to come, and it'd be steep. I finally peaked at 950 metres and rolled into Freudenstadt, which translates as the City of Delights, a name somewhat tempered by its town crest of two depressed-looking catfish and a walking stick.

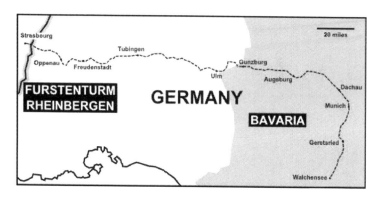

This south-west corner of Germany is Swabia and, while it doesn't have its independence movement, sometimes it feels like the rest of Germany wished it did have. All the stereotypes that exist about Germans in general, the Germans believe to be true of Swabians. According to The Independent, they are "hard workers, miserly and fastidious doorstep polishers". So unpopular are Berlin's Swabian residents that a new word was invented, *Schwabenhass* or Swabian hatred, and "Shoot Swabians!" stickers were stuck around the city. When it's Germans making such statements, maybe we should sit up and listen.

I'd continue my Swabian adventure the next day. My knee had been playing up again and so I called it quits after only forty miles in the fairytale town of Tübingen. You could imagine Rapunzel lowering her hair from one of the higher windows of the half-timbered houses or a thirteenth century Jimmy Savile pied-pipering the local kiddies down the street and around the corner.

Back at the campsite I visited its restaurant, a feature of most German sites. On the menu was a *Schwobateller*, a taste of all the things this area is famous for. As well as a pork steak, it included ravioli-like *Maultaschen* – literally "feedbags" – and *Spätzle* – that's small, misshapen pasta – lentils extensively grown around here, a glass of schnapps and a toy Swabian flag. There was more obvious self-love for the region here than in most of the wannabe countries I'd passed through.

The restaurant was filling up. Another bloke eating alone asked if he could sit at my table.

"Are you a cyclist?" he said.

"Yes. How did you know?"

He pointed to my head.

"Your red face."

It wasn't sunburn, just weather-worn, like the features of a North Sea trawlerman.

This was Dietrich, he was sixty-nine and tonight was going to be his first ever night in a tent. You're never too old to try something new. He was a Swabian and so I asked him about the stereotypes.

"No, we are misunderstood," he said. "Swabians are not unfriendly. We are sincere. In Cologne, people will make friends in an instant, but it means nothing to them. Here, if we make friends, we mean it."

"And what about the other things, like working too hard?"

He laughed.

"We *have* to work hard," he replied. "The land is shit. That's why we grow lentils."

*

After a morning of leaping from one pretty village to another, something happened that made me lose all faith in my technology. The app I was using for navigation showed smaller tracks as dotted lines. So far these had all been easily cyclable and in most cases allowed me to find routes I'd never otherwise have discovered. The B28 was a fast, busy main road and not particularly pleasant to cycle on. Instead, the app suggested a parallel track through the woods.

All was well to begin with. I biked on tarmac, past a small sports stadium, and then a farm with a field in which a woman was feeding her baby goats. The lane narrowed, not alarmingly so, but then became dried mud. It wasn't an ideal surface, but I was already a couple of miles down the path by now and didn't want to turn back. The trees beside the track grew in number until I was in a dense forest.

And then, under the darkened canopy, the flat route became a steep hill, a gradient of at least 25%. The surface was now loose soil with little stones, and the enormous effort of pushing made my feet sweat and slip around inside my sandals. I turned a corner and the track got steeper still. Going back downhill wasn't an option. I'd never have kept hold of the bike with its weight on a hill of this gradient and with no grip for my hooves. The only technique that worked was a quick burst of energy to push forward on the sloppy surface, and then I'd slam on the brakes before rearranging my feet inside my sandals. With the temperature up around 30°C it was physically the hardest half an hour I can remember. By the time I got to the flat bit at the top I was shaking. But my troubles weren't over.

There were two tracks before me, but which one did I need? Unfortunately, with dense foliage overhead, my mapping app couldn't pinpoint my position and showed me dancing all around the forest like a coked up Bez. I had no idea where I was or which of the two tracks to take.

Fortunately, one of them was even steeper than the hill I'd just climbed and would've been impossible in any case. I took the other, but then I turned a corner back upon myself and started to descend. Brilliant.

I cycled around for another half an hour, totally lost, and then luckily a sign appeared. It was just a pity it was for the sports stadium I'd passed right at the bottom of the hill. Choosing escape over living in the woods forever and having to eat my own legs for survival, I rolled downhill and arrived back where I'd started about an hour and half earlier. And then I still had the busy B28 to negotiate and its huge climb all over again.

*

The previous night I'd found a campsite in a sleepy hamlet called Lauberg. I began to pack up around eight, but Gerda, a German woman in the only other tent on the site, had different ideas. While her family quizzed me about what I was doing, she gave me bread and ham and a mug of steaming coffee.

"Can I come with you?" she asked.

Her husband didn't seem too bothered by this request.

The family dog came bounding up to me. I stroked his head and played with his ears.

"I love dogs," I said. "I want a dog."

"Yes," replied Frank, the family grandad, "but you can't have this one."

Their surname turned out to be Bohne, I'd spent half an hour chatting with Mr Bean and his family!

Today's ride took me through the city of Ulm, home of the tallest church in the world. Outside of it were dozens of one metre high, blue Einsteins that could be picked up and moved around, or stolen if you had strong arms and a nearby van. Despite only living his first year in Ulm, the Einstein connection is milked. The local marathon is named in his honour and there's an Einstein Museum, presumably showing his favourite rattle and an old nappy.

I rode out of town along the Danube. It was odd to think I could cycle from here all the way to this mighty river's delta and be less than 150 miles from Ukraine's Odessa, from which I needed to catch a ferry later, and it'd all be downhill. My actual route would take me over the Alps twice more, through the High Tatras and the Carpathian Mountains. Why were independence-seeking nations so inconveniently located?

I found a campsite in Leipheim but more importantly in Bavaria, my next wannabe. There's a stronger desire for independence here. Borrowing a neologism from the UK, their removal from Germany is called "Bayxit". It's unlikely to happen though. The Wannabe Bible gave it only a 2% chance. Later, on that ferry from Odessa, I'd share a cabin with a German lad.

"Are you from Bavaria?" I asked.

"No, thank god," he replied. "They're always talking about independence, but no one takes them seriously."

*

In the centre of Leipheim early the next morning I breakfasted on a magnificent *Leberkäsesemmel*, a thick slice of pink, solidified meat slurry with a dollop of mustard on a bun. It was this dodgy snack that'd made me look forward to southern Germany so much.

Today's ride took me through Günzberg, birthplace of Nazi doctor and "Angel of Death" Josef Mengele, a memory the town struggled to shake off, especially as his dad's farm machinery business, Karl Mengele & Sons, played such an important role for local employment until recently. With this in mind, was it wise for a company with wartime associations to name its sweetcorn gathering machine the Maize Blitz?

Bike lanes and quiet roads delivered me to Augsburg, a

city of nearly 300,000. A fountain on its main square took an original approach to how it spurted water. The four female figures fired liquid from their nipples as well as from novelty lion-headed She-wees.

I found a campsite to the north of the town with an odd payment system.

"There's a ten euro deposit for the toilet key," said the receptionist.

"OK. And do I pay for camping now too?"

She smiled.

"No, tomorrow. That's how we guarantee the return of the key."

No, it didn't. At an expensive eighteen euros a night, a less honest camper could bugger off with the key, lose their deposit and still be eight euros up on the deal.

It was a tranquil evening sitting on the picnic bench beside my tent and working my way through the collection of goodies I'd liberated from the Netto across the road. But then the wind got up and a violent thunderstorm attacked Augsburg in the distance. After five days of pleasant temperatures, had the German Weather Gods finally found me?

*

I was on my way to Munich, the capital of Bavaria, and a slight detour took me for a dose of historical misery in the form of the Dachau concentration camp.

Although Dachau wasn't officially an extermination camp like Auschwitz, plenty of people were still murdered here. Visitors get a chance to see a museum, the prison and a recreation of one of the barracks. All the others have been pulled down with just their outlines sketched on the surface of the parade ground. With the site levelled you didn't get the sense of claustrophobia that must have been ever present.

Even putting the death aside, the daily misery and overly

harsh punishments would have been enough to grind anyone down. For missing a single spot when washing a coffee cup, you'd be hung by your hands for an hour. Over the life of the camp, inmate numbers swelled without subsequent growth in the facilities, which compounded the horror.

It was difficult to imagine just how truly awful it would've been at its most densely packed. Inside the prison section of the camp, each cell had a board with a quotation from one of the former inmates. One complained about only getting hot food every fourth day. This made me think of my own stove-less existence. I then had to chastise myself for comparing my plight to that of a death camp prisoner.

Dachau is also the name of the town around the camp. It must be strange to live in a place so associated with death, that grim face everyone pulls whenever you tell them your address for the first time. For that reason I was amazed to see two other towns had actually twinned with Dachau. Upon closer inspection, one of them maybe wasn't such a surprise. Austria's Klagenfurt is the state capital of Carinthia, once governed by ultra far-right Jörg Haider. So perhaps the twinning on Klagenfurt's part wasn't so much in the spirit of "Let's all move forward together" but rather "Good work, lads! Do you still have the blueprints?"

Afterwards, I fought my way across a hectic Munich to a perfect campsite in the south of the city, only three miles along a riverside cycle path from its central Marienplatz. The site also had a restaurant and a bar selling great German beers. The sun continued to shine, which made the ale taste even better. Those damp, depressing days of France felt a long time ago. I was finally having fun, albeit Germanic fun, which probably isn't as fun as, say, Mexican fun, but I'd happily take it for now.

*

Rather than cycling fifty miles to the next town, I was

going to have a day off and instead do a bike tour of Munich, one that'd probably also cover fifty miles and so not much of a day off at all.

I had a list of places to visit in the city. The first was a plaque marking the spot where Hitler was very nearly assassinated in 1939. Knowing Adolf made an annual speech at the Bürgerbräukeller, Georg Elser planted a time bomb in one of its pillars. The explosion happened as planned, killing eight people and injuring fifty-seven. Unfortunately, none of them was Hitler, who'd cut his appearance short and left the building early. Elser was caught, imprisoned for five years and then shot, whereas Mr Hitler went on to become something of a celebrity.

Munich has a famous glockenspiel that lives in its main square, Marienplatz, and on a fine day draws a large crowd. As I listened to the tuneful chimes, a young fella stood a few metres away, wearing nothing but a pair of blue underpants. When the bells stopped, he started to clap his hands slowly above his head. Performance art or mental illness, the distinction is often difficult to decipher.

Something else I wanted to see were the golden cobbles of Viscardigasse. Hitler made Munich's Feldherrnhalle a national monument. This meant everyone who passed it had to give the Nazi salute, and there were guards outside to ensure this happened. Anyone trying to avoid all the "Heil!" nonsense could use Viscardigasse, a narrow side street, as a way of bypassing the hall. Today, a path of golden cobblestones commemorates the route taken by brave dissenters. I wonder if they chose this colour as reminiscent of the trail left behind by those nervously taking this alleyway.

For the rest of the day I just pootled around the city, visiting the parks, with hoards of locals sunbathing by the river. A circuitous route dropped me on to Maximilianstrasse with its top-end brand stores and sports cars covered with the key scratches of more resentful drivers. This street has the highest rents in Munich.

I followed a tall, slim blonde in white, floaty clothes. She carried a pink handbag and seemed to be walking in heels for the first time. Then she went over on one of them and looked around sheepishly. Transitioning can't be easy.

*

On my last full day in Germany I headed south, down the Isar river. In Grünwald I saw my first evidence that today was special. I came across a gathering of folk in traditional dress. For the women this meant colourful *dirndls* and for the men lashings of *lederhosen* and felt hats with huge shaving brushes stuck in the side, just in case you needed to whip someone's beard off in a hurry.

And then in Geretsried I saw a procession and more dirndls, but this time added into the mix was a lechery of priests. (I honestly didn't make up that collective noun.) Today was Corpus Christi, the Catholic holiday relating to transubstantiation, during which Christians believe they literally eat the body of Jesus, which seems a bit ungrateful.

Cloudless blue skies allowed me to see into the distance, and what I saw were magnificent mountains, loads of 'em, worryingly high and snow-capped, even on this, the last day of May.

A little further down the road these Alpine peaks were made even more beautiful when they were reflected in tranquil lake Kochelsee. I felt a million miles from the bustle of Munich. And then came a second lake, Walchensee, one of the deepest in the Alps and the watery home of two Lancaster bombers. The water was turquoise, and on its far shore chalets were sheltered by tall, tree-covered hills. A large white cross sat atop one of them. Scenery rarely gets better than this.

What on earth could happen to disturb my reverie? I'll tell

you. People, that's what. Lots and lots of people. Don't get me wrong. Normally, I love people. But when a campsite packs them in so tightly you suspect you've mistakenly pitched your tent in Metallica's mosh pit, I'm not so keen.

The site was full for vans, but no such concept existed for us canvas dwellers. You were especially encouraged to come here with a tent if you had loads of small kids who ignored your every parental command. The peace of the mountains was marred somewhat by six-year-olds seemingly on cocaine running around my tent – after all it was a gap into which only a six-year-old could fit – repeatedly tripping over my guy ropes and ripping out the pegs. A couple of them scraped their knees, but they still came back for more. I considered sharpening a few sticks and placing them strategically but figured the blood would've been hell to shift from my tent.

Those German Weather Gods that'd so often smiled upon me did so once again. I could hear the first pitter-patter of a storm that sent the little shits scurrying for cover. So now I just had to contend with their bored screaming and later their parents' farts and snores.

In Britain, most campsites enforce a six-metre gap between tents on the basis of fire safety. If a blaze broke out here tonight, we were all gonna burn, and I wasn't sure I didn't prefer that scenario to my current one.

Chapter 6: Swimming through Italy

Südtirol, Padania, Veneto, Friuli and the Free Territory of Trieste

After an unsurprisingly terrible night's sleep, I'd never been more thankful to escape a campsite. I left at seven in the morning, wiping the Sandman's dust from my eyes and Freddie Krueger-style child-slaughter fantasies from my mind.

After a beautiful day of Alpine cycling I entered Austria. A worrying road sign appeared. Apparently, after the village of Leithen, I'd no longer be allowed on the main road to Innsbruck. What was special about that place? I checked the map, but there was no easy alternative. If the threat were a fire-breathing dragon or a zombie hoard, I could have backtracked and added an additional twenty miles and endless hills to my day, but I'd still have no guarantee I wouldn't be thrown off that route too. I decided to continue and see what happened. It'd be quite cool to see a dragon.

What happened was that, for several miles, the road became exceedingly steep. The signs said the gradient was 16%, but it felt much more than that. Fortunately, it was downhill, but that wasn't necessarily good news. I repeatedly had to stop to let my brakes and rims cool down. It was causing trouble for the cars too, but the road hadn't originally been designed with them in mind either. It followed an ancient route, the traditional one from Italy to Germany. Romeo would've had to come this way had he wanted to buy Juliet a birthday bratwurst.

For some reason a dark thought popped into my head.

That disparaging mechanic in Geneva might have got my bike back on the road, but he'd said the front wheel wouldn't last forever. Without the clanking sound of dodgy bearings to remind me, I'd forgotten I needed to do something about it. I now convinced myself it was going to fall apart halfway down this mega-hill, probably just as a truck came from behind to finish me off. With rims the temperature of Christina Aguilera's underwear drawer, I reached the bottom and headed straight to a bike shop.

Now the gentle German Weather Gods had handed me over to the Austrian ones, I had new forces to deal with. This explained why, once in my tent, a storm blew in with such ferocity it made me question whether I'd arrived not in Innsbruck but Aleppo. It didn't matter though. I'd be in Italy tomorrow, under another god's jurisdiction and surely they'd be kinder. Wouldn't they? Whaddayamean, no, they wouldn't.

*

I woke up to a tent covered in brown slugs so large you could have mistaken them for sea lions. To effect a snappy removal procedure, I pulled on my trainers bare-footed and discovered there was one inside there too. There's no better way to start your day than peeling a squashed gastropod from between your naked toes.

I knew today would involve a lot of climbing, having to get me and my steel monster over the Brenner Pass into Italy, a total of nearly two thousand metres of ascent. That's a Ben Nevis an' half, or a bit less than a quarter of Everest. I was gonna be pooped.

Higher means better views. The route up was inside an emerald valley with snow-peaked mountains ahead. Once the initial steep climb out of Innsbruck was in the bag, the rest of the ascent was at a more comfortable gradient. After a few hours of toil, I reached the top. The pass is also the border between Austria and Italy, not that this matters much in these more enlightened times, unless of course you live in the place I was heading toward.

Right back at the outset I mentioned there was only one country more independence-seeking than Britain and – ta-daaah! – we've finally arrived there. Almost every province of Italy has some form of regionalist movement. This is hardly surprising. The nation in its totality was only cobbled together in the nineteenth century. On top of this, there's a campaign for the north as a whole to leave and, possibly as a reaction to this, one for the south too.

Crossing the border brought me to my next wannabe country or, in fact, two of them. The first was Padania, the northern movement I just mentioned. The name Padania wasn't generally used until 1996, when it was seized upon by the far-right Lega Nord, who want independence for the region. At the last election Lega Nord became Italy's third largest party, and in some areas of the north they're the largest of all. The land of Mussolini goose-steps to the right.

The real reason I was here was to see Südtirol, as it's called in this German-speaking region of Italy. Other Italians know it as Alto Adige, the English-speaking world as South Tyrol. This area, once belonging to Austria-Hungary, was annexed by Italy after the First World War. The locals never forgot, and many want to be reunited with Austria, a country I once heard described as "like a cross between Germany and Italy, y'know, all the fun of the Germans but with an Italian work ethic".

Thankfully, in recent years the more extreme agitators for the independence movement, those in the South Tyrolean Liberation Committee and in Ein Tirol, have stopped blowing up electricity stations and historical Italian monuments, but support for secession from Italy still runs at 46% for all people in this region, not just the German-speaking ones. Prodding the rattlesnake, Austria has recently angered Italy by offering citizenship to Südtiroleans. It's this trip's most credible independence movement since Catalonia.

Cycling down from the pass was fun. I did about ten miles on a great path before the Italian Rain Gods noticed my arrival and sent a watery greeting. I found a woodland campsite in Vipiteno, also known to the more Germanic locals as the less romantic-sounding Sterzing. Most towns around here have two names, with the one you choose depending upon your allegiance, in the same way Jeremy Corbyn is known as "the saviour of Britain" or "that Commie tit".

Dodging the showers that dogged the rest of the day I plundered a large local supermarket and was surprised just how unItalian everything felt. German was the language of choice. And to make matters more complicated, another tongue besides Italian is also spoken up here. Ladin, not to be confused with Latin, is a Romance language similar to Swiss Romansh. In the 2011 census, well over 20,000 Südtiroleans said Ladin was their native language. Europe is a lot more complicated than I could've imagined.

To hammer home that this area was more Austrian than Italian, I got the old assessment gaze from a local while I stood behind her in the campsite's reception. I remembered this well from my days of living in Graz, Austria's second city, back in the mid-nineties. It usually goes something like this: You're standing in a supermarket queue, your eyes wandering about the place in boredom. Suddenly you alight upon a middle-aged woman – it's always a woman and she's always middle-aged – who is looking over every aspect of your appearance. She's really going for it. Her eyeline moves upwards to inspect your head. Now, perhaps because I'm English, at this point I would avert my gaze. She wouldn't. And remaking eye contact does nothing to lessen her desire to judge you entirely. A braver, more gung-ho individual would have flipped her the bird. Or maybe given her the same treatment and then displayed a card saying "3/10".

*

At more than a hundred miles, today was the longest day of the ride so far, but it hardly felt like it as I slowly tumbled down the Alps towards the Venetian Plain. It wasn't all freewheeling though. The cycle path had an annoying habit of taking me up the valley sides to see tiny hamlets still sound asleep on this Sunday morning. Occasionally, one village would be conscious enough to make it to church. Dressed in their finery, and this still being Südtirol, women wore dirndls.

I'm not sure what difference independence would actually make. Everyone lived as though this were already Austria.

At Festung Franzensfeste, to give it its German name, and we probably should since everyone this far south was still speaking German, I found a café for breakfast and had a coffee and two heavenly flavoured croissants. Here I abandoned the flaky cycle path and stuck to the main road so that I had some hope of reaching my destination before my 300th birthday.

Around here, the road quality was awful unless it was a stretch that'd been recently resurfaced. This only seemed to happen though once a car had actually fallen through the tarmac, resulting in someone scratching his chin and then saying, "Mmm, yeah, we should probably do something about that."

Further down the hill I hit one of Italy's most beautiful villages. Its delicate Italian name, Chiusa, was much more fitting than the abrupt German Klausen. Here were more dirndls and, attractively, rose petals scattered liberally on its cobblestones. A castle sits on a high cliff surveying the narrow streets below.

I passed through the capital of Südtirol, Bolzano or Bozen, a thoroughly ordinary sort of place with ugly tower blocks, incongruous in such glorious surroundings. It was here in 1961 that Südtirolean separatists – terrorists or freedom-fighters, you choose – blew up thirty-seven electricity pylons in the Night of Fire, plunging Bolzano into darkness. If your aim is to present your cause to the wider world, turning off all the power seems like a counterproductive way of going about it.

I returned to the cycle path as the valley widened and the sheer cliff faces receded into the distance. Eventually, after one hundred miles, I reached the town of Trento with weary legs. The route here couldn't have been less direct. At one time or other I travelled on every single compass point.

Campsite options on the way had turned out to be fictitious or at least Brigadoon-like in their temporary invisibility, wild camping possibilities looked well-policed and so I found a cheap hotel, or what passes for a cheap hotel in expensive Italy.

At least it had a restaurant. With the budget already blown, I ordered and inhaled a meat pizza and a huge mixed salad. The happy waiter approached my table and its now empty plates.

"Game over?" he asked.

I smiled.

"Yes, game over."

He took my dishes away, but I hung around a while, slurping what remained of my wine. On the next table was a Dutch couple, also in the process of finishing up. The waiter walked up to them.

"Game over?" he asked again.

"What?"

Oh no. This wasn't supposed to happen. Having to explain the mechanics of a joke kills it. Maybe it was time to get another one.

As I sipped my wine I received a text. A deadline had now been introduced into my normally fluid schedule. On June 16th, twelve days from now, was my mate Damian's fiftieth birthday. I hadn't seen him for five years, and I promised to do my best to get to his Austrian home in time for the party. I just hadn't given the logistics much thought. He was seven hundred miles and, more worryingly, one and a third Everests away. And the weather forecast for the next week was miserable, but you'd probably guessed as much.

*

After thirty miles of riverside cycling, I waved Auf Wiedersehen to Südtirol and, still in Padania, entered yet another wannabe country. Veneto stretches from here to the other side of Venice, eighty miles away, and has some serious support for independence. A non-binding referendum in 2017 asked if the people of Veneto wanted out of Italy. With a turnout of 57.2%, a massive 98.1% said yes. Even if everyone who stayed home on voting day were anti-independence, that's still a majority decision for leaving. Like Catalonia, Veneto is the richest region within its own nation and their similarities perhaps don't end there. Maybe they both want out because they don't want to subsidise who they perceive as their "lazy" fellow countrymen. With its typical populist stance, the right wing Lega Nord has said as much. This philosophy, if taken to its limit, becomes every man for himself.

More hills appeared and, like Jacob Rees-Mogg to an offshore bank account, my bike path was drawn to them. I opted for the road until conned into rejoining the cycleway and was then sent down and around a vineyard, and then up and up and up some more. After what felt like months of this nonsense, I was ejected into a village with its sign telling me that Verona, today's target, was fourteen miles away. Yet another thunderstorm was brewing. Could I reach safety before it arrived?

The wind increased and the sky darkened, inducing an almost black 'n' white landscape that appropriately matched the opening "twister" scenes of the Wizard of Oz. I tore down the side of a canal as fast as I could and arrived in Verona dry. Well, apart from the copious sweating. My problem was that the campsite was up another very steep hill just outside the old town's ancient walls and, while pushing my bike up, the skies let rip a month's worth.

I'd visited Verona for an afternoon twenty years earlier, but rainy weather had spoiled that trip too. I'd been looking forward to seeing it in sunnier conditions. I suppose I'd just have to keep looking forward.

I set up my tent in the rain on the site's elegant but slightly claustrophobic walled lawns – it was inside part of an old castle – and then went to its small beer garden where a few others were drinking beneath umbrellas. I got talking to a Dutchman called Denis, who'd arrived here by van. He told me his life story in brief.

"When I was younger I was a hacker," he said. "But I got drunk and did something stupid. I brought down CNN's website."

"Wow."

"And then I got scared. I could be caught. So I decided to go into journalism. I thought I'd use it as an excuse to cover my hacking."

"Did it work?"

"No. I realised I couldn't actually write."

"Ah."

"So I set up a software security company. I figured that gave me a legitimate reason to hack. What about you?"

"I used to work in IT," I replied. "I didn't mind programming something new, but I hated fixing things. Especially when I hadn't put enough comments in my code."

Denis smiled.

"So you'd rather create things?" he asked.

"Yeah."

"I'd rather break them."

The weather eased and so I left Denis to smash the place up while I went to see what the rain had prevented me from seeing all those years ago.

I walked across the bridge over the River Adige that surrounds the old town on three sides. Feeling all Shakespearean, I headed for Juliet's house and the little courtyard that today hosted both her tiny balcony and fourteen billion Japanese tourists. At the far end is a bronze

91

statue of the doomed lover, one exposed breast especially shiny due to its constant fondling by visitors looking for good fortune. It's anyone's guess quite why it's considered lucky to grope someone who stabbed herself to death through the mistaken belief her bloke had snuffed it. Maybe it's not luck those tourists are after. Perhaps they just want to know, like Juliet, how to feel a right tit.

The walls of the passageway into the courtyard are dense with marker-pen declarations of love. The ones added on top of these, scrawled on to Post-It notes, don't seem so sincere.

The campsite had provided a town map for me to locate its other attractions. The guide warned me not to eat near monuments. I'd heard Venice had banned chowing down in its streets but could find nothing online to back up a similar prohibition here. Verona though *had* outlawed any new kebab shops from opening, or any outlets that primarily sold fried foods or *frito misto*, a staple of southern Italy. These were apparently "inauthentic". The map offered further advice: "Do not circulate naked". Fair enough. And there was also a weirder instruction: "Imbrattare e deturpare" had been translated as "Do not defeat and dehumidify". I had no intention of doing either.

After walking back up the million steps to the campsite, I sat outside its bar while someone practised cello from a nearby but hidden room. I'd no idea if they were any good or not, but it felt wonderfully cultured to be sitting in an old castle on a hilltop overlooking Verona's terracotta roofs while listening to such a classy musician. I almost ordered a vodka martini. I didn't though. I had a load of beer instead. You can take the boy out of Blackburn...

*

The road out of Verona was a bit hairy. Despite its supposed wealth, Veneto's highways were an order of magnitude crapper than Südtirol's, and there were no cycle paths here from which to escape them. Add into the mix a load of smelly, fume-belching trucks, and it felt more like how I remembered Moldova.

I'd kept today short, and I soon reached the loveliness of Vicenza's centre. Italy does its old bits very well. Many of the streets were arcaded, and its squares, unlike Verona's, devoid of tourists. I wasn't sure why it was so quiet. Perhaps there was simply too much competition from better known locations nearby, but this city is well worth a look.

The campsite was on the other side of town. Having had nothing to eat all day, I needed a source of food and so I asked the young woman on reception.

"Is there a supermarket nearby?"

"Pricks!" she said, taking me by surprise.

"Why? What's wrong with them."

It turned out the store was called Prix.

It'd been a hot day today. I wanted some ice cold beer, preferably at supermarket prices rather than inflated bar ones. Unfortunately, the silly Prix didn't have anything chilled.

The hunt continued to an out-of-town shopping centre. Mission accomplished, I returned to my bike as a well-dressed couple in their twenties were examining it and laughing. I didn't know if it was the shitness of the bicycle or the bright orangey-pinkness of my much unloved helmet that tickled them. Around these parts I'd only seen lids on professional-looking racing cyclists who rode bikes that cost more than your house. I tended to get a lot of derisory smirks.

Back at the site, I sank the beers while sitting on a picnic bench beneath a little canopy, one that came in very handy when another storm exploded above me and poured bucket after bucket of water from the sky. I remained trapped there for half an hour before deciding upon a splashy Do or Die dash back to the tent. This was France all over again.

Another day, another ancient town or two, another evening cloudburst. I spied pro-Veneto graffiti scrawled on a bus shelter while other cyclists openly sniggered at my helmet.

I'd recently read a magazine article suggesting places you should visit if you want to avoid an expensive touristic cliché but see somewhere similar and cheaper instead. Treviso was mentioned as an ersatz Venice and so I had high expectations. Sure enough I was setting myself up for a fall.

The cycleways into town were so overgrown I actually thought a tree had fallen over, but the entire path was like that. I managed to burrow all the way to the centre without seeing a single canal. Hell, Blackburn had more watercourses than this. Its buildings were attractive enough but, as sure as sea eggs are not eggs, it was no Venice. And then, as promised, with the ominous regularity I'd come to expect from Italy, the sky started to grumble. I jumped on to my phone and quickly booked the cheapest hotel I could find, a couple of miles from the centre. I felt a splash on my nose. My visit to Treviso was over before it'd begun. I legged it towards my bed for the night. I got close.

The skies unleashed the sort of rain that'd drown an elephant and so I hid beneath a shopping arcade's veranda. I knew I couldn't be far from my hotel, but the sheer quantity of water made the soaking my tech bag would surely receive too risky to leave my shelter. While waiting, I checked the weather forecast for the next couple of days and my heart sank. After half an hour, the worst of the misery subsided and I biked the 500 metres to my hotel, feeling stupid for having had to find refuge so close to my destination. A carrier bag wrapped around the tech bag was only effective in a shower. I needed a proper solution.

*

After three hours of easy but tedious cycling on the flat Venetian Plain, I turned a corner, realised I didn't know where I was and stumbled upon a non-motorway-situated Decathlon. A solution was at hand. As well as a mini-rucksack cover that fit over my tech bag perfectly, I bought another large rucksack cover for the one on my rack. From now on I wouldn't fear the rain. I'd still avoid a drenching wherever possible, but at least now nothing would get ruined. This was the set-up I'd have started with if I'd planned this thing properly.

And that was the highlight of the day. The second half of today's eighty miles didn't improve scenically. Showers sprinkled me as I rode. I passed fields of wheat and, since still early in the season, corn as high as an elephant seal's eye.

Approaching Aquileia, I realised I was on EuroVelo 8, the signposted route that stretches from Spain's Cádiz to Greece's Athens. Predictably, the number of bikers increased, and I nearly came to a halt behind a party of twenty elderly cyclists, who moved at such a crawl a couple of them actually fell off due to lack of momentum.

I'd now left Veneto and entered Friuli, the easternmost region of Italy. This province may or may not have an independence movement. It wasn't mentioned at all by the usually comprehensive Wannabe Bible, but Wiki's page entitled "List of active separatist movements in Europe" clearly states that independence is the aim of the Friulian Front, although since the party has never achieved more than 6% in any election it has stood for, it ain't gonna happen any time soon.

Road signs sometimes appeared in Friulian, the area's Romance tongue similar to Ladin, the language we met in Südtirol. One argument I've heard against a European superstate is that it could never accommodate so many different cultures and languages but, if I've learned anything on this trip, most of the countries I've cycled through – Spain, France and Italy – already manage this. It's only the monolingual who find foreign languages odd.

Although today Aquileia has only a population of 3,500, two thousand years ago it housed 100,000 and at that time was one of the world's largest cities. This, however, made it a target. In the fifth century, after numerous other attacks, Attila the Hun swept in and totalled the place. It wisely kept its head down after that.

*

A new language appeared today too. So close to another border was I that road signs were now shown in Italian *and* Slovene. We were moving from a world of Romance tongues to Slavic ones. From now on, more miming would be required.

There were two routes to this evening's campsite, one via the centre of Trieste and another more direct that stayed further north. But if Trieste was on the coast, why was I climbing so much? I arrived at the site and finally understood why. The campsite towered four hundred metres above the city. If I'd taken the other route here, I'd have finished today with a three-mile-long 20% hill climb. I met someone who'd done it like that. He looked close to death.

The only foodie option around here was the campsite restaurant, which involved choosing a dish from a shortlist barked in rapid Italiano. I latched on to the only words I'd understood, *spaghetti alle vongole*. I ate my pasta and drank wine under another leaky sky. I finished my food and, after a second incomprehensible linguistic exchange, thought I'd possibly ordered another course, perhaps a dessert, and so I waited, but nothing arrived. It didn't matter. It was just one of the joys of operating in a language you can't speak.

*

I'd originally decided to have a day off in Trieste, but there was no way I was going to cycle back up that massive hill. Plans were rejigged to find another site on the other side of the city and beyond, somewhere in Slovenia.

The ride down the hill was a breezy, winding descent. I swooped and soared like an eagle, a fat, soggy eagle. But this morning the sun was out, evaporating the drips of the previous week.

Trieste was an impressive place with large squares, one with its own canal that acted as a harbour for tiny fishing boats. Bright, grand buildings crowded around the edge of the piazzas and, outside one such edifice, a young couple were getting married. I wheeled around the centre, soaking up the Mediterranean atmosphere of one of Italy's most underrated cities.

I needed cash. The first ATM didn't offer any language options other than Italian. The second gave a range of languages provided you knew, or could guess, the Italian phrase for "Change Language". Luckily, I managed to switch to English or otherwise I may have inadvertently organised a mortgage or something.

Trieste was my final independence movement in Italy. The Movimento Trieste Libera campaigns for the Free Territory of Trieste, a sort of Athens-like city state, but no one is giving them much chance of success. Like a lot of weaker independence arguments, it relies heavily on "the good old days", a flawed concept, despite its appeal to the older generations. If you're aged forty plus, it's not true that the past – the fifties, sixties, seventies or whatever – were better than today. They just *seemed* better because back then we were young, and attractive people fancied us. And we could also get out of a chair without needing to form a plan of attack. Most of the rest of it was rubbish – the polio, two black 'n' white TV channels, The Nolans – and that's why we left it behind.

So, now you've witnessed five Italian independence campaigns with varying degrees of credibility, but that's not all Italy has to offer on the separatist front. Depending who you ask, there are perhaps twelve or thirteen more. It's a crumbly old continent. And no one knows more about recent independence movements than my next destination, former Yugoslavia.

Chapter 7: Anyone for Dormouse?

Istria, Free State of Fiume and Carinthia

Along a sparkling stretch of coastline I crossed another borderless border into Slovenia. I'd also arrived in Istria. Officially I'd entered this wannabe country a few miles back, somewhere just after Trieste, but it was difficult to know exactly where. It didn't matter. Only a tiny portion of Istria lies in Italy. The majority of its area is in the former Yugoslav states of Slovenia and especially Croatia.

Total Croatia News published an article shortly after the 2017 referendum in north-east Spain with the heading: *"Could Istria Follow Catalonia on Road to Independence?"* Since the answer to any newspaper headline posed as a question is almost always "...er, of course not", the media organisation pre-empted this with the first line of its article. "Not really, at least according to the Constitution."

But the story went on to state why independence might be a possibility, citing Istria's strong regional character and "its above average incomes". It's that every-man-for-himself thing again. Officially, even the Istrian Democratic Assembly, which dominates local politics, doesn't want independence. Still, there's an online campaign, and the Wannabe Bible rates its chances higher than any of the places I've visited so far except Catalonia, but only at 10%.

The thirty-mile coastline of Slovenia is, for the most part, utterly gorgeous. I could forgive the ugliness of the ring of container storage parks around Koper once I'd arrived in the 25,000-strong town itself, sitting today on a sparkling Mediterranean. Its red roofs cluster around an attractive harbour. Backstreets are paved and narrow, crammed with houses prettified by sky blue shutters. It was a fine place to wander around.

Titov Trg is its small Venetian central square named in honour of Yugoslavia's Communist dictator, Tito, who ruled for twenty-seven years. In most countries it's unusual to find a street or monument still celebrating its erstwhile authoritarian leaders, but Tito was a shade more likeable than most. That said, as writer Venko Markovski knew only too well, the dictator could condemn you to five years' hard labour on a barren prison island if he didn't like your poetry. That must have been one hell of an offensive limerick.

There were a couple of dishes from this region I was particularly looking out for, especially as they'd be difficult to recreate at home. The first was *neretvanski brodet*, or fish, eel and frog stew. The second was another stew, *obara*, this time made with dormouse. Yes, you read that correctly. Slovenia has a history of dormouse hunting. I don't know about you, but that summons up a peculiar mental image, one of a pack of men on horseback pursuing a solitary rodent across a Tesco's car park.

"I've got another one, Ivo!"

"Where is it?"

"It's stuck to the bottom of the hoof again."

I was more successful in my hunt for a special frozen dairy product. The internet had told me about a parlour that sold rose flavour ice cream, as well as the weird-sounding combo of pineapple, cucumber and parsley. The latter wasn't available today and so I opted for a scoop of rose with another of pomegranate, and lovely they were too.

I continued onwards with the sea on my right and arrived in Izola, its centre almost indistinguishable from Koper. If you want to see a pretty Italian harbour town without paying stupid Italian prices, come to this often overlooked stretch of coastline. Even in mid-June tourist numbers weren't high and you can get a beer for half the cost of its neighbour. It's the Happy Hour that never ends.

After exploring the town I returned to my campsite and had a drink on its café's terrace. A dozen or so customers were scattered around. I took a table to myself in the corner, away from the others, a decision I'd soon regret. A fat old man set up some loudspeakers, MIDI gear and his electric accordion right in front of me. Anyone just arriving would assume I was his sole groupie.

He started to play a terrible sort of electronic oompah music, making frequent eye contact with me because nobody else would. He finished his first tune to total silence. He looked at me pleadingly. I clapped politely, thereby making an even bigger dick of myself, and a few others joined in. During his next number he started to croon horribly. I lasted three songs and then had to get out of there.

Back at my tent I met Mike and Helen, a young, recently married couple, who'd given up their jobs and set off from Gloucestershire, hoping to cycle as far as China. We went out for a few beers and snacks. Although they'd visited similar places to me, albeit a few days either before or after, they'd had glorious weather all the way. Perhaps the global climate wasn't collapsing as I'd assumed. Maybe I was just cursed. Anyway, we got on well and had a laugh, but I was fairly certain that Helen's opinion of me changed overnight.

*

I don't snore often, but I definitely did last night, because I even woke myself up a couple of times. And the Izola campsite jammed its visitors' tents close together. In the morning a groggy Helen looked like she'd had no sleep at all. Of course, that may not have been my fault. They were recently married after all. She disappeared somewhere while I packed up and then bade farewell to Mike.

"Don't leave yet," he said. "Helen'll want to say goodbye to you too."

I doubted it, but we went a-searching and found her

asleep on the sea wall. So Mike woke her up again. That was definitely my fault.

Today I'd leave this beautiful corner of Slovenia and cross into Croatia, the first use of my passport on this adventure, though no one at the border even glanced at it. It was also a temporary goodbye to the money I'd carried around since I'd started. It's not until you have to repeatedly convert currencies every few days that you appreciate just what a wonder the euro is.

Croatian Istria is a lumpy old place, and with the weather now stinking hot, all thoughts of Italy's rain were forgotten. I cycled through pristine vineyards on entirely empty lanes. It was a world away from the country's crowded resorts. My surroundings looked like Tuscany after an epidemic that had wiped out humanity.

Today I'd planned to get as far as Pazin, Istria's capital, almost at the geographical centre of the Istrian peninsula, but I quit in Motovun, an impressive hilltop town whose origins date from the first century. If Pazin is the actual capital of this region, Motovun is its truffle capital. While Italy's Alba is globally renowned for its truffles, with ones sourced there commanding the highest price, often those found here in Motovun are secretly shipped to Alba in order to increase their value. As a result of this illicit trade, no one is making much of an attempt to raise the profile of Istria's lower rent truffle.

The snack bar beside the pricey and frankly shoddy campsite sold a range of truffle-infused goodies. Because the little balls of fungus are a lot cheaper here than elsewhere they can be used more frivolously. I opted for a cheese and ham toastie. Yes, with truffles. I'd never had them before, and I can't say they blew me away, unlike the reviewer of a local restaurant who claimed her few shavings had induced an orgasm. Truffles got filed in the mental category of

103

"expensive things rich people bang on about that are at best merely adequate", like caviar and champagne. That said, maybe cheese and ham toasties aren't the optimal way to showcase their strengths.

After lunch I cycled up the steep hill to visit the ancient village, the job made more difficult when the tarmac turned to cobblestones. Geckos scurried out of my way into the roadside walls. A lazy cricket hitched a ride, clinging to my handlebars.

Once I reached the top, the old town had a similar number of tourist shops to those traps I'd seen on the way here, such as Spain's Peñiscola and France's Colmar, but without anything like the quantity of visitors. Dozens of stores sold local wine and truffle-based products. The truffle display bottles outside the shops were always empty in case a passing gentleman thief.

If you wanted to see the best views from the village you had to buy a ticket to visit the town's south-facing walls. Except that you didn't, because if you descended about three metres to the local car park you got exactly the same amazing vista for free. Motovun's profiteers must be really angry that they can't charge you to look at some stuff that doesn't belong to them.

In town is the Kaštel Hotel, whose slogan is "up on the hill", because that's where it is. Its brochure includes the line: "Twenty-eight rooms, one stylishly furnished". Presumably, the other twenty-seven are just awful.

*

I'd thought today's was a relatively short ride to Rijeka, but through bad planning on my part and a ridiculously restrictive road policy on Croatia's, it became eighty miles with 2,500 metres of climbing. The whole thing took me eleven sweaty hours and at the end of it I was knackered.

The hills began early. I could still feel the tiredness of

104

yesterday's arduous ride in my legs. It was up and down all the way to Pazin, Istria's capital, a friendly if unmemorable town, with lots of cafés surprisingly full of locals for eleven o'clock on a Monday morning. It's a dot of a place. Only 9,000 people live here and so it lacks the grandeur of most capitals I've visited. Still, when Istria becomes independent, maybe you'll come here for a city break. Bring a good book.

Cycling out of Pazin, I followed a lonely lane that, to begin with, shadowed a flat main road before I was carried off into the hills. My track climbed and fell even more than yesterday's roller coaster ride and contained no bars nor shops nor that many houses. After several tortuous ascents I found myself near the main road again, and it looked a lot more enjoyable than my current hillfest. It was only midday, but I was already pooped. I scrambled over the barrier on to the road. From now on it'd be easy. Traffic on the single carriageway was fast but very light, and I had a wide shoulder. It was as safe as a road could be. I crossed three or four massive valleys on modern, towering bridges in the space of a few short miles. The fifteen minutes I'd spent on this stretch would have taken at least two hours on the old lane. I'd made up my mind. I'd definitely stay on this road all the way to Rijeka!

In a lay-by just up ahead stood two young fellas behind a car. They flagged me down. Maybe they're lost, I thought. But they weren't. They were police.

"You need to leave this road at the next turn-off," one of them said. "This is a highway."

It'd looked like a normal road to me, albeit with some amazing bridges. Oh well.

Back on the crap, older track, the hills continued. I was running low on water, despite starting with four litres. And then came a mountain.

The next three miles were at a gradient of 16%. It would

have been tough in any conditions, but at 30 °C I was a sweat-soaked mess. My leather sandals became slimy and slippery, which didn't help. In fact, they nearly prevented me from getting to the top at all. I pushed the bike from the shade of one tree to another. A shiny black snake slithered out of my way as I tipped my brains from my helmet.

Exhausted, I reached the top. A million miles below, I could see the city of Rijeka sitting on the coast. At least, I thought, it'd all be downhill from here. As I descended, the quiet roads thickened with traffic, dangerously so as I approached the centre. It was like cycling through Monaco on the day of the Grand Prix.

I was starving. It was five o'clock and I'd only had a five minute peanut break all day. I found a supermarket and bought two *burek*, that flaky stuffed pastry available everywhere from here to Turkey. One was filled with cheese, the other with spiced mince and mashed potato. They were both heavenly, but, to be honest, I was so hungry I would've enjoyed a battered badger.

I thought today's work was done, with the campsite just the other side of this flat seaside town. Rijeka looked like a cross between two famous coastal cities, the easy glamour of Nice and the studied squalor of Naples. This was yet another wannabe country. Rijeka has in the past gone under the name of the Free State of Fiume. I could find almost nothing online regarding a current bid for independence, but the Wannabe Bible rated its chances at least as highly as Alsace, Andalusia and Valencia. Let's just say it ain't imminent.

Approaching the other side of Rijeka I hit a tunnel I wasn't allowed to enter. Surely I was going to have to turn around, but a road worker called me over to say that if I could get my bike up the large concrete staircase beside the tunnel, my onward route would be unobstructed. I'd been reading about Shackleton's Antarctic expeditions. Whenever his dogs were too weak or the ice too soft, they had to remove gear from their sledges and go backwards and forwards, relaying their equipment. Shackleton would have got his bicycle up these steps.

I decided on a simpler approach. I pushed the bike fully-loaded one step at a time in individual quick bursts of energy. This worked well for the first four flights of stairs, but then the bungeed rucksack fell off the back, and a bottle of water that had been tucked inside rolled all the way to the bottom. I retrieved the bottle and then continued in a more Shackletonesque manner, carrying each item to the next platform and then fetching the bike. Eventually, I reached the top, an endeavour that, had it been televised, would surely have earned me an OBE just like Shackleton.

I thought today's effort was nearly done, but no. The road out of town went uphill and around a huge bay that stank of petrochemicals. I'd expected another six easy miles or so at the most. I ended up doing three times that distance on tarmac that was anything but flat. Never had I been happier to finally arrive at a campsite.

*

Had I not been rushing to my mate Damian's birthday bash, I'd have taken a day off today, especially as I knew the next few hours would be almost as hilly as yesterday. If I wanted to party with friends, shirking wasn't allowed, and I definitely wanted to party with friends.

Leaving the coast of Croatia behind signalled the end of tourist Europe. With one or two notable exceptions, the rest of this tour would involve the sort of places visitors rarely go, and this excited me enormously.

Fortune favours the brave. I had two options this morning. One was a two and a half hour slog back to Rijeka and a similar time to get me up and over the first of today's big hills. The second option was a sneaky back road suggested by

107

my mapping app, the one that had got me lost up that killer climb in the Black Forest. Let's give it a go.

The steep track started with unrideable but easily pushable tarmac. This deteriorated first to gravel and then to grass. The lane narrowed, thorn-covered trees crowding me on both sides and cutting out today's bright sunlight. I was beginning to lose faith in my chosen path. I remembered a line from my Shackleton book about a short cut often being the longest route.

Just as on the steps by the tunnel in Rijeka, the path got so steep the rucksack fell off the back of the bike. I took a moment to do some serious despairing. But then came a short blob of tarmac as the lane passed beneath a tall motorway bridge, and I popped out on a quiet road high above the coast. By choosing the dodgy option, I'd shaved three hours off today's ride. At the first café I saw, I stopped for an espresso, an orange juice and a little inner gloat.

I still had more hills to conquer, but these were on decent surfaces with little traffic and through thick forests that occasionally opened up to offer breathtaking views of the countryside around. I continued onwards, out of Croatia and back into Slovenia. Hugging both the Kupa river and the border, I cycled beside a serious-looking razor-wire perimeter fence at the very edge of Schengen Europe.

After a pleasant hour on a car-free lane, through flowers and fruit trees and clouds of butterflies, I arrived at the hamlet of Dol and its campsite. I was the only person camping there tonight, a trend that would continue for the rest of Slovenia. Surely I didn't smell *that* bad.

*

Over the next three days I headed northwards through Slovenia. The only nod to an independence movement was about ten miles to the east. A group of Poles, including a man called Kamil Wrona, spotted what they believed to be an oversight. When the Slovenian and Croatian borders crystallised after the war in the nineties, one tiny region had been left seemingly unclaimed by either side, and in that territory lay a single house. Kamil bought the property and christened the previously unclaimed land as the Kingdom of Enclava, another example of a micronation, and took the unassuming title of King Enclav I.

In an article in the Daily Mirror, one of the co-founders, Piotr Wawrzykiewicz, said Enclava had been founded to "create a place where everyone, regardless of skin colour, religion or nationality, will be able to express their opinions, study for free, and earn money without worrying about taxes". Quite where they were going to find all these teachers willing to work for nothing wasn't mentioned.

Unfortunately for Kamil and pals, Slovenia said he was mistaken about the ownership of the area and that it actually belonged to them. So the group upped sticks and moved their kingdom to another piece of unclaimed land, this time on the banks of the Danube and way out of reach of this bike ride.

The route was hilly. None of the three days saw me climb less than a thousand metres. Campsites were unoccupied, at least when I arrived. Sometimes people drifted in later. In an empty field near Novo Mesto a van turned up late, a tent was set up and then the couple inside got down to long and very squeaky sex. I couldn't know that for sure. Maybe it was a bloke by himself doing something obscene to a dog chew toy.

The scenery was pretty throughout, with occasional forays into vineyards. One highlight was the town of Laško, the home of Slovenian beer since 1825. Here, by a brown river, the boxy Laško brewery dominates, out of place amongst the greenery of the surrounding hills, but it was nice to have a pint in the spot where it's made.

In town was also the Elvis Bakery. I'd hoped I'd have to make a themed selection, y'know, perhaps choosing between a *Shake, Rattle and Sausage Roll*, or a *Jailhouse Rock Cake*, or maybe even a *You Ain't Nothing But a Hot Dog*, but the Presley connection went no further than the name. They didn't even sell deep-fried peanut butter and jelly sandwiches.

*

I drifted silently into Austria after a long day. As well as being in a state of exhaustion, I was also in the state of Carinthia, the only independence movement within the borders of Austria, according to the Wannabe Bible, although its time seems to have passed.

Far-right Jörg Haider was once leader of the Freedom Party, a political organisation that cared less about freedom for Carinthia and, with its frequently racist campaigning, more about Austria's freedom from non-white people. That said, he famously declared, "My dream is Carinthia's independence!" Haider died in a car crash in 2008, and his dream died with him.

I know someone who met Haider during the course of her work and, despite hating his politics, she described him as unbelievably charming. With Austria's track record of generating charismatic right-wingers, maybe the world dodged a bullet there.

It was the morning of the 16th, the day of Damian's party, and his house was only forty miles away. Unfortunately, I hadn't reckoned on a 1,350 metre hill obstructing my path. But a desire to see old friends and get myself incoherently merry inspired my weary legs.

The climb out of Lavamünd, last night's base, saw some stunning views. The Drava snaked through a rich green landscape. Austria is effortlessly beautiful.

I reached the top and rolled down the other side. The road was full of black, paper-plane-shaped butterflies, white polka dots on their wings, just lying there trying to commit suicide beneath my wheels. I tried my best to avoid them but occasionally they'd aligned themselves in such a way that by missing one I squashed another. Maybe Austria is the Dignitas for winged insects.

At the bottom I needed sustenance. Outside a bakery in Eibiswald, a sixteen-year-old approached. He was unusually impressed by my useless bike.

"Echt cool!" he said, followed by a bunch of stuff in Styrisch, the incomprehensible local dialect that sounds like a dog barking. The lad clearly knew less about bicycles than I did.

"Nein. Es ist scheisse!" I replied.

It was nice to be speaking German again after the linguistic isolation of Italy, Croatia and Slovenia. Swearing was just a bonus.

A mostly flat twenty miles got me to Damian's house. It was great to see his big smily face again. I gave him his birthday present, a bottle of Slovenian plum brandy, and the rest of the day gladly sank into a fug of good beer, tasty food, familiar faces, happiness and talking utter bollocks.

I was now halfway through my journey. And while there were fewer independence movements farther east, they were more serious, definitely edgier, sometimes even deadly. From now on it was former Iron Curtain countries all the way. After tame and occasionally dull western Europe, this was the bit I was most looking forward to.

Chapter 8: Eastern European Slagheap Adventures

Southern Slovakia, Moravia, Kingdom of Wallachia, and Czech Silesia

I had two utterly bald tyres. Before leaving Austria, I popped into a bike shop in Graz and was surprised to see Schwalbe Marathons, the almost unpuncturable thinner tyres I'd used on all my previous rides. In my excitement at seeing them, I forgot that one of the reasons I'd originally opted for this mountain bike and its thicker wheels was to handle the crappy roads further east, and so now, just as I was about to cross that border, I swapped thick for thin. If I'd started with Schwalbe Marathons back in April, it would've made the first half of the journey a damn sight easier. I'm a moron.

After two days of riding eastwards, I arrived at the Hungarian border. Remember Renata, the cyclist I stayed with in Spain? She'd been in touch again to say she was now back here in her homeland and, if I liked, she'd meet me en route at one of her friend's homes, and we could camp in her garden. I was given directions to the house in Csorna and Renata would be there when I arrived. Except she wasn't.

Apparently Renata had suffered a puncture and would be a while yet. Waiting for me though was Zsuzsanna and her husband Zoltán, their two teenage kids and loveable Labrador Missy, and charming hosts they were too.

Zsuzsi's English was excellent. Years earlier, when she'd arrived in Felixstowe to work as an au pair, she couldn't speak a word. Now she was an English teacher.

Renata finally rolled up to the house.

"You look tired," was the first thing she said.

A mirror told me she was right. In my defence I'd cycled three thousand miles and up nearly six Everests since I'd last seen her two months earlier.

Renata had brought me some presents: a jar of her mum's

cherry jam, a good luck Saint Christopher and a bottle of home-made *pálinka*, the delicious and impressively alcoholic Hungarian fruit brandy. That was very kind of her, especially the booze.

We had a tasty meal sitting in their large garden while Renata and Zsuzsi caught up. They hadn't seen each other for years. I noticed a packet of butter on the table, and butter in Hungarian is 'vaj'. Inevitably, the conversation came around to swearing in foreign languages and I mentioned I liked that the Hungarian word for 'cheese' is pronounced 'shite'.

After the meal, Renata and I set up our tents in the garden. As the sky darkened I gathered the family together and took a photo of them with Renata.

"Say cheese! I said.

With big smiles, everyone shouted simultaneously. "Shiiiiiiiite!"

*

Renata was going to cycle with me today. This trip was her first since she'd finished her mammoth ride a few months before, and she'd lost a bit of fitness. By the time we reached Komárom sixty miles later, she was feeling it and just wanted to sleep it off.

There's no point in being in a new town if you aren't going to explore it – unless perhaps it's Benidorm – and so I went out alone. To be honest, Komárom was a bit of a hole. Cycling through the centre earlier, Renata had described it as feeling like a communist hangover, but to suffer a hangover you first need some overindulgent merriment, and there seemed precious little of that around here.

I eventually found a bar. Peering through its thick lace curtains from outside, I could see a lone drinker pacing angrily about the place, looking like he was spoiling for a fight. I gave it a miss.

Back at the campsite a distant storm was brewing. I

watched it from the entrance of my tent, wrapped in my sleeping bag. The wind howled and lightning flashed on the horizon. And then, with wearying predictability, the rain came down.

*

Renata's original plan had been to cycle off to see her sister today, but she wanted to show me a Hungarian speciality first, although we'd have to cross the border into Slovakia to find it. In doing so we'd enter a badly defined wannabe country called Southern Slovakia or *Felvidék*. This is the chunk that was torn from Hungary after it lost the First World War and still has a Hungarian majority today. Everywhere north of the Danube around these parts was given away to what is now Slovakia. Felvidék is to Hungary what Südtirol is to Austria. Rather than seeking independence in its own right, its residents would simply prefer to be reunited. And just like when entering Südtirol, you really don't feel like you've changed countries when you go there.

The town of Komárom was particularly affected by the post-war split as the city straddled the Danube and was therefore sliced in two. The Slovakian half became known as Komarno. Until 2007, when both nations joined the EU's Schengen Area, there was a passport control between the two halves. It must have been a pain to deal with border checks each time you wanted to go out for a pint with your mates on the other side of town.

A while back, the city of York made a big song and dance about being the first place ever to be twinned with itself when it entered into a partnership with Jorvik, its tenth-century Norse name. Yeah, weird. It must've been difficult to do student exchanges without a time machine. But in any case, York wasn't the first. Komárom and Komarno had already beaten them to it years earlier.

Renata told me how disenfranchised Hungarians, those

115

forced to live outside Hungary here and in another place we'll meet later, behave more Hungarian than the folk back in Hungary itself, more frequently wearing the traditional costumes and sticking more closely to older customs. Acting Hungarian was a more important part of their identity precisely because they no longer lived in their ancient home.

"I'm disgusted that we have to go to Slovakia to buy *lángos*," Renata said.

Lángos is as Hungarian as you can get, but unfortunately they weren't available on the south side of the river.

"Yeah, but you said these people are more Hungarian than the Hungarians. So maybe it's even more appropriate to get one from there."

She seemed satisfied with that.

We crossed the Elizabeth Bridge over the Danube and entered both Slovakia and Felvidék. Komarno, the Slovakian half, had fared better than Komárom since the split. It even had some pubs.

Down a backstreet we hunted out a lángos emporium we'd located via the internet. As well as a café it was also a takeaway. Despite being early in the morning, customers queued at a hatch in the street. Five or six people were already standing in line. We went inside instead. Several tables were occupied by lone men, who nursed small glasses of colourless high octane liquid. Aside from Renata and the kitchen staff, there were no other women in here.

The room was dim and dingy but charmingly so. Its panelling didn't allow much reflected light. Cheap chairs sat beneath little wooden tables covered in dark green cloth. The walls were plastered in ancient boxing memorabilia. A small pile of old magazines lay on a shelf in the corner. Things looked like they hadn't changed in years, and that included the prices. A wall chart listed what was available. A glass of local hooch, Borovička, would set you back 53p, and a small glass of wine half that. If you were considering a new career as an alcoholic but were worried about the costs, you should probably come here.

A serving hatch opened on to the room and provided a glimpse into the kitchen. Three middle-aged women worked in a production line, manufacturing lángos to order. The first took a ball of dough and rolled it out to the size of a small plate. The second shallow-fried this in oil until it puffed up and was lightly crisped. The final woman covered it in a layer of garlic butter and then added a large dollop of sour cream and a good sprinkling of Cheddar-like cheese before delivering it through the hatch to a salivating punter.

I popped out to check the bikes were still locked to their railing and noticed the queue outside had lengthened, with more people turning up by the minute. The place was open from Monday to Saturday, from six in the morning until nine at night. Only on Sunday mornings was it closed. Food-wise, all it produced were lángos. Slight variations on the toppings were available, but the one described above is the classic. The business was a real money spinner, even when lángos cost only around 90p each.

Renata asked the women how many they made every day.

"Probably not a thousand, but not far off," came the answer.

Lángos are a guilty pleasure, Renata told me, the sort of thing you'd more usually chow down on at the beach or a funfair. Komarno clearly didn't care about such conventions. Let's eat 'em now, and lots of 'em! While munching your way through one, you know it probably isn't doing you much good, except filling a hole, but you should do it anyway. They're very tasty.

We went outside and climbed back on the bikes. On the way to the café the town centre had eluded us and so now we decided to ask for directions. And that's when we met Péter.

"Don't ask me anything," Péter told Renata. "I'm a Hungarian nationalist, and once I start I can't stop."

Never has a human been more self-aware. What followed was a lecture delivered in million-mile-an-hour Hungarian.

Péter was a big fella, in his fifties, with short, grey hair. He wore a bright white sweatshirt and black tracksuit bottoms. Expressive arm gestures were not for him. His hands remained tucked into the back of his trackie bottoms throughout.

Renata looked physically drained by the quantity and emotion of Péter's speech. She would occasionally ask a short question and he'd be off again, giving a ten minute answer. His topics ranged from local history to the tragic treatment of Hungarians at the hands of the Nazis, to conspiracy-based nonsense like how the Jews control everything, and how the British royal family are lizards. I nodded sarcastically at this last point and won a finger-breaking handshake and a slap on the back that loosened a couple of teeth.

One admission was that he, Péter, who'd been born here in Komarno, was more Hungarian that Renata, who hails from firmly inside Hungary's current borders. This obsession with degrees of nationality is a form of madness.

"How many of the people in Komarno are Hungarian?" I asked.

"Seventy or eighty per cent," he replied quickly. And then he smiled. "The rest are Hungarian too, but they've forgotten their heritage."

Péter invited us back into the café for more conversation, lángos and drinks, but by this stage Renata's brain was fried. We thanked him for the chat, one-sided though it was. He gave me a huge hug and kissed me on both cheeks. If I'd been a fellow Hungarian, he might have even slipped in a tongue.

We cycled into the centre of town, stumbling upon The Courtyard of Europe. This was a colourful surprise amidst

Komarno's greyness. A central fountain is surrounded on all sides by buildings of different architectural styles, one for each of the nations of Europe. The architects were obviously aiming for an arresting rather than a strictly accurate national representation. The Spanish and English buildings looked like nothing I'd seen in either country, but it didn't matter. The square had a pleasant atmosphere and felt like it had been constructed purely to lure in tourists but very few turned up today. In fact, the whole of Komarno felt under-peopled. The streets of the pedestrianised town centre contained dozens of shops but almost zero customers. It was quieter than a Gary Glitter comeback gig.

One of those shops sold bicycle parts. Renata needed to fix a problem and so we popped in. Once done, we asked the staff for a recommendation for lunch. A customer in his late twenties, a local lad called Jo, told us there was a very special bean soup to be found at a restaurant in the fortress at the edge of town. He had time to spare before picking up his daughter from school and so, like a food-focussed Tenzing Norgay, would lead us there.

After a circuitous tour of Komarno, we arrived. This incarnation of the fortress was built in the seventeenth century and at the time was one of the most modern in Europe. A lot of it is still exceptionally well-preserved, although originally its walls surrounded the entire town. The Communists' destructive tendencies were responsible for the missing bits.

We entered the restaurant. The place looked quite classy, like it'd be expensive, the only other guests well-dressed, unlike ourselves. Within seconds, two large bowls of soup arrived, a red-brown goulash colour with cured sausages poking through the surface, a blob of sour cream on top. They each came with a long, thin strip of freshly made garlic bread to dunk. I had a slurp. It was divine, a tasty, hearty, warming

119

dish of goodness, despite being put together from very basic ingredients. The soup is named after Mór Jókai, a local writer, who supposedly caused its creation. At the back end of the nineteenth century he'd stormed into a Budapest hotel kitchen.

"I want a soup made from the best of what you've got!" he famously demanded.

"Soz, fella," presumably came the reply. "We've only got beans and a bit of old sausage"

"That'll do. I'm starving!"

After lunch, Jo took us on a tour of the town's existing walls, including a place with cave-like hollows he said now often shelters the homeless. He greeted each person we passed like a friend.

"Do you know everyone in Komarno?" Renata asked him.

"There are only 35,000 people here. Of course I know everyone," he replied seriously.

We arrived at his daughter's kindergarten and said goodbye to Jo, thanking him for his guidance and kindness. Minutes later, it was also time to say farewell to Renata as she headed for the station. After weeks of limited human contact followed by a riot of sociability – Damian's party, staying with friends near Graz, the hospitality of Zsuzsanna and Zoltán and two days with Renata – I was, as before, all alone. I hope our paths cross again in the future.

I popped back into town and to the Courtyard of Europe. Jo had described this place as attempting to be like Disneyland, on a smaller scale obviously, and it did all feel wonderfully fake. The touristic aspirations of this place, as well as the unfortunate reality, could be summed up with a single image. An electric tourist train drove repeatedly around the streets. There were no visitors on it, just the same bloke sitting right behind the driver, probably a friend of his, going around and around in circles.

Slovakia is famous for having some cracking scenery, but the west of the country is not where it's at. Today I basically stayed on the same quiet lane all day, fields of corn on one side and sunflowers on the other. After fifty miles I arrived at a campsite a long way from anywhere. There was no one on reception and no other campers. I could hear noises coming from the site's restaurant and went inside. Three blokes and a woman, all staff members, were watching a FIFA World Cup football match. There were no customers. The woman peeled away from the football crowd and spoke to me in English.

"Can I help you?" she said.

"Yeah, I want to camp. Where do I pay?"

She thought for a second.

"This week it's free."

Eh? After setting up my tent, I came to the conclusion the campsite was officially closed. Some workmen were rebuilding distant parts of the site. I think they let me stay for nothing because it was kinder than turning me away.

With entertainment light on the ground tonight and the Germany-Sweden World Cup game about to kick off, I tried my luck again at the restaurant. This time the English speaker had vanished, but two blokes stood up as I entered. Pre-emptive Google translations eased my entry.

"Futbal?" I said in my best Slovak accent, which is surprisingly similar to my Blackburn accent.

One of them held up a pint glass. I hadn't googled the Slovakian word for "yes" and so I just nodded and smiled. Beer arrived. This speaking foreign languages lark is a piece of piss.

*

On a fifty-mile day cycling through untidy villages, the most notable thing to happen was the realisation my bike would require some more attention. The bottom bracket, the device connecting the pedal cranks, had started to get a bit crunchy. That wasn't a good sign.

Arriving in Piešt'any, a town of 30,000, I found a campsite that, uniquely for this trip, had its own aviary, containing about a dozen depressed budgies. Their collective noun may well be a chatter of budgerigars, but none of them was talking. Despite a plumage of a thousand colours, one particularly fat bird looked like he wanted to end it all. He was struggling to tie the noose with his tiny beak.

It had started to rain and so setting up the tent would have to wait. Fortunately, the campsite had what was described as a restaurant, although no food other than crisps was on offer. Inside the prefab stood just two tables, a scattering of chairs and a television showing the England-Panama game. Before the game, I'd promised myself a pint for each goal we scored. It turned out to be England's biggest ever World Cup victory. I don't remember the final result. Everything went a bit fuzzy after we scored our fifth.

*

I cycled out of town keeping an eye out for the bike repair shop the campsite owner had told me about, but nothing materialised. The bottom bracket would have to wait. It was probably fine anyway. The crunching had stopped. Maybe the bicycle fairies had mended it overnight.

A lonely cycle on a rough path that cried out for mountain bike tyres brought me to the village of Čachtice. Here sits the ruins of a castle once home to the world's most enthusiastic female serial killer. Her story blurs the line between truth and myth.

After her husband's death in 1604, Elizabeth Bathory went a touch off the rails, morphing, according to some, into a lesbian vampire feasting on the life-giving blood of virgins. Servants were tortured and murdered for minor misdemeanours. When abusing her staff stopped being fulfilling enough, she started to lure young women from the surrounding villages and had her deadly fun with them instead. Being smart cookies, once the locals had each lost a daughter or two they got wise to this and so she opened an etiquette school for young ladies, presumably with instruction on how to walk properly, use the correct cutlery at dinner and take a dagger in the forehead without squealing. It was amazing it took everybody so long to figure out what was happening. In 1610, local authorities descended upon her castle and found a number of young women dead or dying. It's believed she may have killed up to six hundred. Her next church visit was going to be interesting.

"Do you have anything to confess, my child?"

"Errm, yeah, how long have you got?"

Today, as I cycled through the village, a teacher led a procession of young children up the castle's path. Some people never learn.

I continued on my way, and the crunches and clanks of the bottom bracket appeared just as I rolled into Trenčín, the prettiest place I'd seen so far in Slovakia. Here was another castle, a spooky Dracula-esque one up on the hill in its centre, but that's not the town's only nod to horror. There are fun attractions like the plague monument, a tall column to mark the general itchiness that arrived here in 1710, and there's also the executioner's house. I bet he didn't get invited to many parties.

*

The next morning I was in a café waiting for my bike to be fixed. I'd found a repair shop on the edge of Trenčín. I begrudged spending any more money on this knackered machine, especially since it wouldn't be coming home with me at the end of the ride. The cost of its air fare and inevitable post-tour overhaul would amount to more than I'd originally paid for it. I returned to the shop at the specified time. The mechanic picked up my deceased bottom bracket and simply said, "Katastrofa!"

I was temporarily heading out of Slovakia and into the Czech Republic, now also officially known as Czechia, and before the end of today I'd experience two more wannabe countries.

It was still early morning. Hunting for some breakfast from a village near the border, I parked the now non-clanking bike outside a small supermarket. Apparently, it was beer o'clock, because in Slovakia any time is beer o'clock. Two workmen in bright orange hi-vis were standing near the counter downing lagers while an old duffer gassed away to the woman on the till. While waiting, I noticed they sold a local energy drink called Semtex. That must be bloody difficult to export.

I crossed the border through an endless forest and headed for Valašské Klobouky, a town of 5,000 people and the capital of the Kingdom of Wallachia, a micronation created by photographer Tomáš Harabiš as a way to promote tourism in the area. Bolek Polívka, a Czech comedian, was crowned King Boleslav I in 1997. When Polívka demanded payment for his services, Harabiš refused. It ended in court and King Boleslav was deposed. Even in fantasy nations, politics rarely runs smoothly.

In the town's main square I saw a notice board and thought it might provide me with some information about the Kingdom. And maybe it did, but it wasn't what I was expecting. On the notice board glass – importantly, on the *inside* of the notice board glass – were two stickers, one saying *Fuck Off EU Terror!* and the other *Fuck Off Islam!* Is this the Kingdom's official policy?

This area is also part of Moravia, an area covering most of the eastern third of Czechia. This too is a wannabe country, but like the vast majority of breakaway regions in Spain and

France, enthusiasm for the project is minimal. Independence is the goal of Moravané, a political party that has never come close to winning a seat in the Czech parliament. Their finest moment, and not a particular fine one at that, came when they illegally organised a march in Moravia's capital, Brno, but it only attracted forty people, all party members, and was in any case stopped by the police. The Kingdom of Wallachia has more chance of being taken seriously.

The Czech Republic feels just a touch wealthier and better maintained than Slovakia, but Czechia continues its neighbour's love of the semi-naked woman as a device to sell absolutely anything. You can sort of excuse an excess of female skin when advertising hot tubs, but it's less appropriate for the one I saw today, an ad for wheelchairs.

After seventy frequently rainy miles, I arrived in a mouthful of a town, Rožnov pod Radhoštěm, and found a campsite that immediately sent a shiver down my spine. The place was absolutely crawling with kids. It was like *Children of the Corn*.

At the site's restaurant I got too clever for my own good. From menus I'd seen on previous visits to this country, I'd deduced *knedlik* was Czech for "dumpling", and what dumpling-based meal can possibly be anything other than wonderful? With this one factlet I selected something from the Czech-only menu called *alpski knedlik*. I'd mentally translated it as Alpine dumplings. I imagined a mountain of tasty stodginess, probably accompanied by bacon and cheese and sour cream. I was pencilling in the heart attack for a couple of hours later.

While I waited for my dinner to arrive, I gave it some more thought. The item in question had been the last one on the blackboard. Desserts usually come at the end, don't they? But this dish cost €6, pricier than you'd expect for a pudding around here and the second most expensive option on the menu. Since when is dessert the second most extravagant option on *any* menu? Today, that's when. As soon as the waitress moved in my direction, I could see I'd ordered a mega-pudding, a large, steaming bread dumpling, full of fruit and covered in chocolate sauce. It wasn't bad, but it wasn't the savoury treat I'd been hoping for. And it made my beer taste funny.

I was still surrounded by dozens of children. I'd only seen two other adults on the entire site. Those evil little gits would finish the rest of us off by nightfall. A seventy-year-old cycled past on a bicycle. He'd surely be the first to fall.

I wandered back to my tent and crawled inside. I could hear the screams of children and things being smashed all around me. They'd come for me next.

*

Late last night another adult camper arrived. He clearly had the same concerns about the murderous nature of the site's killer kids and sought safety in numbers. In a field the size of a football pitch he parked his tent right beside mine. After the frequency and volume of his snoring and farting throughout the night, I was sort of hoping the teens would carry him off.

Today I'd leave the half-arsed independence wishes of Moravia and cycle into another equally half-arsed one, that of Czech Silesia. There's also a Silesia in Poland to the north. Some sources claim Silesian independence is merely a Polish venture, while others insist upon rejoining the two Silesias. I couldn't find anyone advocating independence purely for Czech Silesia and so, like the cult of the Kardashians, we can safely ignore it.

In the direction I was cycling today, the sky was acting strangely. Then everything started to disappear, not as though objects in the distance were obscured by clouds or fog, but like they were being deleted, a clumsy swipe of the eraser tool in Photoshop. Maybe life really *was* a computer simulation and I was coming up to the outer bounds of what its creators could be bothered to design.

Needing to perk up my weary body, I stopped at a supermarket for a coffee. Behind the snack bar counter stood a young woman and two lads. When she asked me in shy, stuttering English if I also wanted milk, the boys teased her mercilessly until she clammed up in embarrassment. Another more confident female colleague appeared, determined to prove a point, and asked me in full sentences of flawless English if I'd like sugar and a lid for my coffee cup, the little show-off. The lads shrank back in awe of her competence. The sisterhood took a tiny step closer to its goal this afternoon.

The tussle for female empowerment wasn't doing quite so well in other areas of Czech Silesia. I found a winner of the Semi-Naked Lady Advertising Award. Yes, perhaps that micro-skirted woman pushing the empty wheelchair yesterday *could* be justified. Maybe she just had a penchant for short skirts and was wheeling the chair to the care home to pick up her old dad and take him out for the day. That's plausible, just about. But there was no justification at all for a woman advertising a paintballing company in her bra and pants. Standing in the woods, holding a gun, she'd sincerely regret dressing in such flimsy attire. Those paintballs hurt even when you're wearing overalls. The only thing she'd be modelling for the next two weeks would be welts.

I fought my way through the suburbs of Ostrava. This city of nearly 300,000 has a bit of an image problem. Even locally born singer-songwriter Jaromír Nohavica once did it down.

"This place is a dump in every way," he said. "But we don't care what people say."

Google Ostrava and you're confronted with words like "ugly" and "post-apocalyptic", but often in the darkest recesses of Europe you can find something worth clinging to. Besides, I didn't have much choice. I desperately needed a hotel with decent Wi-Fi. Most campsites fail on this front. I'd planned to download the offline maps for the second half of my ride while staying with friends back in Austria, but I'd forgotten. I had only one more day's worth beyond Ostrava before my digital world really did come to an end, as it'd appeared to do this morning.

As I penetrated the city centre, many of the unflattering descriptions of the town seemed justified, but most places wouldn't look pretty with such a heavy, doom-laden sky hanging a metre above my head. My mood was raised when I stumbled upon what I assumed to be a Frank Spencer-themed hotel called U Betty. Unfortunately, that wasn't the case. At no time did a nutter on roller skates come crashing into my room.

My knees had been giving me some grief over the last few days and so I decided to give myself an unscheduled day off in Ostrava to make the most of this highly unsought after location.

My twin-bedded room had a strange mixture of features. Right outside my front door was a little kitchen with tea- and coffee-making facilities and a handy fridge. That was a plus. Less good was my room's tiny wet cell of a shower, so small that once I got inside I was unable to bend sufficiently to wash my legs. Oh yes, and I wasn't that keen on the free-standing toilet in the corner of the bedroom. There were no walls around it, not even a curtain, just a bog to demonstrate you're so at ease with your girlfriend you don't mind curling one off in front of her. Without a female companion, it didn't much matter to me. Or did it?

I heard someone trying to get into my room. Whoever it was had put a key in the lock and was wiggling it furiously. The silly arse had clearly got our room numbers confused. In a minute, the penny would drop and he'd wander off feeling a little foolish. But then my door opened! A Czech man stood there, looking at me stonily.

"Are you 26?" I asked.

I wasn't enquiring about his age. That was my room number. He understood what I meant and checked his hotel key fob.

"Yes," he replied.

Oh dear god! The woman on the counter had spoken no English and only a smattering of German. In our linguistic confusion, had I inadvertently taken a shared room? Would I now have to spend the night watching Pavel evacuate his bowels at disturbingly close quarters? It'd be like a prison cell.

"Me too," I said, holding up my own key.

He turned around and walked away, presumably to ask reception for a room without a smelly biker in it. I breathed a sigh of relief.

*

This was a good day not to be cycling. Despite the drizzly, grey weather, I was determined to explore the city. My wardrobe wasn't really suited to this sort of venture. I had a flimsy, bright yellow jacket, but it had the breathability of rubber sheeting and meant the condensation created inside made me wetter than if I wasn't wearing it at all. My fleeces would get drenched in this rain, taking ages to dry out, and so I opted for the simplicity of one of my black t-shirts. I got some weird looks from the more suitably attired locals, but it was certainly very refreshing.

I wandered aimlessly, attempting to soak up the city's atmosphere, as well as its precipitation. I stumbled upon the tourist office, completely empty except for its two staff members. In 2008, the city unveiled its new logo, something displayed in abundance here in the office. The logo is basically **OSTRAVA!!!** written in a bold Arial typeface, the three exclamation marks supposedly symbolising the dynamism, energy and self-confidence of the city and definitely not someone screaming its name in terror.

With a free paper map – my tablet didn't like the rain – I could now walk more purposefully. I discovered Stodolni, the centre of Ostravan nightlife. The party street was in rehab this morning. I was alone amongst its amenities: the ubiquitous Irish pub, several seedy strip joints, multiple kebab shops and a casino. There was also an English bar called Sherlock's. Around here, Mr Holmes wouldn't have had a problem scoring an armful of heroin.

It was close to lunchtime and I was seeking something specific, a meal I'd had several times before in the Czech Republic and which has never failed to be anything less than amazing. *Vepřo-knedlo-zelo*, or roast port, dumplings and sauerkraut, is deservedly the national dish and so I was disappointed it took me an hour to find anywhere that sold it. Lunch options were filling up fast with the city's workers requiring sustenance. I dived inside the place, taking the last table, and gave my order.

"Sorry, that's only available in the evening."

Bollocks! Instead, I was presented with a list of seven lunchtime set menus in indecipherable Czech. No problem, I thought. I can use my tablet's Translate tool to render into English the entire list automatically. When I'd heard about this facility at first, it'd sounded like witchcraft. I'd never used it before and so was a little excited. And in some ways it *was* very much like witchcraft in that it didn't work at all. In the end, the waiter provided a more traditional, oral translation.

I could understand why this place was full. The food was cheap and filling. I had a tomato soup that cost a whopping 35p and a bowl of potatoes, fried cheese and tartar sauce, which I ordered thinking the waiter had said something else, but was great all the same.

I checked the weather forecast and tomorrow was supposedly worse than today. I'd long since stopped being surprised by this. There was one outdoorsy sort of thing I wanted to see and so I'd better do it now, I thought, while conditions were merely rubbish rather than tomorrow's terrible.

The Czech Republic and their former Commie neighbours no longer like being lumped together as Eastern Europe. It associates them with Russia and the USSR when most of them are in the European Union or hoping to join soon. But if you were forced to imagine what a typical day out in the mythical Eastern Europe of Old might have consisted of, could it have been any grimmer than a walk in the rain up a giant smouldering slag heap?

The heap in question is called Ema, and it lies a short distance from the centre of town hidden within some muddy-laned woods. This man-made hill stands 315 metres above sea level and was created from around 1920 by piling up millions of tons of waste material from the city's coal mines. Its interior still burns at 1,500°C, which gives the area some bizarre properties. Snow never settles on Ema, and it has a subtropical microclimate, enabling species of plants to thrive upon it, ones that don't appear anywhere nearby.

I stomped through the woods, leaping puddles as I went, following signs to the top. The directions dried up as I reached a junction that gave me four, equally slippery options.

A Labrador bounded up, shadowed by his walker, a young bloke with a bald head and built like a cage fighter, in a white t-shirt and camouflage trousers. He was lost too.

"I think it's this way," he said.

Having no better system to determine the way to the top I followed him. The smell of burning tar grew stronger, the

131

trees became less dense and smoke leaked copiously from the earth. Higher we went. A pile of rocks held together with barbed wire appeared over a particularly steamy patch of land as we approached the summit. It was a surreal experience.

From the top I could see the chimneys of Lower Vitkovice, once the site of ironworks and coke furnaces, now reimagined as a science and technology centre. I snapped a few pictures and, seeing this, my walking companion asked me for a favour. Would I take a photo of him and his dog atop this smoking giant and send it to him via Facebook? Of course I would.

His name was Charlie, and he was twenty-eight. He'd lived just over a mile from Ema his entire life and had never been here before. I can't imagine what it was about today's weather that inspired him to go exploring now. No one else from Ostrava thought it a good idea.

*

The awful weather forecast for today turned out to be mistaken. Instead, we had bright sunshine and summer heat. It would've been a good day to cycle and so was a pity yesterday I'd paid for an additional day in Ostrava. While I was itching to keep moving, seeing the city on a pleasant day presented a different side of it. Under a sunny sky, its grittiness evaporated. Once grey and beige buildings showed their true colours, pale yellows, greens and pinks.

I sat on a bench in the huge central square. Kids played happily in the fountains, cooling themselves down. A young female clown danced up to me and gave me a leaflet. She looked directly at me, pointing first towards her eyeball, then at me and finally clasped her heart passionately. That's nice, I thought, she loves me. Or maybe she's *in love* with me. Or maybe...Ah, she's gone. That was quick. Still, it wasn't the worst relationship I've ever had. She danced off to fall madly in love with some other sap. It would never have worked. I hate clowns.

After the disappointment of not finding what I was looking for yesterday, I harnessed the internet to locate a restaurant capable of providing my pork and dumplings. It was quite a schlep to the diacritically-overloaded Dvořáčků, and I was glad I'd memorised their online menu because the real one contained no English.

A waitress came out to the sun terrace to ask me what I wanted, and when I ordered in my best Czech – best is relative here – she smiled. I obviously had the unwarranted confidence of someone who'd chosen something off the menu completely at random.

On the internet my starter had been rendered in English as "bread and pungent cheese". And it wasn't kidding. This bit of the Czech Republic is noted for *Olomoucké tvarůžky*, a cheese unlike any other. At first, before I'd tasted it, I mistook it for chunks of rotten pineapple, so squishily translucent was it. But the ammonia kick when I put it in my mouth put me right. It tasted like it'd been pickled and then allowed to go bad.

The pork, dumplings and sauerkraut that followed, plus the beer in the sun, gave me happy lasting memories of a city that doesn't deserve all the negativity it attracts. It's no Barcelona, but it doesn't pretend to be. It's OSTRAVA!!!

Surely at least one of those exclamation marks is for that freakin' cheese.

Chapter 9: That Bit When the Nazis Turn Up

Silesia, Ruthenia and Western Ukraine

Today I was cycling into Poland and from one unregarded city to another. This stretch wasn't ugly, just utterly bland. I headed northwards, through villages of boxy, grey houses and little else. You'll understand how unmemorable this leg was when I tell you the most interesting thing I learnt today was that in Poland an off-licence – that's a liquor store for American readers – is labelled as an *alcohole*, which seems appropriate. Even the border crossing was disappointing. There wasn't even a sign to say I'd arrived in Poland, or in my next wannabe nation, Silesia.

This evening I made it to Katowice, a city almost exactly the same size as Ostrava and just as unlikely a holiday destination. As the capital of Silesia, it does have a few fans and has even been called "the most underrated city in Poland". But to be underrated, you need to be rated fairly badly in the first place.

Desire for independence is stronger here than in Czech Silesia. In 2010 the Movement for Silesian Autonomy won three of the forty-five available seats in the local parliament, despite the country's Office for State Protection warning that the political party were a threat to Poland's interests. They even gained an additional seat in 2014 after a potentially damaging controversy. Their website had posted a photo of a young fella standing in front of an Iron Cross and a plaque saying, "In memory of the fallen, 1939-45". With such Nazi sympathies, the party was accused of wanting to break up Poland and return Silesia to Germany, to which this area used to belong. The photograph was quickly removed. They appeared to be using the same PR company as Harold Shipman.

Over at Debate.org, a website seemingly designed for the criminally uninformed yet unwaveringly self-assured, a fight broke out over Silesian independence. "Should Silesia be a country apart from Poland?" was the topic. Despite the meagre election results a few years ago, 57% of those taking part answered a solid Yes! OK, so there were only fourteen votes in total, but a movement has to start somewhere.

As in most cities, the edges of Katowice were fairly grim, like a downmarket Ostrava, but then I burst on to its main shopping street and it morphed into a dishevelled Vienna, with an open, pedestrianised boulevard. In one of its larger squares a giant screen had been set up for the World Cup. Hundreds of people were watching the first knockout game between France and Argentina, with a similarly-sized, heavily-armed police presence. The situation felt a little tense to me, but maybe I just wasn't used to the combination of football fans, alcohol and machine guns.

The grandeur of Katowice's centre quickly disintegrates on the way out, with buildings becoming grubbier and a few looking like they could fall down if the wind got up.

A mile or two further, by a park with a pretty lake, was the city's campsite. Beside it was a restaurant, and it was time for food, Silesian food. The service was very attentive, but that's understandable when you're the only person in the entire place. In fact, it was a little too attentive. As soon as the last mouthful of one course was swallowed, the waiter brought the next one. At times, it felt like an eating contest.

I started with Silesian Żurek, a tasty sour rye soup containing mushrooms, bits of sausage and half a hard-boiled egg. This was followed by "Herrings Done Three Ways", a description that definitely oversold itself since the plate only contained two herrings, both prepared identically. I'm sure Greg Wallace would've had something to say about that at the same time as gurning his massive shiny head.

The main course was Silesian beef roll on red cabbage with potato dumplings. It tasted alright, though the beef was a little overcooked, but maybe that's how the Silesians prefer it, to contrast with their independence ambitions, which are merely half-baked.

*

I pushed on and left Silesia behind me, passing a sign for Oświęcim, the home of Auschwitz. I figured one death camp per bike ride was probably enough and so continued on to the magnificent Krakow.

My right knee was giving me grief and so it wasn't a good idea that, on the way to the city campsite, I turned up a steep road to visit a huge pile of soil. The Kościuszko Mound was built in 1823 from dirt carried from the four corners of

Poland. More interesting was the route there, one that took me past some of Krakow's more expensive homes. Each one looked like something from *Grand Designs* and sat inside grounds protected by both metal gates and a company called Solid Security. It must be terrible to have so much stuff you're terrified of having it taken away from you, a life of fear. Better to have nothing worth stealing and to sleep more easily. My bike had now gone several weeks without being locked at night and clearly no one wanted to nick it. How was my knee going to heal if I had to cycle all the way to the end?

After a quiet evening to rest my joints, I biked into the city centre and it was quickly clear why I was back in a world mostly populated by tourists. Krakow is simply gorgeous. Everywhere you look, but especially in Rynek Główny, the main square, there's one beautiful building after another.

For the lazier visitors, white horses sporting equally white plumes pulled even whiter, highly camp wooden carriages along the cobbles. The city had obviously hired an image consultant. I was just surprised they'd employed the ghost of Liberace.

I couldn't just hang around here. I had places to go. I cycled five miles east out of the centre to Nowa Huta, once a communist utopia – I suspect that's a good example of an oxymoron – with gardens and housing estates of scruffy apartment blocks, some complete with lookout towers. This was a planned city, built from 1949 for the local heavy industry workers. More than 200,000 people still live here. Now there are even shops were you can buy bread and stuff.

Within Nowa Huta is the Church of the Arc. The Communists didn't have time for religion, but some of the locals were into God and sin and wafers that magically become lumps of human flesh when the right spell is uttered. They wanted a church. The authorities grudgingly allowed this, but offered them no help whatsoever, not materials nor equipment. The residents mixed their own cement and made their own bricks, gathering whatever else they needed from wherever they could. From laying the foundation stone to consecration took eight years, but they got there in the end. Amen.

It's an odd building, not particularly attractive, and it only looks like an ark if you see an aerial photograph. And the lifeboaty replica clearly isn't actual size. There's not even enough room for every species of insect on the planet, including all those Noah knew about but which still elude every single modern naturalist. Standing beside it, it's an awkward black lump atop a round, grey building, but it's a triumph of humanity over repression.

Near the church was a little market. Around its edges impoverished unofficial sellers glumly sold a punnet or two of garden-grown berries. More heartbreakingly, old women hawked their old clothing and handbags. Life looked hard.

I was feeling up for a linguistic challenge. I cycled back towards the centre of town with a rumbling stomach. While here, I'd promised myself a plateful of *pierogi*, Poland's own stuffed dumplings, working-class ravioli. A blackboard covered in Polish scrawl stood on the pavement outside a basic-looking place. Attempting to read it, "Pierogi" was the only word I could understand. I peered through the window and saw a rough 'n' ready canteen. This should be fun, I thought.

Inside, it had the feel of a 1970s school assembly hall, at once both sterile and a bit grubby-looking. On the right-hand side was a large plain counter behind which stood a fierce matriarch, edging sixty in years and probably kills. Little islands of mass-produced tables were scattered around the room, half of them empty. The others contained a lone male diner, head down, ingesting. No one talked. Every footfall and scraped chair echoed. It looked like the sort of place you came to refuel cheaply rather than to enjoy, a discount service station for humans.

On one wall a huge list displayed the potential items on offer. I assumed only those labelled with prices were available today. What those items actually were though was a mystery. My Polish was at a similar level to my Venusian. That wasn't actually true. In Polish I knew the words for "thank you" and "dumpling". But, confusingly, there were about ten different pierogi options. I didn't want to order the wrong type and get disappointing ones, stuffed with broken dreams or something.

Use logic. The cheapest dumplings would be the ones filled with the least costly ingredients, like cabbage or potato. I went for the hopefully meaty, pricier ones called *pierogi z mięsem*, though they were still only about £1.60 a plateful. Sure enough, a bowl of dumplings stuffed with unspecified meat was delivered shortly afterwards. Or rather, its name was shouted and I had to think, "Damn, is that the meal I ordered?" before confidently fetching them from the counter and hoping I wasn't nicking someone else's lunch. But at least I got to practise my "thank you". *Dziękuję!* Like the restaurant, the dumplings were a little basic. Unlike the restaurant, they were also covered in a thin gravy of onion juice, but they filled a hole, and I'd enjoyed pretending to be a lonely Polish bloke for twenty minutes.

After an afternoon unsuccessfully hunting the Schindler's List film set, there was one thing left on my checklist, and it was to see something my mum would approve of. On the opposite bank of the Vistula River is a shrine to Elvis as well as a street named after him. Well, I say "street" but in reality it's a strip of tarmac in a muddy park. The shrine is a large stone, today covered in bunches of flowers, that contains a hollow inside of which is a severed head, vaguely reminiscent of Mr Presley, preserved in a clear resin. It looks not dissimilar to when Han Solo was frozen in carbonite.

My day was done. I'd enjoyed my time here. Although this location had no current independence movement, back in the early 1800s, it was known as the overly wordy Free, Independent and Strictly Neutral City of Cracow with its Territory. And it was so "Strictly Neutral" it became a centre for smuggling arms into Poland. But that was all in the past. On this journey we're only interested in the future. And very soon my future would take me back into Slovakia.

*

After a dreary fight through the suburbs of Krakow under another grey sky, the drab buildings fell away to be replaced by houses that looked more alpine. Unfortunately, so were the gradients.

The sky cleared, and the scenery improved with each passing mile. The gorgeous views were tarnished somewhat by dozens of huge, incongruous, gaudy roadside hoardings that advertised breast enhancements and other cosmetic procedures. Maybe the marketing tossers' theory was that amongst all this natural beauty you, poor unthinking sap, will realise just how ugly you are and want to make some expensive adjustments. Instead I just silently despised the clinic responsible for blocking out such scenic wonder.

By the time I reached the small town of Nowy Targ in Poland's deep south, the distant horizon revealed a long line of gigantic, craggy peaks, the High Tatra Mountains, the natural border between this land and Slovakia. I found a cheap guest house and checked in. The young woman on reception was being chatted up by a guy in his late twenties or early thirties, a Polish Danny Wallace lookalike with short hair and glasses. He turned out to be another guest here.

"Are you watching the football later?" asked Danny once he'd determined my nationality. Tonight was a big game for England. We'd made it to the knock-outs and this evening were playing Colombia. "I'll watch it with you."

I popped out for food and to visit the local alcohole. As you know, football requires beer. Back at the hotel, a few minutes after kick-off, there was a knock on my door. It was Danny Wallace from reception.

"I have cold beers!" he announced with a smile.

We chatted for a bit. His actual name was Lukasz, an electrical engineer from Krakow, working here on a contract for a few months and living at the hotel during the week. I mentioned I'd enjoyed his city.

"What did you see there?" he asked.

I reeled off a list of places.

"Oh, and a church in Nowa Huta, built by the people to look like an ark."

He shook his head.

"Never heard of it. I'll have to go. You've taught me something about my home town."

Lucasz was a happy fella who smiled easily, and he was nothing if not honest.

"Your shoes smell not good," he said, wrinkling his nose.

He meant my trainers, and this was very true. I'd worn them all day every day since giving up on my sandals three weeks ago. In truth, they'd smelled none too fresh when I'd first set off. This was the reason my windows were wide open.

"Yeah, sorry about that."

He gave it another thirty seconds before he cracked.

"No. It's too bad. Can we watch it in my room?" he asked meekly.

So we relocated to his less pungent quarters and I cheered on England from there. We also continued to chat.

"Your English is very good," I said.

"I've worked in England. Once near London, and once in Manchester."

"Did you like it?" I asked.

His expression said not.

"In Manchester it rained every day for a month."

"That's Manchester for you."

"The weather destroyed two umbrellas."

Not long after half time, England scored. I punched the air and pulled a Gloaty McGloatface.

He told me how he'd worked in Leatherhead for a Georgian businessman and serious politician, one who'd been murdered shortly afterwards, back in 2008. This was Arkady Patarkatsishvili, who went by the nickname Badri. At the time I spoke to Lucasz, Badri's official cause of death was from a heart attack. Although British police had treated it as suspicious – Badri had met some Russians in the City of London that day – they eventually concluded there was no foul play. However, in mid-October 2018, ten years after the event, the Georgian government accused their former President Mikheil Saakashvili of ordering Badri's assassination. The recent poisonings in Salisbury might have been one of many such attacks on British soil.

We were into injury time and England were strolling into the quarter finals, but they never like to make it easy for themselves. With only seconds to go, Colombia equalized. Lucasz howled with laughter.

Then came the penalties, normally England's Achilles' heel. After scoring our first two penalties, we missed our third, and it looked like football was coming home, or at least the England football team was coming home. But Colombia fluffed their next two and into the quarter finals we progressed. Lucasz smiled and shook my hand.

"I always wanted England to win," he said.

"The whole tournament?" I asked.

"Yeah."

"Why?"

"They are Europe," he replied.

"But you have France. And Sweden. And Rus..."

He held up a hand.

"Don't say Russia," he said seriously. "Russia isn't Europe. We don't like Russia."

*

Lucasz and I arranged to meet for breakfast the next morning. A table was laid out with cheese, tomato, cucumber and bread. And then the hot food arrived.

"Normally at this hotel," he said, "it's eggs *or* sausage." A waitress came out carrying two plates that contained both items. "But I told them, no, we have a special visitor today."

"Me?" I wasn't sure why I was special, but I'd take any privileges it bestowed, especially a sausage. "Well, thank you."

"I tried to get some baked beans for you too."

Lucasz tucked into his eggs and then delivered a non-sequitur.

"Why are English girls not looking good?"

"You don't think so?" I asked.

He shook his head.

"Worst in Europe." Then he had a rethink. "Nah, maybe Germany is worst. But everyone thinks so."

"I can't answer that," I said. "They look alright to me."

He smiled, and then came another quick shift in the conversation.

"After breakfast, if you have six minutes," he said, "I can show you something very special."

We finished up and jumped into his car. He drove away from town, up a long, steep hill and parked up.

"Look!" he said.

Those Tatra Mountains I'd spied yesterday were much clearer from up here, a seemingly impenetrable ridge, stretching over 2,600 metres into the sky between where I was

143

now and where I intended to go later today.

Lucasz had to go to work while I continued rolling towards the hills. Today's ride was one of those that make you glad to be alive. The sun shone all day, but being at a high enough latitude and altitude it wasn't so hot that I needed to seek out the shadows. The Tatras were in view the whole time, their handsome jagged peaks showing their treelessness as they came closer and exposed their rocky brawn. The roads were wide and quiet, the gradients barely noticeable. I reached the top of the pass with ease. And the fifteen mile descent was, of course, orgasmic. It was mid-afternoon when, after sixty glorious miles, I rolled into Slovakia's Levoča.

I took a walk around town. I liked the lived-in feel of it. The houses were all pastel shades, but the plaster was usually peeling. Most homes were eerily quiet except for the ones full of screaming babies or moaning toddlers. A bottle blonde came to her front door for a smoke. A drying rack containing an unfeasible amount of washing stood outside her house, loads of tiny t-shirts and shorts, as though she'd had an extended visit from Ant and Dec.

Near a supermarket a late teen puffed away on something you couldn't buy from any shop. He was obviously not the only one. I noticed on the back wall of someone's garden the words "I love ganja".

Unusually, in the town's main square is the Cage of Shame. Whereas Britain had stocks for its wrongdoers, Levoča had this thing. And you didn't have to commit much of a crime to find yourself inside it. Gossiping, infidelity or public drunkenness would see you locked up for a couple of days, during which time your neighbours could hurl rotten vegetables at you, or rocks, or just spit in your face. That must have made your next meeting with them down the Post Office awkward.

Assuming a bad meal would see the restaurant's proprietors locked up for a bit, I was expecting something decent from the local snazzy hotel. Their menu contained a couple of things I'd been recommended by Jo back in Komarno. First came a goat's cheese soup he'd suggested but here, pretentiously, it was covered in "bacon dust", at least according to the menu. It must have blown off somewhere between the kitchen and the table.

The main course was *bryndzové halušky*, tiny dumplings with goat's cheese, bacon and sour cream. Yes, two goat cheese dishes in one meal was a mistake, but I was only following orders. Besides, they tasted great, and I couldn't complain when both courses with a pint came to about eight quid. Come to Slovakia for great views and fantastic value for money. Especially if you like goat's cheese.

*

I was enjoying myself a bit too much. The weather had picked up, and with the low prices of the east I could afford to eat out, and eat out well, every day. No more cold tins of lentils! And in all but one location between here and the end of this adventure I'd stay in a hotel, albeit sometimes comically shoddy, or somewhere that pretended to be a hotel, sometimes for less than the price of an airport sandwich.

Over the next four days, I remained in Slovakia, cycling from Levoča through Prešov to Košice, the country's second city. Some of that time was spent resting my ailing knee and watching the World Cup. Meanwhile, as I moved ever eastwards, the countryside withdrew some of its earlier splendour and so let's leap over this period. Besides, there are no independence movements around here.

I cycled out of Košice via a huge Carrefour shopping centre. On its door a sign listed all the things you weren't allowed to take inside, including revolvers and bombs. Are the people carrying such weaponry likely to be put off by these prohibitions?

"Foiled again, Ahmed. Apparently, we can't take 'em in. It turns out God isn't willing after all. Fancy a pint instead?"

Today, I'd planned to leave Slovakia, but it didn't work out like that. I was now into the country's far east. Elderly Romani men and women sat on the grass at the side of the main roads selling small tubs of wild mushrooms they'd collected. Some of these fungi-mongers would have lived in the tumbledown slums on the edge of Sečovce. As I approached the town and drove through them – that's through the slums, obviously, not the mushroom sellers – Romani kids and their dogs raced backwards and forwards across the main road, seemingly unaware of traffic. This part of Slovakia felt markedly poorer than Košice and the places I'd seen further west.

By the time I reached Michalovce, home to 40,000 people, I'd only cycled forty-five miles but, even after two days' rest, my knee was painful again. Although its outskirts were a touch grim, the town's central street was pleasant enough and so I considered giving up for the day. I pootled around for a bit and discovered a Greek Catholic church, the Nativity of the Blessed Mother of God. This got me thinking. This mother was obviously Mary, mother of Jesus. But according to the Bible, Jesus *was* God, which means, logically speaking, Jesus impregnated his own mother. It's a pity Jeremy Kyle wasn't around back then.

As I examined an information board, an older bloke approached me. He shook my hand and, just like Péter back in Komarno, nearly broke my fingers. We determined he spoke Czech, Slovak, Polish and several other Slavic languages but unfortunately none of mine. A small detail like this wasn't going to stop him. Off he went in rapid Slovak while I nodded and smiled in what I thought were the right places. At one point he suddenly looked angry. Shit, perhaps

I'd just grinned when he'd said his ex-wife had strangled his beloved dog. But then his smile quickly returned, so maybe he didn't love his dog so much after all. Perhaps it was a rubbish dog, probably a poodle. Then he introduced himself as "Gee-org-eea", or George, crushed my hand a second time and disappeared. I hope he got more out of that interaction than I did.

I'd made up my mind. Michalovce was a friendly sort of town and so I'd stay the night. I cycled back to a place I'd seen advertising rooms for only £8 but found its business model hadn't been too successful and the hotel had closed. With a complaining knee, I continued onwards the twenty-five miles to the next border crossing. The Ukrainian town of Uzhgorod lay just on the other side. I'd stay there tonight. Well, that was the plan.

I got in the queue behind some vehicles and waited. After a minute or two, a border guard with the charisma of a testicular wart came out and told me only cars were allowed to cross here, not bicycles. I didn't ask why. I assume he would've just screamed, "Those are the rules!" while struggling to hide the massive erection induced by this exercise of his authority.

I really didn't want to cycle any further today, but a search of nearby hotels found absolutely nothing. The nearest place was in Vel'ké Kapušany, another twenty miles away, very close to the next Ukrainian border crossing, one I could possibly use, unless that one was restricted to, I dunno, mobility scooters and people on Space Hoppers.

The ride to my new hotel was flat and uneventful but wearying. Today hadn't been far off a hundred miles in total.

Upon arrival, I was given three choices of room, all in Slovak. The first was even cheaper than the place in Michalovce, but its description included the word "*robotník*". Some distant recollection told me the English word "robot" had originally come from the Czech word for "slave". Through perhaps a misguided sense of self-importance, I figured I deserved better than the servant's quarters. As it turned out, I'd been wrong on both the language and translation. "Robotník" is actually Slovak for "worker", but maybe I'd still dodged a bullet. The "Premium" room didn't need any translation but cost £22, a fortune around these parts, and I certainly didn't deserve *that*. Instead, I went for the indecipherable option in between at £13, and it was worth every penny. Read that as you will.

My chosen bed for the night was at the Hotel Družba, the same name as the oil pipeline, the world's longest, that passes here on its way from the eastern part of European Russia through 2,500 miles all the way to Germany. In order to manage your customers' expectations, it's always best to associate your hotel with something dirty and smelly that's buggering up the planet.

It was the hotel's clients who'd be dirty and smelly though. The shower didn't work. And neither did the Wi-Fi. When you tried to connect, you merely got a message from a communications company saying the hotel hadn't paid its €43 internet bill. So close to the Ukrainian border, all this malfunctioning hardware was just to get you attuned to what was the norm a few miles away.

The hotel had a restaurant attached. I figured I'd eat there later and so went to explore the town of Veľké Kapušany to see what it had to offer. The answer was "very little". Returning to my hotel's restaurant, I found that, this being the ungodly hour of six in the evening, the kitchen had now closed for the day. Today wasn't really working out too well. At least they were still serving large glasses of beer and for only 68p. Calorifically, how many pints are equal to chicken and chips?

I ordered a beer, sat down and had a think. There'd been

another foodie place on the way back from town. I'd down this drink and go there pronto. It was entirely in keeping with the spirit of today that, as I emptied the glass, the deluge chose this moment to come crashing down. Deep joy.

I bought a second beer and emergency nuts and settled in to watch the rain. The barmaid gave me an alternative by switching on an old television, the size of a Renault Clio. Miss Hungary 2018 appeared. It wasn't only the parade of female flesh that made this experience feel like the 1970s. The price list on the wall advertised four centilitres of gin, almost a double by British standards, for just 56p. What should I do? Stay here and drink away my hunger or put on some Speedos and swim to the other restaurant?

A little later, but not *that* much later, a group of old boys in the bar moved on to shots. The thirty-something barmaid looked over to me and smiled, not a gesture you can take for granted in Slovakia. It was the sort of grin that suggested she may have been lacking most of her teeth.

At half eight, already with several pints inside me, the rain finally eased. I left the revellers to their bargain gin and sparkly bikini-clad Hungarians. I limped slowly to the other restaurant. Inside was as dark as a night club, but through the gloom I located a member of staff. As I'd forgotten to download Slovak to my tablet's translation app, I successfully acted out the international mime for eating food. It turned out this place was just a pub. The barmaid showed me around the corner to a pizzeria living in a hole in the wall.

As is the norm everywhere I've been behind the former Iron Curtain, the exact weights of my dinner options were listed on the menu. I'd always assumed, historically, this was so you couldn't argue about how small your portion was when eventually served with half a potato and a grimace. Although I was starving, the Family pizza weighed nearly a kilo and that was too much even for a greedy sod like me. I opted for the more standard-sized Diabolo at around £3.50. With these higher prices we'd now moved into the 1980s, but I still wasn't complaining.

After a few minutes, the pizza arrived at my table, one of the picnic variety, outside the unlit pub. Even to someone used to spicy food, it was damn hot. Although I could barely see what I was eating, the pizza didn't last long. I gave the kitchen staff a "thank you" in something hopefully approaching Slovak and then mimed a chilli mouth. I like to think of myself as a sophisticated international traveller, but really I'm just a shit Marcel Marceau with a phrasebook.

*

As luck would have it, yesterday's enforced detour to Vel'ké Kapušany helped me discover another story of how the USSR despised humanity, one I wouldn't have otherwise known about. It was the tale of Big and Little Slemence.

Before I could see the place for myself, I had to reach the Ukrainian border, five miles away. Just as my hotel had only provided services if they were in some way broken or deficient, to make a smoother transition into my next country the government of Slovakia had thoughtfully cluster-bombed all the roads leading to Ukraine, the Pothole Capital of Europe.

As I got closer to the authorities, the wealth of the region was sucked drier and drier, barely feeling European at all. I couldn't see how anyone made money. Businesses of any kind were in short supply. Unemployment around here is high.

And then I reached the border town of Vel'ké Slemence, the larger brother of the two Slemences. It retained the air of poverty, surrounded by flat, open countryside, and seemed in every way unremarkable, a school, two churches and a football field. But this is the luckier half of town.

I cycled up to the border's passport office, waiting to be told I couldn't cross here unless I was entering on the back of an elephant. The Slovak side spent ages perusing every aspect of my document – a large queue of locals built up behind me – but eventually they let me through. One down, one to go.

To be honest I'd been expecting some trouble with this passport. I'd had to renew it while living on the Isle of Man. They process their own passports there – on the front it says "British Islands, Isle of Man" – and only inside, on the page with the photo and holder details, are printed the words "British Citizen", but only if you *are* a British citizen. Manx-born residents aren't. The Isle of Man is not a part of the UK and neither is it a member of the European Union. The only thing that turns this Manx passport into an EU one is the inclusion of those two little words. Could I expect officials on an obscure border crossing on the very edge of the EU to know this? And it didn't help that, having been in my bag for the last three months and jostled around on a daily basis, most of its gold writing had worn off the front.

So, on to the Ukrainian side. At first it looked like no one was about. In these situations I've found the best approach is to walk across the border slowly until someone shouts "Stop!" They always do, and then they're usually in a great panic to process you, as though someone nearly slipped through illegally. Either that or they shoot you. Today I got lucky.

The woman inside the Ukrainian office spent about a month checking my passport, even asking over another official to help her. She looked at me suspiciously and took out a magnifying glass, examining my documents like Sherlock Holmes.

Ukraine's borders once had a terrible reputation. The extraction of bribes was almost a national sport. Now, however, the passport office contained a large sticker that provided a telephone number I could call in English to report dodgy behaviour. Ukraine, or at least some people in

Ukraine, want to join the EU. To do that, they have to clean up their act. They were starting with the eradication of bribes. Absolutely everything else would have to wait.

Finally, Sherlock let me through and so I continued towards the customs office. In this one were two male guards. The younger of the two called me over and so I stepped through the office's open door. Apparently that wasn't what he meant and so he screamed loudly at me to get out. I wondered what previous psychological horrors or penile deficiency had led him to apply for a job in the border force but felt this would be the wrong time to ask. As was the Ukrainian way, he spent quite an age with my passport. Fine. I looked around, absorbing the emerging details of this new land. He coughed to get my attention and handed the document back to me, but when I went to take it he snatched it away again. He was only one step from chanting, "Na na na-na naaaaa!"

Once through, I arrived in Mali Selmentsi, or Little Slemence, and was faced with a mass of naff-looking temporary shops selling knock-off sports brands and the products you'd find in an airport duty-free. Ukrainians need an expensive visa to visit the EU, but it costs nothing for Slovaks to cross here. Ukraine is both cheaper and less concerned about the sale of illegal goods. As a result, this centre for cigarettes, booze and faux-branded tat has developed. Slovaks come here to buy their allowance of knock-off tradeables before taking them home to sell on at a profit. So that's how the people in that poor corner of Slovakia made a living.

The two Slemences were once a single entity, but during the night of August 30th 1946 the Red Army put up a six-metre-high electric fence that cut the town in two, the USSR on one side and Czechoslovakia on the other. For several years, family and friends were kept forcibly apart, unable to visit one another. They weren't even allowed to talk through the barrier. Instead, to fool the guards, they'd wander close to the fence and sing news-filled songs in Slovak.

"Happy birthday to you, happy birthday to you, Auntie Valerie's snuffed it, and your grandad's dead too!"

After Stalin died in 1953, it became possible to travel from one side of the village to the other, but it wasn't easy. You needed a visa – these were strictly regulated – and you had to make a forty-mile round trip via Uzhgorod to cross the border there, but obviously not on a bicycle. The necessary paperwork became easier to obtain after the collapse of the USSR, but it wasn't until 2005 that a crossing was added here, between the two Slemences, allowing former neighbours to walk from one side of the village to the other. But with only one half belonging to Schengen Europe, the town still isn't united. Maybe one day, in the distant future, Ukraine will join both the EU and the Schengen area and then Slemence can finally become a single entity once again. But then how would anyone make any money?

Beyond the twenty or so shops the village was much poorer even than the Slovakian side. The houses here looked knackered. An old woman in black was bent double, supported by a gnarled stick. The Ukrainian roads were awful when I was last here in 2013. Clearly not a penny had been spent on improving them since then. But five additional cold winters, filling potholes with water that freezes, expands and splits the tarmac further, had made them even worse. I'd have had a smoother ride on the surface of the Moon.

Having managed three months without a dog attack, a small hound chased me within a minute of arriving, just to warn me this would now be a daily occurrence for the rest of my journey.

Down the centre of the misshapen road walked a middle-aged man, guiding a herd of ten cows with a branch. But these animals didn't belong to him. Every now and again, as they passed a house, one cow would peel off and head towards it. Its owner came out and opened his gate, and the cow would be home. Some families even had two cows, the stuck-up buggers.

After another fifteen miles of quiet but challenging country lanes, picking my way through the labyrinth of potholes, everything went a bit mad. I was on the edge of Uzhgorod, the capital of wannabe nation Ruthenia, and home to over 100,000 folk. The traffic was crazy. The badly cobbled road surfaces didn't feel safe. I got off the bike and started to push. There were also masses of people. It all felt like Delhi.

Ruthenia, also sometimes called Transcarpathia, is a region that stretches beyond this corner of south-western Ukraine, into the eastern flank of Slovakia. On March 15th 1939 it even declared a short-lived independence. It was occupied by Hungary the very next day before dissolving into the cruel swamp of the USSR after the war. They speak their own language here, called Ruthene or Rusyn, and even have a poster child in the form of Andy Warhol, born Andrij Warhola to parents who came from here before emigrating to the US. The artist never visited though. Despite that, one restaurant in town offers a starter of a bowl of Campbell's Tomato Soup.

The Ruthenians see themselves as something apart from modern Ukraine, and some people want another chance at independence, hopefully this time lasting longer than a single day. Worryingly, Ruthenia's bid for release is supported by Putin. His gas lines run through this region, and anything that destabilizes Ukraine, or anywhere for that matter, is a bonus for him. One commentator has even suggested that, like Crimea, Donetsk and Luhansk before it, this area is ripe for Russian annexation. By the way, you'd better get used to this sort of Russian involvement from now on. They have their grubby fingerprints over almost every independence movement from this point eastwards. This is that bit in the Sound of Music when the Nazis show up.

There's another wannabe country here too, one that stretches over a larger area than just Ruthenia. This is Western Ukraine. Their independence claims have also been motivated by Russia, but here it's a bid to free themselves from what is happening to eastern Ukraine and its Russian tyranny. Western Ukraine was never as pro-Russian as the east, preferring to look westwards for salvation.

The Wannabe Bible puts both Ruthenia and Western Ukraine's chances of gaining independence higher than most, certainly higher than anywhere on this ride since Istria, but they are still fairly low compared to what lies ahead.

There is also a different sort of nationalist movement hiding in Ruthenia, although it makes no claims for independence. Remember CONIFA, that football association for wannabe nations I mentioned right at the beginning? Within it is a team called Kárpátalja. It represents the Hungarian minority in Ruthenia. Ukraine's Sports Minister, Igor Zhdanov, got himself rattled when he heard the club had won the CONIFA World Cup in 2018, beating Northern Cyprus in the final.

"I call on the Security Service of Ukraine to respond appropriately to such a frank act of sporting separatism," Igor squeaked. "It is necessary to interrogate the players of the team, as well as to analyse in detail...ties with terrorist and separatist groups."

C'mon, they were just playing a game of footie, you chump! Congratulations to Kárpátalja on their success.

Back to the ride. From here on in, the euro would be no more. The super-currency that worked equally well from the western shores of Portugal to the eastern border I crossed earlier today was no longer how I'd buy what I needed to fill my face. Between now and the end of the ride, I'd use seven different currencies, losing money on every transaction but giving my mental arithmetic a good work-out as I translated all prices into a value I could comprehend. One day, the whole of Europe, maybe even the whole world, will use a single set of coins and notes. It's just a question of when.

I looked for a hotel. Instead I found the one building in town that appeared to be finished, a bright, blue-and-white church with shiny gold onion domes, Christ the Saviour Cathedral. And, as luck would have it, just across the road was somewhere to stay, a concrete monster the Communists specialized in, one in which you'd only find yourself disappointed if you expect anything to work. From outside, the hotel seemed to be on its last legs. It was only when viewed beside the nearby tower blocks that, comparatively speaking, it didn't look too bad and carried off an air of squalid grandeur. In any case, these places were usually fun in a grimly amusing sort of way and, more importantly, it had started to rain hard. I legged it inside.

Once in my hotel room, my phone beeped. It was a message from my network provider, Three. Whereas their internet rate within the EU cost only 1p per megabyte – the European Union had recently prohibited phone companies charging for roaming throughout its territory – Three still had no issue with profiteering once out of the EU. Here in Ukraine it was a brain-melting £6 per megabyte. I switched my phone to Flight Mode in case any rogue app tried to connect to the outside world.

The rain had ceased. It was time to explore the town and get some food. In the hotel corridor on my way out of the room I noticed another door directly beside mine, almost unfeasibly close. I attempted to open it with the most gentle of touches, but after a strange cracking sound the door, which appeared to have been screwed to the wall, came off in my hands. This wasn't good. I leant it against the wall as closely as possible and walked away, whistling innocently. Any security cameras wouldn't have seen me. The corridors were pitch black, like something from an asylum-based video game.

I strolled into the centre of town and crossed a bridge over its mediocre river. A smattering of love locks were attached to its railings, but they'd all gone rusty. Was this a statement on the level of affection here? Regardless, a man leant over those same railings and dropped bits of bread down to the fish circling below. At least *they* seemed to love him.

On the other side of the river, even the pedestrianised shopping streets had potholes, which was impressive. It wasn't an attractive town by any means but had a sort of rough charm, like Danny Dyer doing an impression of those price comparison meerkats.

I was hungry. I saw a place advertising "Transcarpathian Specialities" – the real food of Ruthenia! – and figured if the blackboard was in English, the menu would be too. The young waiter inside spoke neither English nor German but, when met with a "Nyet!" to his question of whether or not I spoke Russian, he beamed widely and kept beaming throughout the rest of the meal, and that's a rare trait for a Ukrainian male of any age.

Many of the food choices were a bit pedestrian – I didn't come all this way to have macaroni cheese – but then I spied a section offering "Favourite Dishes of our Guests" and so I decided to take a punt. For my main I ordered something called "Kremzluk of Drugetti Family", which could have been literally anything. I would have googled it but, with the current charges from Three, finding that information would've cost more than the meal itself. To ensure there would at least be some food in my stomach at the end of all this – after all, maybe Kremzuk was Ukrainian for dog shit and chips – I also opted for a safe starter of chicken soup.

As expected, the soup was ordinary, but the Kremzluk was a potato pancake, folded in two and filled with sausage, pork, peppers, mushrooms and a creamy chilli sauce. It was the nicest thing I'd eaten in days. And the low prices continued here too. The entire meal with three pints of decent beer came to less than £6. A bargain, eh? Er, not really.

Throughout my time here, I was the only customer in the whole restaurant. I dreaded to think how little my smiley waiter was paid and so I dug around for some figures. The average monthly salary in Ukraine in 2015, the latest numbers I could find, was little more than £150, with a minimum hourly rate, almost unbelievably, of 29p! That meant my two courses and drinks would cost over twenty hours of minimum wage labour, an equivalent in 2018's Britain of around £160. Suddenly things didn't seem so amusingly cheap any more.

*

The next day started well. My £16 a night Commie hotel included breakfast, although the menu only showed the options in Ukrainian. I picked the description with the most words in it, assuming more words equalled more food. My meal turned out to be two fried eggs, ham, cheese, tomatoes and a few slices of bread. Just when I was finished, a second plate arrived. It looked like cheese covered in jam and cocoa powder, which would have been an odd combination in any country. The cheese slices were actually pancakes, and that made much more sense.

There was a twitchy moment at reception. The day before, I'd had to pay a hefty deposit for my door key for some reason. Maybe it was my face. I mean, my beard *was* getting a bit trampy. Upon checking out, I handed in the key, but the woman on reception had to make a phone call before she'd give back my deposit. I'd read about this practice last night on a TripAdvisor review of the hotel. The receptionist was calling to get someone to check the room, to see if anything had been damaged or stolen. I can't tell you how tempted I was to sneak their non-functioning, three-ton, eighties telly into my panniers. I assumed crimes committed, albeit accidentally, in the hallway also resulted in punishment. She waited a good five minutes for someone to answer but was left disappointed. She rolled her eyes and begrudgingly handed back my deposit. There'd be no Ukrainian jail for me today.

The next part of the day – Day 100! – didn't pan out quite so well. The onward journey from Uzhgorod to Khust, continuing through both Ruthenia and Western Ukraine, was stressful, in fact *eighty miles* of stressful. Ukraine wasn't helping my blood pressure.

It had all started so well. The sun was shining and on the edge of town I found a cycle path. What the hell was this? Ukraine never used to have cycleways. But, in reality, it still didn't. A quarter of a mile later it ended. My only onward option was a dual carriageway. Roads of this size are sometimes fine, provided they have a wide enough verge. This one occasionally did, but usually not. I spent the next three hours with huge, sweaty trucks and their screaming engines mere inches from my head.

On my way through Mukachevo, slightly smaller than Uzhgorod but in better condition, a large metal gate opened to reveal a troop of soldiers in a courtyard. If you had to be in the military in troubled Ukraine – and, thanks to conscription, all able-bodied males did, or they'd lose the right to a passport – I suppose it was much better to be one in the far western side of the country rather than out east, where the war with Russia had now topped 10,000 casualties.

From Mukachevo onward, the road was even more unpleasant, like being on the cracked, suicidal highways of

Russia. Today I had the lot: broken tarmac, traffic both heavy and fast, cars overtaking cars that were already overtaking, especially when they were coming towards me, forcing me off the road if I didn't want to end up in a YouTube compilation of dash cam death videos.

On the positive side, the scenery improved marginally. That said, every house looked like it was either falling down or half-built and abandoned. Ukraine was on its arse, and it didn't help that it had to funnel much-needed cash to a senseless war in the east.

A "No Cycling" sign appeared, but with no alternative available, short of turning around and going backwards, I ignored it and pedalled faster until I came to another junction, one without such a sign to give me a good get-out if I was stopped by the police. I wondered what they'd do: fine me a quid or two or take a crowbar to my teeth.

One stretch of road towards the end of today's ride was notable for its smooth tarmac, but this merely increased the speed of the traffic as well as the local mortality rate, if the higher frequency of roadside memorials was any indication. An old man walked down the side of the road carrying a huge scythe. I suspect he may have been the Grim Reaper.

Finally, I arrived in Khust, a small town of about 28,000, my nerves frazzled. Cycling through the centre, a mountain of a man in army fatigues stared hard at me. Uh oh, I thought, where was this leading? He then smiled warmly and wished me happy travels.

I found a cheap hotel and needed food. There didn't seem too many options in Khust. I chose one with an outside terrace on the central square. It sat opposite a large 3D sign saying "I Love Khust" in Ukrainian, a sentiment clearly not shared by everyone here. In 2016, vandals smashed up the thing not long after a young fella was videoed urinating on it, earning himself a fine of £1.43. I turned my attention to the waitress and asked for a menu. Helpfully, she brought me an English one. Why hadn't my perfect Ukrainian accent fooled her?

Walking back to my hotel, I stopped at a shop. The woman behind the counter had a hard time finding enough change for me. It was only about 5p and so I told her it didn't matter. She smiled, stuck her hand in a jar of sweets and paid me in candy. The country might be buggered, but its people are lovely.

Tomorrow I'd leave Ukraine. I'd only been here for two days, but my stay felt a lot longer. This, however, wasn't the last time I'd see this impoverished land. In just over two weeks I'd find myself in another corner of it, even less visited than this one.

But before then comes Romania, a country that last time had tried to kill me on a daily basis. Would it still be equally murderous? Well, yes, it would.

Chapter 10: A Hundred Ways to Die

Székely Land

It was another hot day on terrible roads. At least the traffic reduced as I headed towards the border. Somewhere along the way I heard a girl's laughter and looked left to locate its source. She was standing next to five teenage lads, one of whom shouted me an "Ahoy!" I waved in their direction, inducing a group chuckle. I was the butt of this particular joke. It was probably the helmet again, this poncey orange-pink lid. Or it could simply have been the bike. I hadn't seen any other cyclists in Ukraine except frail old men, and they'd chosen their rickety two-wheeled machines because a car was financially out of reach. In a land where wages are low, status matters. I read that in the USSR it was alright to *be* poor, but a social crime to *look* poor. Maybe it's the same everywhere, the reason rappers cover themselves in so much naff bling, aiming at appearing rich but unfortunately ending up more like African American Jimmy Saviles.

After fifty flat miles I arrived at Solotvyno, the border town, and followed a sign pointing me in the direction of Romania. But immediately this felt wrong. It took me down a dried mud lane lined with dozens of cheap-looking market stands. People milled about, picking things up from stalls and putting them down again. And why the hell were portly middle-aged men walking around in Speedos? At least that question was answered quickly enough. At the bottom of the lane stood two hotels, one either side, each with a swimming pool and each devoid of swimmers because they'd all gone shopping in their pants.

I continued. The path took me towards greenery. I felt like I was heading into the wilds. Then I passed a giant quarry full of water a disturbingly chemical shade of blue. Chunks of wood, plastic and other debris floated on its surface. Decaying mining equipment stood silently nearby. Regardless, a couple of people were sunbathing on the lake's barely accessible shoreline. If they went for a swim here, I reckon their limbs would have quickly dissolved. And then my path disappeared completely.

I decided I'd keep going in the same direction. A track of sorts eventually re-appeared and led me towards a collection of dilapidated factories. I soon found myself in a courtyard, ringed by crumbling industry. In front of me was a huge metal gate, thankfully open. I cycled through it, watched by a bemused security guard. He returned my smile with a blank stare. Outside the gate – praise be! – I was in a town again. I saw an old woman at the side of the road and met her gaze. She looked at me sternly and then crossed herself. I didn't know what I liked least, the mocking laughter of those teenagers or the fact I was now obviously Beelzebub.

After that bizarre ending to Ukraine, I joyfully rolled down the hill to the border that straddles the Tisza river. I waited with the cars until someone else biked past me. He seemed to know where he was going. The driver in the car behind me gave a shout and told me to follow the other cyclist. I'm not so British that I won't queue-jump if it's officially sanctioned by a local.

Together, we went to the window at the head of the six-car queue. But then someone else turned up on a bicycle and went into one of the nearby offices. My cyclist leader decided to follow him instead. Maybe he was as clueless as I was. I went after him.

We stood in a small group of steadily increasing numbers, waiting silently for anything to happen. After ten minutes, a door opened and a guard told us all to return to the original window at the head of the car queue. There's nothing like a clearly defined system.

While standing outside again, I looked skywards. Stupid, uncivilised sparrows flapped overhead, crissing and crossing the border over and over again like it didn't actually exist, as though it were just an arbitrary line drawn on a map, merely invented by intelligent, civilised humans.

Processing was slow. After forty-five minutes it was my turn. First I had to see the customs bloke. He studied my documentation briefly and then slipped a ticket inside. I moved on to passport control. Again, no one said a word. He gave me a stamp and a nod. That was easy. I cycled onwards, out of the border compound. At its edge, a final guard checked my passport and removed the ticket.

This last guy was fascinated by the compass dangling from my handlebars. He held it in his hand and then shook his head. He thought it didn't work, but compasses tend not to be too accurate when in close proximity to a massive lump of steel such as – oh, I dunno – a bicycle. I unclipped the compass, held it away from the bike and showed him the direction he knew to be north was indicated correctly. He was a little too impressed, which perhaps tells you something about the quality of Ukrainian military hardware.

I was out of Ukraine and now in no man's land or, as those stupid sparrows would have called it, land. I crossed a wooden bridge over the river and joined another queue, the one to enter Romania. This was all very tedious.

I showed my passport and got nodded through immediately. While waiting, I'd noticed the customs official ahead had checked the satchel of an earlier cyclist. Would this be the first time I'd have to explain my huge sackful of blood pressure medication?

"What's inside the bags?" he asked me.

"Clothes, toiletries, tools," I replied.

"No cigarettes or alcohol?"

"No."

Should he perform a search or not? Nah, he couldn't be arsed to take all the luggage off my bike and look through it. It was no skin off his nose if a kilo of heroin or a dirty bomb made it inside Romania on his watch. No one would know it was his fault.

What a palaver, but I was finally in Romania and also today's destination, the smallish border town of Sighetu Marmației, home to 37,000. I found a cheap, clean place to stay. Another customer, a Romanian bloke with excellent accent-less English, was in the process of checking out. He asked me where in Britain I was from.

"Near Manchester," I always said first. And then narrowed it down, usually to a blank look. "Blackburn."

"Ah, I know Blackburn," he replied. "Blackburn Rovers."

"Really?" I said incredulously.

"I've bet on them often. And lost every time."

Many Blackburn fans have done the same.

After a much-needed shower – the Ukrainian hotels I stayed in didn't offer this service – I went for a walk and was puzzled. When I'd cycled around this country in 2013, the route Austria-Hungary-Romania-Moldova-Ukraine had been one of steady decline, each land poorer and more buggered than the one before. But today Sighetu Marmației seemed a world away from what I'd experienced in Romania last time. Was this merely because I was travelling in the opposite direction to 2013 and that, after Ukraine, anywhere would look cleaner and less decrepit? It might have been. But I didn't think so. Romania felt much wealthier than I remembered, not like it had recently won the lottery jackpot or anything but maybe a handful of decent scratchcard prizes.

Sighetu Marmației's buildings appeared similar in style to those in Austria – this place was, after all, on the outer edges of the Austro-Hungarian Empire – but perhaps a shade shabbier. But money was clearly being spent on the town. For one, a gigantic new cathedral was in the process of being built, and how many towns with a population fewer than 40,000 can say that? None, at least none with any sense.

Walking around, I was accosted by a sixty-year-old bloke, the beefy eastern European type. I suspect he was a bit drunk. He wore a sailor's cap, held a carrier bag and smiled a lot. We shook hands and he pulled mine towards him, Donald Trump-style, keeping hold of it tightly and for way too long. We had no common language and so, like that fella in eastern Slovakia, he burbled relentlessly at me in his local tongue. The only thing I could understand was that he liked to refer to himself as "capitan". Maybe he wasn't drunk. Perhaps he was just mad. Or both.

He talked and I nodded, and I sometimes replied in English that was as incomprehensible to him as his Romanian was to me. I very quickly got bored of this conversation and so insinuated I had to leave. I wrestled my hand free, said goodbye and he followed me. Great.

I headed for the nearest bar. My thinking was that if he was an old alcoholic, then he probably did most of his drinking at home where it was cheaper. He'd avoid expensive bars. Wrong. Somehow he managed to convey that he wanted to buy me a beer. So now I was freeloading off a nutter.

We sat at a table outside, but with no visible waiter my new friend decided to go inside to order. With him gone, I considered just legging it, but I couldn't bring myself to do that, to imagine this Romanian ambassador's little face when he returned to the beer garden, two bottles in hand, to find he'd been stiffed. Future British visitors to Sighetu Marmației might have suffered his wrath because of my cruelty.

The Captain came outside again and plonked two beers on the table. We clinked bottles, said cheers in various languages and then his boring lecture resumed. I amused myself by chipping in with random, nonsensical comments.

"Yes, capitan, that's what my old mum always says."

Whatever he was talking about, he was very passionate. Throughout his presentation he kept trying to grab my hand and I kept twisting it away from him.

"Well, y'know me, I blame Thatcher."

He started to get a bit over-animated, waving his arms around, almost swiping our bottles off the table a couple of times. And then, to emphasize a point, he slapped his hands on the tabletop, sending both beers flying. I managed to grab mine without losing too much liquid, but half of his leaked into his carrier bag. He didn't seem too bothered by this. I kept hold of my bottle after that.

"Have you had some work done? You have the most beautiful nose."

His passion upped a notch, his face more inflamed. This was stupid. At any minute he could turn violent. Romania still had the power to confront you with life-threatening

167

danger. I had to get out of there.

I finished my beer. While the Captain rambled on I took out my phone, stared at it intently and, using all the acting skills I could muster – rather than Laurence Olivier, think early eighties *Grange Hill* – gestured that I had to leave immediately. I stood up, thanked him firmly and marched away from the bar. I felt bad abandoning him, but he'd be alright. He could sit there and finish his beer and then slurp the rest from his carrier bag as a bonus.

After an unremarkable meal outside another bar, keeping one beady eye open for a rampaging Captain, I walked back to my hotel. My, there were a lot of people wearing t-shirts sporting vacuous English phrases, such as "Not my problem!" or "Now is now".

In the time it had taken me to eat dinner and waste my life in the company of the Captain, there had been a change of hotel staff. Gone was the non-English-speaking receptionist of two hours ago. She'd been replaced by someone much more sparkly and chatty, a woman in her early twenties. She knew who I was before I opened my mouth. They probably don't get too many Brits staying here. Or more likely I was their only customer.

"Hi. Steven? Pleased to meet you," she beamed. "Would you like a fan in your room?"

This might seem normal anywhere else, but this type of attentive service didn't usually make it so far east in Europe, not in cheap digs at least.

"Er...no, it's OK, thanks."

"Oh, and there might be some noise later. We have a lot of new guests arriving."

"That's alright. I won't hear. I'll be watching the football."

Today would be the day Croatia put England out of their misery, beating them in the World Cup semi-final.

We chatted for a bit. She told me her name was Kinga, one

I thought I'd never heard of before. But then some distant memory of *Big Brother* popped into my head, one involving another Kinga and a bottle of wine inserted into her body, and I don't mean her mouth. I didn't think it was right to bring this up so early in the conversation.

"I like your town," I said.

She smiled.

"It's OK for families. But it's too small for me."

"Where would you rather live?"

She'd no need to consider this question.

"Cluj!" she replied immediately.

This was short for Cluj-Napoca, the city of 300,000 people about eighty miles away. It was also the birthplace of the Cheeky Girls. (My detail, not Kinga's.)

I could see what she meant. She seemed too big for this place. She'd had a taste of working abroad, having done a stint in the US, where she'd learnt her perfect English. Still, the world's loss was Sighetu Marmaţiei's gain. Every hotel, nay, every customer-facing business, needs a Kinga. In case there's any misunderstanding, I mean this Kinga here, not the one off *Big Brother* with a wine bottle stuck up her vadge.

Back in my room, I noticed a detail I'd missed earlier. In my bathroom was a second door made from the same pale pine as my hotel room's, but it was tiny, too small for any adult human, except perhaps Tyrion from *Game of Thrones*. To add to the schlock horror B-movie weirdness, the door had a number on it, the number thirteen! If the Captain couldn't do me in tonight, maybe Chuckie would.

*

Today I had this trip's first real taste of Romanian roads, and I couldn't believe the progress made in just five years. Back then, the tarmac throughout this country had been nearly as potholed as Ukraine's. Every square metre had had more holes than the Ryder Cup. Now they put French ones to shame.

To begin with, the roads were flat. I passed through small villages, seemingly populated entirely by tanned, stout women in shapeless dresses and headscarves. Occasionally, a scrawnier old dear in black would be sitting by the roadside, chewing her gums. In between these places were many large homes, and they often had the most over-sized, dark wood gateway. The house's surrounding wall would be a metre and a half tall but the Gothic archway would stand four or five metres high and wouldn't look out of place on Dracula's castle.

I eventually started to climb, and high. The villages melted away and I found myself on long slopes in deep forest. I passed a lay-by whose bins had been ripped open. Was this the work of brown bears? They can easily develop a taste for human food. Apparently, Romania has 6,000 of the animals, the largest population of anywhere in the EU. More quickly now, I cycled a little farther. Other bins had also been attacked. I looked around, scanning the woods. The idea of being ripped apart by a bear didn't appeal much. To be honest, I've always felt that. It wasn't just because I was now trapped in a forest, almost certainly with scores of 'em only holding back while they decide whether it's red or white wine with human.

The wiggly nature of the roads ahead, according to my map, suggested a further steep ascent was coming. I estimated I had a climb of at least six more miles. Bugger. Moving through these dark woods so slowly felt creepy. There are also 4,000 wolves scattered throughout Romania. Being from Britain, not known for its flesh-eating monsters, made me a little wussy about these things. I wondered where the nearest large carnivore was. Was something in the woods already eyeing up its lunch? Romania likes to keep you on your toes.

As you've probably guessed, it started to rain, a slow trickle to begin with before becoming harder. I found a dry patch beneath some trees and waited it out. I peered into the dark forest behind me. Every rock and old stump became a hungry bear ready to pounce. I tried to look farther into the gloom, but the foliage was so dense that beyond twenty metres or so it was impenetrably black. And then the Rain God climbed out of the tin bath from which he'd been splashing me and upended the entire thing from the sky. Sheets of fat raindrops bounced half a metre from the tarmac. Thunder rumbled violently. It's not wise to shelter under a tree in such weather conditions, but the chances of mine being hit were slim when surrounded by four million others.

Twenty minutes later, the storm calmed a little. Frantically searching the shadowy woods for instant death was making me twitchy. I'd have to go for it. It was only water. What was that compared to having your face ripped off by a couple of huge claws?

I made it to the top. Halfway down the other side I saw another cyclist puffing his way up the hill. As he biked past, I gave him a wave, which he returned while shouting something in Romanian that sounded like "ursa". It probably just meant good luck or something, but, as I continued rolling, I thought about it. I'd read that Romanian is the Romance language most unchanged from its Latin predecessor. And The Plough, that one constellation everyone can recognize, is also called Ursa Major, or The Great Bear. That cyclist had just shouted something about a bear to me! And, thinking about it, he *had* looked perturbed. Was he telling me he'd just survived an ursine encounter, or was he merely inquiring about bear activity up ahead? If he was asking if I'd seen any bears, then, yes, I had. I'd counted hundreds of the bastards, although obviously later they'd all turned out to be tree stumps.

I arrived in Baia Mare, relieved and by now completely dry. Approaching the place, it was a town of spires, the fourteenth century Stephen's Tower being the most handsome. The atmosphere of the place was less manic than those of the last few days. It felt chilled, with gentle traffic. I arrived in its generous main square, its edges loaded with cafés, people sipping coffee in the sun. I was back in Italy.

Maybe it was the same sunny weather that had made Baia Mare's womenfolk go crazy back in 2004. The town's mayor set up a special hotline for local residents to call with their civic complaints. But complaints weren't what he received. In one week alone, the major claimed he was pestered for sex by over a hundred different women. He had to make a public appeal for them to stop. Perhaps he should have just gone for it and serviced them all. I mean, he wouldn't have been the first politician to screw an entire population.

At one end of the square, two temporary beach soccer pitches had been fenced off. Four teams were playing beneath speakers pumping out a thumping bassline. A teenage girl took a penalty and smashed the ball so far wide it disappeared over a nearby house. A barefoot lad ran out of the fenced area to retrieve it, hopping from one foot to the other every time he stood on something sharp.

For all its loveliness, Baia Mare's name could have had the same horror connotations as Chernobyl. An accident that happened here in 2000 had the good fortune, as far as tourism PR goes, not to have involved nuclear radiation. Even so, it has been called the worst environmental disaster in Europe since that distant part of Ukraine went a bit glowy back in 1986. A dam holding 100,000 cubic metres of toxic water spilled over and infected the local river. Cyanide contamination levels were seven hundred times higher than the acceptable limit. That poisoned water then fed into the Tisza river – the one I crossed at the Ukraine-Romania border

– and eventually into the Danube. In the Tisza, absolutely everything was killed. Even as far away as Serbia, 80% of all aquatic life in the Danube was terminated, amounting to two hundred tons of fish. But it wasn't just fish that suffered. Foxes, otters and ospreys died after feasting on the contaminated creatures. To make matters worse, just five weeks later, another nearby dam burst, leaking 20,000 cubic metres of heavy metal-infected water into the Tisza. There was nothing left to kill.

Despite its woeful environmental record, I really liked Baia Mare. A piece of me wanted to stay for a fortnight, but I doubt I'd have been doing much swimming in the river.

*

The next morning's ride was through more challenging terrain and scary forest that I'm sure was full of bears. I found some suspect excreta on the tarmac. Maybe bears don't shit in the woods after all. But then came a road sign for deer. Perhaps it'd just been gazelle poop. I checked online later for photos. Both flavours of dung looked identical to me, but I'm obviously no dirtuoso.

Bears were also a problem for shepherds in Romania. Occasionally, I'd see a field containing a flock of sheep, with both a makeshift tent for the sheepdogs and a more substantial, but still tent-sized, corrugated-roofed building for the human. The shepherd could take refuge inside his solid shelter while his dogs sorted out the predators outside. Some of those sheepdogs looked utterly terrifying. I think I'd prefer to take my chances with the bears and wolves.

I trundled the long seventy miles towards Dej. Near the end of today's journey I passed through one village in which a sixty-year-old woman was pushing a heavy wooden cart, a cigarette dangling loosely from her lips. Well, I'm guessing she was sixty. She may have just been an extremely over-worked woman in her twenties. In any case, she was a right

173

little bruiser.

The men around here had it much easier. In the next village a man of a similar age slept on the ground next to the tarmac, his hat part-covering his face, while he snored contentedly.

You have to get used to sharing the road with animals here. On the outskirts of Dej, a young lad rode a white horse. It clearly didn't want him sitting on its back if all the bucking was any indication. And then another horse, this time attached to a cart, passed me, veering wildly all over the road, generating an orchestra of honks from the other cars and trucks. Romania is never boring.

Entering Dej, I realised immediately it was a different animal to Baia Mare. If Dej were a child, even its own mother couldn't love it. In fact, if it were a child, its mother would probably leave it on a hillside and never mention its name ever again.

I noticed another one of those cheap Commie messes soon after arriving and thought that, given how the rest of Dej appeared, it was only appropriate to stay there. But was it even open? It looked derelict.

I entered its enormous foyer, past a broken window, and went up to the old desk. The geriatric receptionist was bizarrely proud of his Romanian-only monolingualism, an odd source of contentment for a man whose line of work in any other hotel would have put him in front of foreign visitors on a daily basis. But, in his defence, I doubt the international jet set pop in here very often.

My first challenge was the lift. In most countries, elevators are very solid, built to reassure you. For good reason, there's never any indication you're basically entering a metal box dangling from a very, very thin thread. Not here in Romania. Merely stepping through its doors and making contact with it, my foot caused the whole thing to wobble worryingly.

Holding my nerve, I selected the third floor and, after a violent jolt, headed skywards at the same pace that would have been achieved if Grampa Simpson were personally winching me by hand. I was delivered to my destination with a second, vertebrae-loosening spasm.

The corridors had the odour of stale cigarettes but luckily the room didn't, or at least not as much. My quarters were, on the whole, fine. Well, obviously the bathroom light didn't work, but I was prepared for anything. I'm just not sure how other guests would have successfully managed their daily ablutions without a head torch.

And then there was the room's principal reflective surface, which I can only assume was sourced from a failing Hall of Mirrors. Depending on my angle of approach my body type could range from Barry White to Live Aid-era Ethiopian, although it was more fun to bend at the knee, moving up and down, to see how large I could make the gap between my eyes and nose.

Against all the odds, the massive, Reformation-era television actually worked. Well, sort of. There were three buttons on it and no remote control. Two of the buttons changed the volume while the third selected the channel, although it preferred just to stay on the current one.

My hotel room wasn't a place to make me want to linger and so I hit the town. Surely there was a better side to it somewhere, I thought. But I was completely wrong. Whereas Baia Mare had been constructed around a fine pedestrianised central square, Dej was just a smashing together of various unpleasant main roads, populated by boy racers, who judged the quality of their automobiles on the number of achievable decibels.

According to the Urban Dictionary, "Dej is a synonym for poop, shit or crap". Just sayin'.

*

Morning came and it was time to check out. The uncommunicative receptionist wasn't at his post and so I strolled into the bar beside the foyer, a bar I hadn't even noticed yesterday. The waiter was pouring out two large brandies for a customer, not a double or a triple but about two hundred millilitres, nearly seven US fluid ounces. I hope neither of them was operating heavy machinery later.

It had been a couple of days since I'd visited a wannabe country, but one was on its way today. Székely Land, pronounced something close to CK Land, is a piece of Romania that clung on to its Hungarian roots as Hungary shrank after the First World War. The Wannabe Bible places its chances of achieving independence as more likely than anywhere I've visited on this trip so far outside of Catalonia but still a lot less than all but a couple of those that follow. The big guns are coming soon.

If you're American, or a big fan of comedy, the name of this region may have reminded you of a certain performer, Louis CK. That his surname matches the pronunciation of this place is no coincidence. He was born Louis Székely – his paternal grandfather was a Hungarian Jew – and wisely thought he'd struggle to win fans if they couldn't even say his name. It worked, but given the recent accusations of sexual misconduct against him, maybe he now wishes no one could remember it.

The flat roads of today provided landscapes less inspiring than of late, at times mile after mile of sweetcorn fields. This monotony would be replaced by another, this time endless fields of sunflowers. How would Romania try to engineer my death today? Perhaps through boredom. No, of course not. It chose electrocution. As I biked through Beclean – a town as well as practical advice – a thick cable, with its twisted metal core visible, hung at exactly the right height to frazzle a passing cyclist. Luckily, I saw it just in time to swerve.

The electricity hadn't worked and so they sent the dogs in. A field contained three medium-sized canine savages. They saw me and started to charge. Unfortunately, the road ahead began to climb and outgunning them wasn't an option. I leapt off the bike and roared at them as loudly as possible. They whimpered and ran away. I started to push. After all, getting back on the bicycle would have given them a fresh invitation. With my back turned, they came after me again. I yelled a second time and they disappeared for good.

But it wasn't all aggression in Romania. Cycling along once again, a malnourished Romani lad, probably about ten years old, saw me from his house and ran to the roadside, a blur in red shorts and lime green t-shirt. He held up his hand for a high five. I stuck out my right paw while holding the bike steady with the other and we connected solidly. He gave a little whoop of joy.

"Ah," said one of the Romanian Death Gods, "have we tried anaphylactic shock before?"

"Good idea. Send him a wasp!"

The air vents in my rubbish cycling helmet were designed perfectly to trap any adventuring buzzy things. I thought I'd seen something flying towards me, but I couldn't be certain until it stung the top of my head. I yelped, slammed on the brakes and ripped my hat from my noggin before it could do me a second time, the little bugger.

After eighty-five miles and the dogs and the cables and the wasps I arrived in Târgu Mureş, a city of 130,000 and the unofficial capital of Székely Land. According to the Wikipedia page for Târgu Mureş, this town also has the honour of being twinned with Bournemouth, a fact curiously missing from Bournemouth's own Wiki page. Someone's fibbing.

I found a hotel. It cost only marginally more than last night's wreckage but was utterly lovely. The England third-place play-off was due to start in half an hour and that meant one thing: more beer. And local rules meant I had to get plenty. The Hungarians around here have an expression: "A beer is not a beer, two beers is half a beer, three beers is a beer."

I strolled to a nearby off-licence and scored me some cans. As I walked back to my room, I laughed to myself. With my Romanian as woeful as my Hungarian, and obviously being unable to read anything on the tins I'd just purchased, how funny would it be if I'd bought alcohol-free beer instead? When I reached the hotel and tasted the first one I discovered the answer: not funny at all. I had to go back to the shop and negotiate an exchange, missing the first goal of the game in the process.

After the match I thought about Székely Land and how Hungarian it was, or rather wasn't, at least not so far. I'd expected to see a lot of Hungarian flags today, but hadn't. However, many village name signs were in both Romanian and Hungarian. When I'd bought the beer in the off-licence the woman before me in the queue had spoken Hungarian, while the one behind gabbled away in Romanian. You might ask how I knew the difference. Well, Romanian sounds a bit like Italian. Hungarian sounds like whatever they speak on Saturn.

A walk through the centre of Târgu Mureş didn't turn up much more evidence of rampant Hungarianism, although I did see some more of those pointless English-language t-shirts. "Too bad to be good" on the chest of a sixty-year-old woman didn't seem particularly convincing, unless she just meant bad at picking decent t-shirts, but at least it made more sense than the shirt simply containing the words "My shoes".

The town itself was attractive enough, with a grand cathedral on its main shopping street. A tourist poster advertised the region's highlights, but the impression I got was that there weren't many.

There's a blog written by a British man, Andy Hockley, who lives here in Székely Land. It's a useful and humorous source of information about the local psyche. In one post he told of their legendary carefulness with money. Apparently, Lidl is considered expensive around here. They're also extremely conservative and treat with deep suspicion anything that comes from outside – Andy mentioned basil or tofu – always choosing the local alternative instead. And in line with what Renata said, he told of how they see themselves apart from other Hungarians, as somehow more Hungarian.

Maybe here they now keep their allegiances less overt. This town was, after all, the setting for violent clashes between ethnic Romanians and Hungarians back in the nineties, which left three hundred injured and six dead.

As someone who happily left his homeland in the mid-nineties, I struggle to get my head around any form of nationalism. One massive positive in moving to another country is that you see your birthplace through new eyes. Neither your old land nor your new one is the best place in the world, not because either is bad, but because there simply isn't a best place in the world. Everywhere has good stuff, but everywhere also has problems, whether that's Britain, the US, Australia or anywhere in Europe. A strong nationalism almost demands you wrongly believe your country to be the Chosen One. It's this naïve attitude that sits at the root of most of the independence dreams we've met so far on this ride, and this will only continue later but to a more devastating and tragic end than the handful of people killed here in Târgu Mureş. So you've got that to look forward to.

*

A few days ago, I cycled past an old bloke enthusiastically emptying his mucus glands in any direction he was facing.

This got me thinking. I haven't had a cold in years, I thought. I came to the conclusion this must mean I'm extremely healthy, almost superhumanly robust.

I now had a cold.

Waking up to a thick throat I hung around the hotel as long as I could, putting off the inevitable. The traffic out of Târgu Mureş was unpleasantly heavy and then as the city receded into the distance I had to negotiate a few small hills. By Bălăuşeri, only ten miles from my starting point, I was knackered. Was this down to my cold, the lack of a rest after yesterday's long ride or to the general weariness you'd expect after several thousand miles on a shit bike? Whatever it was, I didn't like it.

I kept moving, slowly. Another kid, maybe about eight years old this time, stuck out a hand for a high five. Sorry, lad. I apologise if I passed my cold on to you.

Today there wasn't as much forest as I'd experienced earlier this week. Sure, there were small clumps of trees in the distance, but it was mostly open country. Unfortunately, I'd read only this morning that brown bears actually prefer this sort of terrain rather than the woods, but at least I'd be able to see them coming. Obviously I wouldn't be able to outrun them, but I'd have a minute or two to say a mental goodbye to my loved ones before having my head turned inside out. Small blessings 'n' all that.

And bears are a real problem around here. Back at the end of 2017 the Guardian reported how in the village of Atid, only ten miles from today's destination, children weren't allowed outside after dark for fear of the big brown carnivores. The number of attacks is on the rise. In the first half of 2016, forty were recorded. Over the same period one year later, numbers had nearly doubled. But, anyway, what could I do about it? Unless I planned to end it all here, I just had to push on through until I reached Moldova in five days' time. Brown bears are extinct there. That shouldn't make me happy but, y'know.

After a route that took me past thousands of wild fruit trees, I landed in Praid, a small town of fewer than 7,000 inhabitants. It felt a long way from anywhere else. Immediately, I found somewhere to stay. My room was at the end of a staircase of about twenty steps, each one a dagger in my kneecap, whether going up or down. Rather than walking, I decided to give this small place the once-over by bike before the inevitable thunderstorm hit.

I might have mentioned elsewhere how extremely cool I am, but I can't prove this to anyone because as soon as human eyes are upon me I tend to fall over or do something else that makes me look a bit of a knob. Today was no exception. All day long, all alone, you'd probably have mistaken me for The Fonz, except that if your eyes had seen me then I would've instantly crashed into a lamppost. This evening, I rested my bicycle against the wall of a hotel, outside of which were perhaps a dozen tables, full of people happily eating their dinner. The bike wasn't close enough to the brickwork and so I picked it up by its seat to inch it forward. I must have carried out this manoeuvre at least five times every single day on the trip, but the difference was that on all those other occasions there weren't fifty people watching. My bike was pretty heavy and, for this reason, but mostly because of those fifty pairs of eyes, today there was a loud pop and my saddle came off in my hand. I looked over towards the diners, making eye contact with a handful of smirkers.

In order to prevent serious internal injury, I decided to push my bike for the rest of today's exploration. Praid had more daily visitors than I was expecting. This was because there's a major draw here, the Praid Salt Mine. I'm sure it would have been very interesting to visit, but the site map showed endless staircases and the way my knees were behaving today there was the possibility I'd get to the bottom of the pit and have to live there forever.

Instead I looked elsewhere. The town's single main street was lined with stalls selling pointless crap and fast food. Lángos were once again available. This region was starting to feel more Hungarian.

I found a restaurant specializing in local food and thought I'd go for the weirdest thing they had. For my starter I went for potato and tarragon soup with pigs' trotters. Unfortunately, this choice exhausted their oddball options and so the main course was mincemeat-stuffed pancakes, breaded and fried – it wasn't a million miles from something *Findus* used to make in the 1970s – covered with cheese and sour cream and served with chips. Both courses were tasty, and I certainly needed all those calories. Tomorrow would bring another 800-metre climb and my knees weren't looking forward to that. And neither was my arse, unless I could solve the problem of my broken saddle.

*

I cycled out of Praid into the countryside beyond. The saddle could still sit happily upon its supports, but I was certain it'd fall off without much persuasion and so I gaffer-taped it into position, a solution that allowed me to keep moving without turning my bike into an accidental proctologist.

Today was short – less than forty miles – but tough because of the hill, a fifteen mile climb. Eventually, at a pass somewhere close to 1,300 metres high, I reached the top and an unexpected party atmosphere. There was a handful of stalls, including a lángos merchant and another selling *kürtőskalács*, a spit cake, which isn't as disgusting as it sounds. At a picnic bench was a cycle tourer, Ivan, munching on this Székely Land speciality. He offered me some.

Kürtőskalács is made from a sweet dough rolled in sugar

and spun around a ten centimetre-diameter cone baking spit. As it cooks over charcoal, it is basted with melted butter until the sugar caramelises. It tasted nice enough – I mean, how could butter and sugar *not* taste nice? – but its consistency was similar to 3M double-sided foam tape.

I tried to chat with Ivan, but he spoke only Ukrainian. Still, I managed to discern he was from Chernivsti, the capital of wannabe country Bukovina, a region I'd originally planned to visit, a few tens of miles north of where I was right now. A knee-saving diversion had put paid to that.

Bukovina straddles a small part of northern Romania and an equally little bit of south-western Ukraine. It's another of those regions Russia sees as ripe for destabilization. A plan was formulated to provoke friction between the Romanian and Ukrainian communities that live there. In the spring of 2018, Putin's henchmen hired an arsonist to burn down two Romanian schools in the Ukrainian half of Bukovina, the age-old technique of divide and conquer. Luckily, the scheme was discovered by security services before the attack could happen.

While I chatted, but mostly mimed, to Ivan, a Romani family gathered around. Using my tablet to explain my route meant extracting it from the thick sock I carried it around in. This show of pauperism amused the seven-year-old member of the family, who laughed mockingly at me. I was being dissed by a gypsy. I didn't care. The sock was lightweight, cheap and absorbed the not infrequent raindrops that fell upon it. I can recommend it, provided you can handle the abuse from the Romani community.

I rolled down the other side of the hill. Despite the ease of the final hour I'd worked up an appetite. I entered the small town of Gheorgheni and found a cheap hotel with its own restaurant that smelled so good I had to eat immediately.

I've never understood why Wetherspoons displays the

calorific value of each meal on its menu. The reality of imminent obesity takes the shine off the anticipated gluttony. The restaurant here took the same approach. On each table was a flyer offering something called a "megaschnitzel", a main course that surely demanded an exclamation mark. From the photo this option looked like a three square mile slice of breaded pork, all covered in a thick cheese blanket. It cried out to the place where my soul should have been. My mouth salivated while my stomach rumbled audibly. But then I perused the menu. On its Specials page was the megaschnitzel, and its description confessed to containing 1,900 calories, an entire day's worth, although that huge hill today must surely have given me some wiggle room.

Worryingly, the megaschnitzel was the second *least* calorific dish on that page. They also sold a Peasant's Platter – sausages, a chicken breast, a skewer of pork, strips of bacon and various other meats, fried cheese, chips, rice and fried eggs with maybe a gherkin and a handful of veg thrown in – which came in at 4,000 calories. And their Kentucky Chicken Bucket – a name surely unsanctioned by the Colonel – maxed out at 4,200. Those two options made my megaschnitzel seem positively katemossian.

After my meal, I walked some of it off with a look around town. Unfortunately, this place was more akin to grotty Dej than lovely Baia Mare. It was basically a scruffy hole with lots of five-storey grey apartment blocks, crumbling and flaking their way to eventual non-existence. At its centre was a ratty bit of park ringed by a road and a bank of tatty shops. Given the scenic beauty of today's route, it was a shame it couldn't have been extended into the town.

I still hadn't seen many nods towards the Hungarian majority here in Székely Land. That said, of the nine towns with which Gheorgheni is twinned, seven of them are in Hungary and so the folk around here are clearly hankering for the old country.

Giving up on exploration, I headed back to my hotel. Something of a show was taking place across the road from my temporary home. A young bloke was violently throwing up his guts on to the pavement. His mates stood around him, clutching cans of beer to demonstrate this was entirely self-inflicted and so no sympathy was required. Two of the hotel staff were outside, monitoring the situation, their faces a cocktail of pity and disgust.

Romania may have changed for the better in the last five years, but it still sometimes had the ability to feel grubby.

*

Over the years, Székely Land has had different boundaries. Whatever its current position, at some point today I'd leave it behind and head back into plain old Romania.

Once again the land folded challengingly, and I had to regain almost all the height I'd lost yesterday afternoon. The pine forests thickened but, on occasion, I could sneak a peak through the dense foliage and the views were magnificent. A moody, cloud-heavy sky glowered at the thin strip of tarmac that fought its twisted way through these wild hills. Today would be my final day in the Carpathian Mountains.

I'd been looking forward to seeing the Red Lake this morning, otherwise more spookily known as Killer Lake. It was formed in 1838 during an earthquake that caused a natural dam to collapse. There's a myth that the quake killed most of the inhabitants of the village below and that the lake's eponymous colour came from the villagers' blood. But today, as in every photo I can find on the internet, the lake was a murky brown. It doesn't mean the legend wasn't partly true. Maybe it wasn't the villagers' *blood* that ended up in the pond.

If the lake was a disappointment, the stretch of road that followed definitely wasn't. I descended through the steep, narrow gulleys of the Bicaz gorge. At times, speeding through the slender passageways made it feel as though the walls were closing in, ready to crush the life out of me. The narrowest part is known as "The Neck of Hell". Occasionally, the limestone would open up and reveal craggy, free-standing mini-mountains a couple of hundred metres tall. This was easily the most impressive natural feature I'd seen on the ride so far.

At the end of today's seventy miles and well over a Ben Nevis of climbing, I rolled into Piatra Neamţ, a town of 100,000, just as it started to rain. The wetness wasn't unexpected. Rain had been forecast every day this week. This was the middle of July for God's sake. It looked like we were jumping straight from spring to autumn.

The depressing skies didn't do much for the town's appearance, and neither did its thick traffic. Grey predominated. People shuffled along unhappily, their collars turned up.

Oh, how I love to hunt for accommodation in the rain! I eventually found a cheap and basic place in what felt like the rougher part of Piatra Neamţ. It was run by an old woman no bigger than my thumb with a voice that suggested she was closely related to Joe Pasquale.

The rooms – hotel is too grand a word – had its own bar. If you sat outside on its miniscule but thankfully covered two-table terrace, you looked out upon a forest of minging concrete flats. With the addition of today's awful weather, everything felt a little Soviet.

The rain eased and I had a hollow belly to fill. My digs were on a small road that ran parallel to the town's main thoroughfare, and it was on that larger street a restaurant lived. I set off blindly, hoping to find a short cut to the main road, but before then I'd meet Maria.

Walking some fifty metres ahead of me was a slim woman

with waist-length blonde hair. She wore clingy, black leggings with a tight, black sleeveless shirt. Occasionally, she'd turn around and look in my direction while wildly flicking about her flowing locks. That's odd, I thought. According to some behavioural psychologists, a woman playing with her hair means she's attracted to you, but even if I'd been Tom Hardy I would've been much too far away for her to see me properly. The possible conclusions I could draw were that 1) she fancied everyone – we'll come to that later – or 2) she was mad or 3) she had a problem with head lice.

I was still searching off to my left for an exit on to the main road. When I turned back to look in the direction I was walking, Maria was standing in front of me, waiting for me, sucking on a cigarette. Apparently she'd flirted enough. Now she was going in for the kill.

She held out a hand and introduced herself. I don't want to be mean, but the package advertised from fifty metres away wasn't the one delivered. She was a wasted-looking sixty-year-old, but could have been twenty years either side of that, with the worn skin of someone who'd smoked too many cigarettes, necked too many bottles of whiskey and God knows what else. She smiled frequently through thin lips covered in a pale red lipstick that looked like it'd been applied while cycling over cobblestones.

She was also quite a long way down the merry road to the happy town of Roaring Drunk. I was suspicious. Women don't need to act like this to get male attention. If the #*metoo* thing demonstrated anything, it's that men are constantly pawing women whether they want them to or not. Sadly, everything about Maria screamed hooker.

She took the same approach as the Captain back on my first day in Romania. She didn't let a little thing like lacking a shared language get in her way. She talked and talked. Maybe there's a belief that, because it'd be unusual to find a foreigner who speaks Romanian, the visitor can learn the local tongue by osmosis over a period of ten minutes as long as a constant stream of words is fired at them. Sure, this approach might work if you were imprisoned in a Bucharest jail for a decade, but it wasn't very successful today.

I carried on walking, Maria happily by my side, although she'd occasionally glance around nervously. While moving, she got so close our bare arms rubbed. I was definitely in here if I wanted it, but I really didn't. At one stage she pointed out a decomposing apartment building. Was this an invitation to make the beast with two bad backs? Maybe there was a more innocent excuse. Perhaps she just wanted me to repaper her lounge. Nope, she was definitely an ageing prostitute, a.k.a. a Tenner Lady.

After a few minutes of walking we came to a bar beside a stone staircase that led up to the main road I wanted. I turned to climb them, but Maria grabbed me and unsubtly suggested we go for a drink in the bar instead.

"No, I'm going up the stairs now," I said pointlessly.

She kept gesturing towards the bar and jabbering away in rapid Romanian.

"I'm going!"

I turned around and started up the staircase. She followed me, but after three or four steps the effort clearly became too much. She stopped dead and threw her cigarette away. I felt bad for her. I gave her a smile, walked the few steps back to her, unintentionally giving her a second of renewed hope, and shook her hand again.

"Goodbye, Maria," I said. "Nice to meet you."

"Bye bye," she replied sadly in English.

This was hardly *Pretty Woman*, was it?

*

The next two days covered a drizzly and uneventful hundred and twenty miles. Well, I say uneventful, but there was one highlight. At the bottom of a dip, an oncoming lorry nearly knocked me off my bike with the wall of air it pushed before it but, y'know, that's just Romania. I'd survived the country's final attempt to kill me.

I overnighted first in the scruffy town of Roman and then the more attractive city of Iaşi, close to the Moldovan border. This is the point where everything gets more serious, including places the UK and US governments warn you not to go. No longer are we just talking about *wanting* independence. We're going it alone and *claiming* independence. And because of this decision, people will die.

Chapter 11: Don't Mess with the Sheriff

Transnistria

I had arrived in Moldova. The route from the border was almost entirely traffic-free, containing more goats than cars. Large rustic houses lined the country lane that acted as one of the few main roads into Moldova's west, but there were no businesses of any kind. The tarmac started smoothly but became progressively more broken as I reached Ungheni. This is the sixth largest town in the country, despite only having a population of 30,000. As such, hotel options would be limited, but before I could find one, I first had to get some local cash, a currency with the international respect of Piers Morgan.

On Ungheni's long and scruffy main street I located one of Moldova's few shiny objects, a gleaming branch of Victoriabank, and its cash machine. Normally I won't use an ATM abroad unless its attached bank is open, just in case something goes wrong. But today was Saturday and this branch, as well as all other banks in the country, had closed an hour ago. I didn't fancy waiting until Monday morning, camping wild and surviving on the single chocolate bar in my panniers plus whatever else I could forage. No, I wanted a cheap hotel and a pizza and so I had to chance it. Another reason I didn't need a delay was that, ten days and over five hundred miles from now, I had a very sporadic ferry to catch.

In went my card and I requested a few thousand *lei*, which

isn't as much as it sounds. I heard the whirring and sorting of cash, and then the screen told me to take back my plastic. Unfortunately, in the slot, only two millimetres of it reappeared. I made a pincer with my fingers and tried to extract it, but on a hot day like today my hands were sweaty. The machine also had a weirdly firm grip on my card. After thirty seconds of increasingly frantic snatching, the electronic Pac-Man re-devoured it. Oh no! The ATM then made another attempt to return my plastic meal ticket, although without resolving any of the issues that had prevented me from taking it the first time. I wiped my hands, but even minus a film of sweat, it wasn't coming out. Once again, it sucked the card back inside, beeped insistently and then the screen reported itself "Out of Service". Wonderful. I was stuck here with no money until Monday morning after all. I wondered what the market was for overweight, middle-aged male prostitutes.

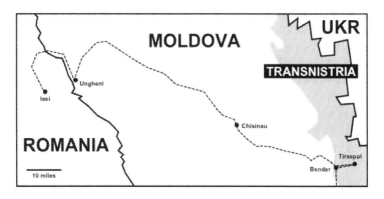

Not really knowing what else to do, I wandered around the outside of the bank, looking through its tinted windows. No one was inside, but then a company employee appeared from nowhere over my shoulder, a man with a sticking plaster on each cheek, a look that's very difficult to pull off with any dignity. With no common language, I used the medium of Charades to explain what had happened. A woman then came out of the bank. Where had she been hiding? Plasterface said something to her, and she mimed she was making a call. A minute or two later a policeman arrived. I'd caused quite a palaver.

The policeman, it turned out, was married to the woman from the bank, and he spoke a little English, if shyly. Unsurprisingly, he told me I'd have to come back on Monday. So far, so every bank in the world.

But here's when a Moldovan customer service story kicks in, and that's a sentence you're unlikely to have encountered before. Another phone call was made, this time from the woman to the bank's head office in Chişinău, Moldova's capital. She relayed a message to her husband.

"The boss is going to come from Chişinău, and she'll open the machine for you," he said.

"Really? Chişinău?" I replied incredulously. That was more than sixty miles away! And on her Saturday afternoon off.

"Yes, she is driving here. Come to the police station in two hours."

"And where's that?"

It was a good job I asked. There were two different stations on this one road alone. The copper walked me the short distance to his base and then had me show my fizzog to the desk sergeant, who stared hard at me. I couldn't tell if he was trying to memorize my face or burn a hole through my head.

I thanked Mr Plod and told him his English was very good, which earned me a huge grin. Before we parted, he stuck out a hand to shake.

Just up the road was a large hotel. Assuming I'd soon have money, I checked in and was told there were two options, economy rooms priced in Moldovan lei and deluxe priced in euros. Obviously, foreigners were steered towards the more expensive.

"What's the difference?" I asked.

"Economy is really noisy," the receptionist replied. "We have two discotheques. You won't sleep."

Wasn't that a design oversight? Aren't Moldovans allowed a snooze? I went for deluxe because the price certainly wasn't.

Two hours later, I returned to the police station. Unfortunately, the lone desk sergeant from earlier had been replaced by four others, terrifying-looking humans with thick necks and squashed noses. There was a barrier inside the room to prevent getting too close to the counter. They were obviously sick of having their hooters punched in. We stared at each other in silence for about ten seconds before I realised what I had to do. I'd mime what I wanted to the most intimidating panel possible. It was like an *X Factor* audition where the judges were all KGB agents and failure meant a crooked smile and a bullet in the back of the head. Just as I was about to launch into my act, my new policemate appeared through the front door with my debit card in his hand.

"If it is blocked," he said, giving it back to me, "then call the number on the back."

"Why would it be blocked?" I asked.

"You typed in the wrong pin three times."

"No, I didn't."

"Then you must have snatched at the card."

Eh? I could barely touch it. And, in any case, how could an ATM judge someone on how they retrieved their plastic? Was there a sensor to evaluate artistic merit?

He took me to another ATM around the corner and I got the money I needed. I suspect the bank was looking for a way to make this seem like my fault, but I didn't care. They'd gone out of their way to help me and to return the card, and I appreciated that. Can you imagine Barclays doing something similar, having a local branch manager drive from London to Cambridge – it's the same distance – to save a lone Moldovan tourist?

After all the excitement of near destitution, I found somewhere to eat, a place called Andy's Pizza, one of Moldova's few chains. The large photo menu had a smattering of English, but the Moldovan language is the same as Romanian and so, as with all Romance tongues, foodie items are often guessable. Weirdly, when the dishes arrived, their contents looked *exactly* like the photos on the menu. Clearly, the Moldovan model for fast food chains is different to the rest of the world. Didn't they know you're *supposed* to be disappointed by the experience. That's how it works. How else would such massive profits be made? I remember a particular KFC Tower Burger, the photo for which showed an architectural masterpiece standing close to one foot tall. The wobbly, taste-free, squashed reality would more accurately have been labelled a KFC Condemned Tenement Burger.

Finding food that is specifically Moldovan is a challenge since this region was just a small slice of the USSR. I started with *okóshka*, a large bowl of cold Russian yoghurt soup loaded with bits of meat, quails' eggs, sour cream and dill. It was tasty but made drinking my equally chilled beer seem wrong. I followed this with a mighty fine Diabolo pizza. We were still in the realm of economical eating, the whole lot with two pints coming in at less than £7. But that wasn't much of a surprise. At around £120 per month, the average wage here is just three-quarters of Ukraine's miniscule amount. Maybe Moldovan ATMs are *supposed* to operate like the one I used this afternoon to help you stretch your money further by starving you for a few days each month.

Returning to my hotel I leaned out of my window to look

at the facilities behind the building. It was dark, but I could see what would once have been a swimming pool out there, now a concrete hole with a central platform, presumably for splashing up to and then ordering a cocktail, but it was empty and grimly derelict. No one had been in there for years. Now all was peaceful. There was nothing to disturb the sense of decay but the cicadas chirping in the warm evening air. Hang on a minute. What happened to those too-noisy-to-sleep discos?

*

The next morning's ride took me back on to the tatty shopping street, where I loaded with pastries from a stall. Every other male customer had a broken nose. I guess that, around here, with my untwisted beak, I was the freak.

Today would be a long eighty-five mile trek. Moldova doesn't really do mountains. Its highest peak, although peak is perhaps the wrong word, is only 430 metres above sea level. But what the country excels at are short and frequently repeated hills. This lumpiness should've ground me down, but with the continued sunshine, all the more appreciated given this trip's soggy history, I moved along with a smile on my face. Keeping my spirits high, a middle-aged man beamed at me and punched the air while several children called out from their houses and waved. I felt like the prophesied god they'd all been waiting centuries for, except no one slaughtered a lamb in my honour or offered me their nubile womenfolk.

The scenery was unlike any other European country. The rolling hills could be covered densely or sparsely with trees as anywhere, but there was a sense that a lot of this place simply didn't belong to anyone, as though it had just been left to head in whichever biological direction it chose. Whereas everywhere west of Moldova is parcelled up and fenced off, here vast tracts of land were given over to the production of nothing more than wild flowers. Goats and cows wandered around unfenced and untethered. Heavily loaded walnut trees slept by the roadside. Whether or not my observations were near the truth didn't matter: It all *felt* very free. The oppressive world of twenty-first century control seemed a million miles away. The ignorance was bliss, like being seven years old again.

On this toasty Sunday afternoon, everyone had their own way to pass the time. Within this bucolic paradise, an incongruous white stretch limo barrelled down the empty highway. More fitting was the mad fiddle music that leaked from the windows of a house. Farther along the tarmac, in a fancy Soviet bus shelter, a man lay still, presumably asleep, or dead drunk, or just dead.

The roads were a lot better than I remembered from five years earlier, at least in part. The larger arteries were being resurfaced piecemeal. One minute I'd be screaming down the smoothest surface in Europe and the next I'd be back on something that would raise eyebrows in Ukraine.

There was clearly no one whose responsibility it was to remove roadkill. I found it in all states of decomposition, from freshly struck to fetid decaying fly hostel to just the merest residue of fur. There were dogs, cats, foxes, hares, polecats and one that looked suspiciously like Captain Caveman.

Throughout the whole of those eighty-five miles I didn't come across a single other town worthy of that label until I reached Chişinău, possibly Europe's least visually appealing capital. Its wide avenues would normally be bumper to bumper, but I'd got lucky by arriving on a Sunday evening. I felt like I had the place to myself. I still had to outrun a couple of savage hounds and to negotiate huge piles of sand lying casually on the road's edge, but it was a more pleasant entry than I'd expected.

I found a shabby hotel in the south of the city. Preparing myself for my morning exit, its location was more important than its facilities, which was just as well because it didn't have any. Being in the middle of an industrial estate, there was nowhere nearby to score food except a petrol station. Tonight's dinner was particularly unhealthy, mostly crisp-based.

On the wall of my hotel room was a list of fines that'd be imposed should any object go missing or get broken. The list contained twenty-three items although, looking around the room, I couldn't see twenty-three different things. They wanted £150 for the telly and it didn't even work. Damaging a cup would set you back £2.50, but luckily there weren't any. Strangely, there was no fine relating to the bed and so, since there was nothing else to do around here, maybe I'd spend the evening smashing that to pieces.

Tomorrow was a big day, one I'd been looking forward to for months. On this trip there would be three places you're warned not to visit by the UK and US governments for various reasons, because of, say, chronic corruption or the possibility of abduction or generally just, y'know, death. Tomorrow's wannabe country was one of these places. But it wasn't really a wannabe. In every respect that mattered, it was a *real* country. Unfortunately, no other recognized nation agreed. Tomorrow was Transnistria.

*

Sunday evening may have seen empty roads in Chişinău, but the same couldn't be said for Monday morning. It was a horror show. The streets narrowed and hosted a procession of fast-moving, fume-belching trucks that roared by, inches from my ear. Shredded juggernaut tyres lay at the side of the tarmac, each one a monument to a trucker's nightmare. If a tyre exploded as its truck passed me, I'd be shredded too. Since I couldn't do anything to prevent this from happening, I wouldn't worry about it. Death, a necessary end, will come when it will come.

But as the grimy city slowly faded away, so did the cars and, under another welcome sun, the tranquil mood of yesterday returned. Stretching from the capital through Transnistria's twin cities of Bender and Tiraspol and on to Ukraine, this road links the largest population centres in Moldova, but the traffic stayed light. A sense of joy rose within me, and excitement.

I was a few miles from the border with Transnistria. Yes, that's right, a border, a real one. This is the first wannabe on my voyage that acts as though it already exists. Its government and the 469,000 people who live there *believe* it exists, but no UN country has recognized it. According to everyone except Transnistria, this region is merely an unruly bit of Moldova, one that just happens to have its own military, police force, postal system and currency.

As I was taking a breather, another cyclist came in the opposite direction and stopped for a chat. Meet Bruno, a twenty-something Brit. He'd started in France, biked all the way to Azerbaijan's Baku via Albania and was now on his way home again.

"You looking forward to getting back?" I asked.

He pulled a face.

"I can't be bothered with everything that's happening there right now," he said. "I think I'll get a job, save some money and then set off again. Maybe South America next time."

"How was Transnistria?"

"Yeah, it was good. I had a bit of trouble leaving."

When you enter the *de facto* country you have to get a visa. It doesn't cost anything, but you need the right one. If you tell the authorities your final destination is outside Transnistria, they give you a transit visa, which is good for ten hours, easily sufficient to cycle across Transnistria's narrow strip of land. If you say you want to visit Transnistria in its own right, then by default you get a three-day visa, although you can ask for longer. Bruno didn't know this. In fact, before he arrived there, he'd never even heard of Transnistria. Not many people have.

"I told them I was heading to Chişinău and so they gave me the ten-hour ticket. But I stayed over in Tiraspol. Things got a bit sticky on the way out, but there was a queue of cars behind me and so they waved me through anyway."

"That was lucky. I've heard if you've got the wrong visa you sometimes have to pay a bribe."

"Not sure how that'd work."

He didn't have any Transnistrian money. Bruno hadn't known you can't use Moldovan currency in Transnistria.

We chatted a while longer. He seemed like a nice lad, but I was itching to get inside this weird part of the world. After about twenty minutes, we said our goodbyes and I headed up a hill towards the border.

Unlike the other two dodgy places coming up later, warnings about visiting Transnistria have reduced in recent years. It once had a terrible reputation for corruption, with border guards extracting bribes from everyone. Stories suggest this is still the case at some of the more remote border outposts. But the one on the road from Chişinău – this is Transnistria's main entry point – has made a big effort to clean up its act, in the hope the country will be taken seriously. Nowadays, the UK Foreign Office doesn't specifically tell you *not* to go there, but it does warn you that, since Transnistria is unrecognised, the UK has no representation – in other words, there's no embassy – and so if you get into trouble, it's up to you to get yourself out of it.

I cycled up and over the hill. At the top, various police officers and soldiers stood around languidly. Yes, guns were visible, but it wasn't the tense situation I'd been expecting.

Moldova itself doesn't have a border post here. After all, according to them, you aren't leaving Moldova when you enter Transnistria. I wheeled up to the Transnistrian authorities and was waved to a shed by an official with a hat twice the size of his head. He looked like a six-year-old wearing his dad's uniform.

The hut contained a desk behind which were sitting three people in battle fatigues, two men and one woman. She was clearly in charge. I showed her my passport and said I wanted to visit Tiraspol, the capital.

"Prime Rose Schmitt, Stayvan Peter," she said, reading from my documentation. Inexplicably, she added a "Wow!"

Within a matter of seconds I'd received my visa – little more than a bus ticket – that told me how long I had inside this oddity's borders. She smiled kindly and wished me a good trip, not the former Soviet intimidation I'd read about. I rolled into Transnistria and felt a tingle of anticipation about what lay ahead.

Drowning in a reputation for knuckle-headed masculinity, Transnistria has recently been placing women, particularly young, physically attractive women, in prominent positions to soften its image internationally, as here at the border. In 2016, eight of the fourteen government roles were filled by females. Between 2013 and the end of 2015, the Prime Ministers were also women, along with many of their deputies. But don't go thinking this is some sort of feminist utopia. Transnistria has a reputation for sex trafficking.

That's not the only dodgy thing it's been accused of. There's a former Soviet weapons dump in the north of the country. It's believed to be from here that a rogue lump of weapons-grade uranium turned up in a shopping bag in Chişinău in 2010.

"Unexpected item in the bagging area!"

It's not the first time that radioactive material has been smuggled from the weapons dump. An entire nuclear bomb's worth once went missing. Worryingly, no one knows where it is now.

After the rustic joys of the ride here, Transnistria felt surprisingly brash, appearing brighter and more modern than the rest of Moldova, as though the larger country had been given a good shake and then had its rough edges chipped off. A lot of older sources describe Transnistria as an eighties-style Communist museum, but it didn't give that impression today.

Transnistria is a particularly impractical shape, long and thin, and one that seems designed to facilitate cross-border smuggling, something it excels at. From north to south it's around 120 miles long but only a handful wide in some places. I cycled the seven miles from the border to the capital Tiraspol, over halfway across the country at this point.

I needed to get my hands on some Transnistrian rubles, the official currency, unrecognised internationally or even within the rest of Moldova. It can't be traded at all outside Transnistria, where any value it once had quickly evaporates. I popped to a bureau de change and gave the cashier a fifty euro note, about £45. She asked if I wanted to change it all and was surprised when I did. I was going to be here for a couple of days after all. Let's go mental! I was handed back a bundle of tatty-looking paper. There are some coins in use here, but there's not much call for them when a one rouble note is worth less than five pence.

On the outskirts of the capital and its 133,000 inhabitants, I passed the gleaming home of FC Sheriff Tiraspol. Sheriff is a company that more or less owns Transnistria. Created by two former KGB agents, it now has fingers in more pies than Mr Kipling. They have a virtual monopoly on Transnistrian supermarkets and petrol stations and they also own the phone network, radio and TV channels, a publishing house, a construction company as well as the prestigious Kvint distillery, the manufacturer of the highly-regarded local brandy. Oh yes, and the football club is theirs too. In a land where GDP per capita is only two-thirds that of on-its-arse Moldova, there's clearly some inequality here, but Sheriff is doing alright, thank you very much, as is their footie team. Given the dearth of Transnistrian clubs to compete against, they play in the Moldovan league. Since 2000, the club has won the Championship every year but two. Ominously, the corporation is known locally as "Big Brother".

As I reached the centre of the city, the traffic thickened and the previously smooth road surfaces started to crumble. My accommodation tonight was a campsite, not far from the Dniester river. It was also close to everything else worth seeing in Tiraspol. Depending on who you ask, this isn't a particularly long list.

The site was small and basic but had everything you needed. The shower was solar-powered but effective, and the toilet was an outdoor squat-style hole in the ground. Various fruit trees, vegetables and sunflowers grew there too. It couldn't comfortably host more than about eight tents, but it was a tranquil spot, even with the distant music floating in from a party boat on the river. One of the friendly owners, Yuri, was also a keen cycle tourer.

"Are you actually from Transnistria?" I asked him.

He laughed.

"Yes," he replied. "The country that doesn't exist."

I needed food. Given my inability to read Russian, the local language, I'd been relieved to see a branch of Andy's Pizza near the campsite. It wasn't like they only did pizzas, but I felt a bit weak for not being more adventurous. Right now though, I required calories rather than a badly ordered bucket of goat tripe.

The restaurant's service was provided by two young

women in black, who couldn't manage a smile between them. I took a seat on their outside terrace and, after waiting for approximately one Ice Age, the most sullen server of the two gave me a menu. Not wanting to miss my opportunity, I placed my order for a beer at the same time. She typed it into a device that sent the request to the kitchen about ten metres away. She could have just shouted for it. Then she went back to chatting with, but mostly scowling at, her mate. The beer arrived ten minutes later. The staff inside were as slow as those outside. Their Marxist practices may have withered and died, but here at the Tiraspol branch of Andy's Pizza the quality of service remained distinctly communistic.

Andy didn't live up to the standards he'd set in Ungheni. The sour and spicy *solyanka*, a Russian soup, didn't start too badly, but the fungi ravioli thing I ordered for main course was like pasta drowned in a lukewarm tin of condensed mushroom soup.

As I ate my substandard meal, two young boys stuck their heads over the glass barrier separating the dining area from the street and screamed at me for money. I couldn't remember having any cash on me when I was nine years old and so I declined their request. Given my scruffiness, I wasn't sure what singled me out as a supposedly wealthy tourist, probably just that I could afford to dine at a restaurant at all. There was, after all, no one else eating here. By the way, Tiraspol Andy's, well done for conforming to the low standards of international restaurant chain norm. This is how it's meant to be done, another sign of the encroaching commercialism here in Transnistria.

I went for a tour of the city's sights. In most parts of the former USSR, statues of Lenin have been dismantled. Here though, outside the parliament building, there's a very special one, a goliath looking every inch the superhero, wrapped in a cape and about to leap from his plinth to save the world from capitalism, although it seemed to be doing well enough here, at least for the KGB owners of Sheriff.

Next up was the statue of Alexander Suvorov, the founder of Tiraspol and one of Russia's most popular military leaders, a man who won sixty-three major battles and never lost a single one. He's not the only Russian connection the place has.

When the USSR fell apart in the early 1990s, its constituent nations scrambled to assert their independence, often, as we shall see, with deadly results. Traditionally, Transnistria had been a part of Ukraine, and it saw no natural reason to remain connected to the newly liberated Moldova to which it now belonged. When war first broke out in 1990, Transnistria was backed by the Russian army. It still is. Transnistria couldn't have survived without them. Even so, several hundred people died on both sides. Russia's strength prevented Moldova from reclaiming Transnistria and eventually a ceasefire was negotiated, a stalemate that continues to this day and suits Putin perfectly. Officially, Moldova is occupied and therefore cannot join NATO, and its fragile state means it's unlikely ever to be invited into the EU. European instability is the name of Putin's game and in this corner of the continent he's winning.

Remnants of the war can still be found nearby. Across the road from the Suvorov statue stands a church and a small tank positioned so that, with the right photographic composition, the military hardware looks like it's attacking the religious, just as Communism liked to do.

I couldn't see everything Tiraspol had to offer today. I needed to save something for tomorrow. I walked back to the campsite via the Dniester river, which further north acts as most of Transnistria's border with Moldova. The sun was still out and around three hundred folk had dragged their bodies to the sandy shores at the water's edge. It was a happy scene.

People laughed and danced. Lovers were entwined. Drunks were drunk.

Transnistria has a reputation for being an early-eighties Communist museum, a frozen time capsule of how the USSR used to be. This isn't true though, not these days. That said, it's always hard to compare somewhere you are just seeing to somewhere you never saw in the first place. Modern Russia, at least the small and medium-sized towns I've seen, is a crumbling hole. I can't imagine it was much better under Communism. Parts of Tiraspol have this dilapidated appearance too, but not all of it, although maybe it did before the Sheriff company put a superficial gloss on things.

Certainly the stories of people in Moscow queueing around the block for bread aren't replicated here. Sheriff sees to that. Its supermarkets are as bright and product-packed as their British, American or European counterparts. The only things that seem reminiscent of the eighties are the prices, even though locals complain they are still too high. You can get a half-litre bottle of vodka for a pound and a packet of twenty cigarettes for sixty pence. It's cheap to be addicted in Transnistria.

Maybe there *is* one other similarity with the old USSR, and that's its lack of tourists. As I walked around the city today, I didn't hear a single non-Russian or Moldovan voice. I'd entered Transnistria at the country's busiest border crossing and was through in a matter of seconds. Before I came here, I'd assumed people would visit simply for its novelty value, but perhaps not. Maybe its geography puts visitors off, sandwiched as it is between two unfortunate nations. Moldova, the West's poorest country, is probably the last most people would remember if asked to reel off a list of every European state. And then you have Ukraine, unappealingly mysterious as well as at war with, and occupied by, the world's current bogeyman. Nah, we'll stick to the Italian

Lakes or the Spanish Costas if it's all the same to you.

Back at the campsite I sat in its yellow outhouse, a comfortable, open-sided shelter from the sun. The site's second owner, a young fella called Dimitri, introduced himself. We talked about Transnistria's future.

"Will it become properly independent?" I asked. "I mean, will it ever be recognized?"

"It's unlikely because it's not self-sustaining," he replied. "We rely on free oil from Russia." Fuel is just one way the Great Bear keeps instability stable. "It's more likely we'll join Moldova, Ukraine or Russia. But there's no appetite for Russia. No one wants to be another Kaliningrad," he said, referring to the isolated exclave of Russia, crushed between Poland and Lithuania.

I'd recently read about one possibility.

"Perhaps Russia will snatch a part of Ukraine to link Russia and Transnistria together," I offered.

He shook his head.

"I doubt it. That would be a *big* war. We're more likely to join Moldova."

I wasn't sure if this really was most likely to happen or just what Dimitri personally wanted. I suspect it was the latter because it flew in the face of recent referendum statistics. In 2006 the populace was asked two questions: Should we rejoin Moldova? Should we join Russia? 96% of voters were *against* the first possibility, while 98% were *for* the second one. That's about as unanimous as you can get. And let's not forget the Transnistrian flag still includes a hammer and sickle. Unfortunately for the Transnistrians, Russia wasn't as interested.

"Perhaps increased tourism would help," I said.

"It can help, but it's not enough. We are in the wrong part of Europe. But things are much better for tourists here than they were ten years ago. Corruption is less."

I mentioned Bruno, the cyclist who had the incorrect visa and how I'd read in the past he'd have been invited to pay his way out of his hole.

"Yes, he was still lucky though," Dimitri said. "There's probably a 25% chance that today he'd be asked for a €20 bribe. Ten years ago, the chance would've been 90%. The guards don't go for the locals because we know the law."

But amid this pessimism, Dimitri saw one solution, although I wasn't sure how serious he was.

"Maybe Transnistria could be sustainable as a low-tax haven," he said, "with casinos and prostitutes."

That's right, Dimitri. Keep it classy.

*

The next morning I walked back into the centre of the city. For a place with such cheap cigarettes and booze it was strangely short on laughs and smiles. I headed for the bit of town that always provides something of interest, even somewhere with no tourist infrastructure, the main market.

On the way I ambled through a small park. Some beggars sat at the side of the path, playing recorded music as an incentive to win a few coins. One scrawny young bloke had gone a step further and sang karaoke-style over the top of his tunes, rocking quickly backwards and forwards, out of time with his music, less an innovative dance technique and sadly more reminiscent of mental illness.

Outside the market a street dog slept soundly. Inside it was a huge, single expanse of trestle tables but limited to just fruit, vegetables, flowers and honey as far as I could see. Things were cheap. Tomatoes were down to thirty pence a kilo, about one-sixth the price of the cheapest I could find at Tesco.com. There were so many people inside, it was difficult to move about, especially when they kept stopping to stare at me.

Seeking space again, I went back on to the street, past a

huge, yellow tanker selling draft *kvas*, the barely alcoholic beer made from fermented bread, and to the Church of the Nativity. It was a reverse TARDIS, large on the outside but small once within, plushly decorated with chandeliers and paintings. It seems wealth in Transnistria is shared out between Sheriff and God.

I was quickly exhausting what Tiraspol had to offer. I decided to wander freely, unencumbered by the need to tick a box. I passed the famous Kvint building. Formed in 1879, the company now produces twenty million bottles of the hard stuff every year. Its youngest cognac is just three years old, and a half-litre can be picked up locally for about three pounds. Obviously, as the brandy increases in age, so does its price. The most expensive generally available is forty years old. There's also a limited edition fifty-year-old that sells for two thousand quid each. The first two bottles, numbered one and two, were sent to Russian President Putin and Prime Minister Medvedev although the company wouldn't be drawn on who got number one. I think we all know who.

The day was heating up. I stopped at a city centre shack and bought a large kvas from a Russian momma. It tasted both sweet and savoury at the same time, much more satisfying and thirst-quenching than Coca-Cola on a hot morning. I slurped from my plastic cup while sitting on a bench and wondered if this constituted drinking alcohol in public, illegal here, despite Moldovans being Europe's most prolific boozers. I reckoned I was safe. Usually it's considerably less than 0.5% alcohol, twice the strength of a can of Foster's.

I realised I was near a special bookshop, the one place in town you could buy Transnistrian souvenirs. Two local lads came past, guiding an American towards it. A woman walking in the opposite direction did a comedy full-body double-take when she heard them speaking in English.

Unlike some of the places on this huge bike ride, no one could accuse Transnistria of selling its soul for the tourist dollar.

The two Transnistrians and the American disappeared into the bookshop. I went inside too. In the long, dark, narrow store, another young fella in his twenties was weighed down with a heavy rucksack. It seemed that every one of today's visitors to Tiraspol had assembled here at the same time.

I continued to stroll around the city. Tower blocks were disintegrating before my eyes. Some of the smaller buildings were even older, and odd-looking too, seemingly made of clay by the thicker kids from Year 3.

A little further along, a snack bar sold kebabs. On its sign the word "shawarma" was written phonetically in Russian. Its initial consonant sound in Cyrillic looks not unlike a W. The shop had used the golden arches of an upside-down McDonald's M instead. This is not a country worried by trademark infringement.

I was hungry and luckily stumbled upon a branch of Fornetti, the closest thing east of Europe has to Greggs. I took my picnic to the wall opposite the Ministry for Foreign Affairs, a sleepy government office with a noticeable lack of comings and goings. Outside the front of the building were the flags for South Ossetia, Abkhazia and Nagorno-Karabakh, three other breakaway nations we'll be meeting again later, the only places on the planet that reciprocally recognize Transnistria as a sovereign state. If this bike ride had an HQ, this building would be it.

Back at yesterday's church-tank combo I noticed a monument I'd missed the first time around containing an eternal flame and the names of all the people killed in Transnistria's war of independence. A rough count suggested about five hundred died on this side of the battle lines. All that death and where did it actually get them? The locals are trapped here in limbo between a country they don't want to be a part of and a much larger one who only associates with them in order to mess things up politically in Europe, a pawn in a smarter man's game of power chess. Meanwhile, the economy is sucked dry by two former KGB agents.

The day was refusing to cool down. I found an outdoor café by the river and decided to grab a cold beer.

"Do you want a bottle or draft?" asked the young waitress.

"Draft, please."

A minute later her boss appeared.

"Are you sure you want draft?" he asked.

"Yeah."

"Draft isn't working."

I had to smile.

"A bottle then."

In the former USSR, you've got to expect a certain amount of stuff is going to be on the fritz.

I sucked my bottle of beer as an overweight guy walked past. He wore camouflaged army trousers and no shirt. His huge pale belly hung meatily over his belt. Soldier of Misfortune? Inaction Man?

I finished up and strolled back to the site. The roads in Transnistria, at least the ones I'd seen, were generally better than Moldova's, but the pavements were just as awful. Sometimes I felt like I was drunk given the number of times I stumbled over cracked concrete. One advantage is that you don't have to negotiate people walking in phone-comas here, eyes glued to a screen, brains in the Cloud. To do that in Transnistria would be lethal.

I'd selected somewhere local for dinner. Although the prices were almost comical by any western standard, Dimitri told me this place, Shinok Kumanek, was where they took visitors they were trying to impress. And the food was great. My chicken noodle soup came with a lovely minted potato samosa. This was followed by a second starter – I was using up the useless Transnistrian money I had left, OK? – a pile of potato rostis in a mushroom sauce. Main course was a chicken breast stuffed with spinach and cheese with a side of yet more potatoes cooked with onions. There were no taste explosions, but everything was delicious. And when it's all washed down with three dark pints of local beer before you're presented with a bill for less than a tenner, you realise why that woman on the exchange desk didn't think I'd get through a full fifty euros.

On the way back to the tent I blew the few notes I had left on a low-end bottle of Kvint brandy. This was a better, if only temporary, memento of my time here than any throwaway plastic flag from that souvenir bookshop.

Transnistria had been an experience, which was all I could have hoped for. There are some places you visit for fun and some you visit for interest. Ideally, your destination would provide both. Although it had its moments, Transnistria was definitely in the latter camp for most of my stay. And despite its no longer being the planet's best preserver of the former USSR's way of life – Belarus wins on that front – it's genuinely unique. Don't believe anything you read about it – not even this book – but go and see it for yourself.

*

My time in Transnistria was at an end and I had to move on. Today's first job was to escape the unrecognised country. I approached a more low-key border post on the broken road that headed towards the south of Moldova. Another large-hatted teenager stood outside the border office. I handed him my passport and he looked at its front cover.

"Money," he said firmly.

"What?"

Was this Transnistria's famous bribe extraction system?

"Money?" he repeated.

This wasn't a command though. Was he asking me a

question? I was confused and shook my head.

"Manny?" he said again, the sound changing slightly as he pointed to the front of my passport.

The penny dropped.

"Ah, Man," I said. Russian words sometimes end in a soft Y sound, turning man into something like manny. "The Isle of Man."

He looked perplexed.

"Britain?" I tried.

Nothing.

"UK?"

Still nothing.

"England?" I offered for the sake of comprehension.

I don't know whether he finally understood or he'd just had enough of this foreign-speaking moron. He waved me on to the official passport guy, sitting inside his box. He inspected my document thoroughly but wasn't interested in why I was travelling with an Isle of Man passport. He nodded, and I was finally free of Transnistria.

Now, you've every right to think Moldova has been exhausted in my attempt to mine wannabe countries from within its borders, but you couldn't be more wrong. It has another *two*, and one of these, Gagauzia, another Russian-backed region, I'll reach this evening.

Yes, I know, Moldova's a right mess, isn't it?

Chapter 12: Comrat, Your Next City Break

Gagauzia and Taraclia

In Moldova, accommodation is sparse. There's no problem to find somewhere to stay in its larger towns, but these are few and well-separated. A search of Booking.com returns 1,452 hotels in similarly-sized Belgium but only 121 for Moldova, and ninety-eight of those are in the country's four most visited cities. That leaves just twenty-three hotels for the rest of the entire nation. As a result, I had to put in the miles today if I wanted to find a bed. In the end, I topped a hundred, but at least this took my total to a nice round five thousand.

The roads this morning were flat, wide, sufficiently smooth and usually entirely empty. A car might occasionally trundle by, but it'd be well over fifteen minutes before another came along. Even better, trucks didn't bother this poor, forgotten piece of Europe. And weather-wise, a duvet of dull cloud kept the sun's heat at bay. These were as near to perfect cycling conditions as you'd find anywhere. It could only have been improved with a machine every half mile dispensing complimentary cold beer and bacon sandwiches.

So empty were the roads that at times it felt post-apocalyptic. Occasionally I'd pass a small collection of tumbledown houses, perhaps with a solitary shop but usually not, and then the buildings would fade away and I'd return to car-free, walnut tree-lined lanes, low distant hills and wild flowers again. Life had slowed to a standstill. Never has cycling a hundred miles been so relaxing. It felt like meditation. I nearly nodded off.

Somewhere around Cimişlia, I joined the road that forms the non-Transnistrian link from the capital Chişinău to Ukraine's Odessa. This highway would also deliver me to today's destination, the sexily named Comrat.

Hidden in the hills a few miles north of my target is the

little town of Bugeac. Despite a population of fewer than two thousand, the stench of heavy industry hung in the air as I cycled through. This is an area rich in shale gas. I wasn't going to stick around. Environmental destruction wasn't Bugeac's only problem. Villagers were recently warned to stay indoors, not due to the pollution but because of packs of hungry, child-munching wolves. As if this place didn't have enough to feel glum about.

In reaching Bugeac we'd arrived in our next wannabe nation, Gagauzia, the poorest region of the poorest country in Europe. I pushed on through a sudden shower to its 20,000-strong capital Comrat, a place that, on first viewing, had all the charm of an abandoned oil refinery. I wondered whether the town's name was a contraction of "Communist Rathole", but apparently it isn't.

Gagauzia is an autonomous region of Moldova, but unlike Transnistria it hasn't yet broken away, although there were fears it would when the USSR collapsed. This is another pro-Russian corner of the country. The locals had a referendum in 2014 to determine what would happen if Moldova chose union with either Romania or the EU. A whopping 98.9% of residents said this would be grounds for Gagauzia to become fully independent, just like Transnistria isn't. In a separate question they voted with similar certainty to increase the area's ties with CIS, the Commonwealth of Independent States, basically all that remains of the USSR. All this anti-EU/pro-Russian support comes despite only 3.2% of Gagauzian residents being ethnically Russian. This Putin love-in followed Russian meddling in the months before the referendum. A detachment of Russian Cossacks appeared in Comrat and sought formal recognition as a public organisation to "support the motherland". By not being official Russian forces, the Cossacks could stir up trouble that would effectively help Russia but from which Putin could distance himself if things got ugly, a similar strategy to that so successfully employed in Ukraine's Crimea.

At first glance, Comrat isn't much of a looker. That's still true even after a second and third glance. Its one main road, Lenin Street, was lined with businesses whose shopfronts were all obscured by the dense foliage of overgrown trees. Driving or cycling past would provide no hints at all as to what lay behind. The only way to tell which shops were hiding there was to walk down the smashed pavements. Unfortunately, these were so badly broken that if you turned your head towards the shop windows and took your eyes off the ground, that's where you were liable to end up.

The side roads perpendicular to Lenin Street were invariably sandy, stony lanes. If you've ever seen photos of what the now tarted-up white villages of Spain looked like back in the late 1800s, you'll have a good idea of how a lot of Comrat appears today. But with less paella.

Before finding my hotel I passed one of the town's few tourist attractions, at least according to TripAdvisor, a small statue of Lenin. Usually, when carved from rock, Lenin cuts a powerful figure, glowering down at you from on high, like that giant Superlenin in Tiraspol. Here in Comrat, he's human-sized, only slightly raised from ground-level and wearing a worker's cap, looking less a communist revolutionary and more like a left-leaning geography teacher. Facially, he was familiar, less angular than normal, bearing a distinct resemblance to Jeremy Corbyn. Not being too well up on the variety of Communist theory, I don't know whether or not Jezza would see this as a compliment.

My hotel was called the Altin Palace. After seeing my room I suspect the establishment's naming department had a keen sense of humour. "Altin" is the Turkish word for "gold", although it would've been more fitting if it meant "Definitely not a".

My room didn't have any windows or even a fan. Luckily it had an air-conditioning unit on the wall. Unluckily, this wasn't wired in and its mains cable hung limply, too short to reach any power outlet.

Despite today's general mugginess, the room's temperature level was acceptable at first, but then I had a hot shower, which increased both the room's heat and its humidity and introduced the sort of conditions you'd expect of a rainforest. There was a scratching sound coming from a cupboard and then a couple of orangutans climbed out.

With a dearth of hotels in Moldova, rooms are usually over-priced. Compared to the bargains in Ukraine and Romania, the thirty pounds-plus I paid for this natural light-free hole was daylight robbery. Well, not daylight obviously. It was single electric bulb robbery, and I'd stupidly booked it for two nights!

As you might expect in a poor town in an impoverished land where the number of foreign visitors is close to zero, restaurant options are minimal. Of two recommended places, I couldn't find one of them and the other was yet another branch of Andy's Pizza. The requirements of my stomach demanded I give Andy another chance. Best of three seemed only fair.

The menu for this incarnation of Andy's didn't bother with any English, but the pictures were the same as before, and by now I'd picked up the odd Moldovan word. This wasn't as much use as you might imagine. Most people here speak Russian or Gagauz, a language derived from Turkish, hence the "gold" in the name of my terrible hotel. My waiter spoke zero English and at first crept around me uncomfortably. He soon relaxed once I dipped into the few Russian words I knew, a vocabulary list that extended little further than "thank you", "beer" and "another beer", which was all I needed.

I shuffled back along Lenin Street towards my hotel after dark. With my head down to avoid falling into any pits, and because of the detail-obscuring properties of the dense foliage, I managed to walk half a mile past my dwelling before I discovered I was on my way out of town. I turned around sheepishly and trudged back towards my airless cave.

The room was like a blast furnace when I entered. What I need right now, I thought, is a nice glass of cool water. It was then I realised that, reversing all tradition of hotels in former USSR countries, there *was* no cold water, only bubblin' hot. Alright then, I continued positively, go and lie calmly on the bed and dick about on the internet until it's time to fall asleep. Ah yes, of course, the Wi-Fi didn't work either.

Comrat was a bit of a hole, and my hotel room was a perfect match for it, but I had a day off tomorrow and I was determined to enjoy myself. Happiness is a state of mind. I set myself a challenge. I would "complete" TripAdvisor by visiting every single one of the Things To Do in Comrat. This wasn't so much of a challenge if I'm being honest. I mean, I'd already managed to tick off a quarter of that list with that Jeremy Corbyn statue. Let the good times roll!

*

I woke up with the pillow case welded to my sweaty brow. I needed to cool down, but having a cold shower wasn't an option. Its water temperature defied physics. By rights it should have shot out of the tap as steam.

Better to get outside as quickly as possible and go for a refreshing walk. I looked at my less-than-overflowing list of Things To Do: the pretty church, a statue of an old tank – gotta love them! – a second viewing of Jeremy Corbyn just in case I missed something last time and then the *pièce de résistance*, the showstopper, the cherry on top, the Gagauz History Museum. And then, to finish it all off, a world class dinner at Comrat's fine-dining establishment, er, Andy's

Pizza. You want to be me, I can tell.

I was heading out of the hotel through the bar area. This was the one nice element of the place, an airy terrace containing comfortable chairs, the whole space draped in linen, giving it a Middle Eastern feel. I was just about to leave the premises when the female owner asked me if I wanted breakfast. Why the hell not? After all, such a heavily-laden sightseeing day required a solid lining of the stomach.

"Can I have a coffee, please," I said.

She shook her head.

"It's finished," she replied.

"Ah."

Oh well. I could always get one in town when I...

"Espresso or Americano?" she asked abruptly.

Was she using a new definition of finished? It didn't matter.

"Americano. And do you have any food?"

She didn't understand that and so I did a Feed My Face mime.

"*Omlet?*" she asked. This is the Latin transliteration of a Russian word. Can you guess what it means?

Ten minutes later I'd wolfed down my ham and cheese omelette – see, you can speak Russian too! – and she asked me how it was. I'd rehearsed this part.

"*Ochin harasho!*" I replied. This means "very good", which was a bit of a lie. It had been mediocre at best, but I didn't know how to say that, and probably wouldn't have in any case for the sake of Anglo-Gagauz relations. For my meagre attempt at Russian, she smiled at me patronisingly.

I continued on my touristic adventure. If you leave the building through the hotel's bar area you're thrown on to a broken lane at the back of the establishment and experience a rustic return to the centre of town. A gang of teenage chickens scuttled along the path and squawked at me as I passed.

219

Full daylight didn't help Comrat's looks. Even by Moldovan standards this place was ropey. If you want a mental picture of the condition of its pavements, imagine making a tray of toffee and then smashing it to bits with a sledgehammer. Because of the street's roughness, prams weren't the preferred method of transporting babies around here. Women tended to carry their sprogs. I did see one burly chap attempting to wheel a pushchair around town, but it was a struggle even for him.

My first job was to find the tank monument, but unless the internet had supplied the wrong address it'd been replaced with an altogether less macho eternal flame. It stood in a tiny park the size of a tennis court and I was the only person present. If there's a time when Comrat receives the tourist hoard, it isn't the end of July. Maybe visitors prefer the frigid -10°C of winter instead. At least by then my hotel room might have fallen to a temperature slightly less than the sun's core.

From the eternal flame I walked down another pebble and grit path to Lenin Street – again! – and to the cathedral. Dimensionally, it was merely a small church, but its shiny golden domes were attractive, their grandeur only diminished by how shabby the building's yellow paintwork was, peeling like a jaundiced Mancunian in Magaluf.

Leaving the cathedral I noticed a second road running parallel to Lenin Street, a find that excited me more than it probably should. I'd thought I only had the museum to amuse me for the rest of the day. Now I had an entire new thoroughfare to explore. Ah, this was living!

This second road – it was named Kotovsky Street after Grigory Kotovsky, a Red Army commander and occasional bank robber, such are Gagauzia's role models – had fewer trees than Lenin Street and so it was easier to see what was actually on it. And what was on it was a hundred billion stores – OK, probably about thirty stores – gaudily attired with the colourful, garish feel of commercial Turkey, which made sense because, ethnically, that's where the Gagauzians originated from. A lot of the people around here had a Turkish look about them, but the women certainly didn't dress in that staid, buttoned-up Islamic way. Some of the skirts wouldn't have been out of place on a Saturday night in Newcastle.

As yesterday, it wasn't particularly sunny, but it *was* very muggy. A lot of people buzzed about and only a few dozen of them stared at me. Was this simply because they didn't know me, or because I looked different in some way, or because I was the only one sweating like a penguin in the Punjab? Probably all three.

Disappointingly quickly, I came to the end of Bank Robber street. I appeared to have arrived at Comrat's bus station. Well, that's what I assumed this untidy bit of land with two old, knackered-looking buses sitting on it was. I imagine many a visitor would be ecstatic to locate it, if only to escape, but there was something about Comrat that was beginning to grow on me. It was unpretentious and honest, rough and ready, and the people smiled at each other and occasionally at me. This is not the norm in the former USSR. A withering death stare is the default and I liked Comrat for bucking the trend.

And what was this? Back on Lenin Street I passed a statue commemorating the soldiers who fought in Afghanistan, presumably a hangover from the eighties when the USSR took its own futile, ill-fated turn at fighting them. This monument wasn't even listed as one of Comrat's Things To Do. It was a wonderful bonus!

But that wasn't all. I found a sixth attraction. Comrat was proving to be something of a miniature Rome. A fountain gurgled, surrounded by a series of steps and black plinths, commemorating various Russian celebrities and super-tsars.

221

The only name I recognized was Pushkin, but this wasn't built for me. There were also benches were locals could sit and wallow in the splendid plinthiness of the place. Under one of them was an empty bottle of vodka, a crushed packet of ciggies and a kebab wrapper. Presumably this was the happenin' spot in Gagauzia, Comrat's Heaven and Ministry of Sound all rolled into one!

I'd now nearly exhausted the city's paved streets. Not wanting to burn myself out, I decided to save the museum for later. I fought off the urge to dive right into its dusty corridors by stalling for time with a cold beer, but I was only putting off the inevitable.

Beer dispatched, I entered the museum's foyer. A dour version of Norman Wisdom was sitting behind the desk near the door. He wore what looked like cleaner's overalls and was surprised, nay, confused, that anyone would come in. Via sign language he communicated to me the forthcoming visual feast would set me back a full ten lei, or around 50p. I was sure it'd be worth at least that much.

The next few minutes saw me follow his shuffling skeletal frame as he opened one door after another. Each time, he walked into the room, switched on a light and beckoned me inside. Clearly, there weren't enough visitors to justify keeping the place permanently illuminated.

In the main room I whipped out my camera to take some photos to serve as reminders of the crazier exhibits. Photography, apparently, *was* allowed but carried a fifteen lei surcharge. I got the impression this fee was going straight into his pocket. It was 75p well spent.

There were musical instruments and folk costumes and a crocheted Gagauz peacock. All the exhibits were labelled in Russian and so I was reduced to staring and trying to work out what things were. The army medals and old farming implements were self-explanatory. Less easy to explain was a poster of three soldiers in full battle uniform standing behind guitars and synthesizers, clearly Photoshopped on to a backdrop of a military hardware-strewn Afghan mountainside. The expression on the faces of Right Said Vlad suggested they couldn't explain what was going on either.

Later, the museum ran out of Gagauz-specific exhibits and had to get a bit more general. There was a model of a typical nineteenth century farmhouse scattered with any old toy farm animals the curator could find at the local market. As a result, scale was all over the place. Either that or in the olden days Gagauzian pigs were the size of elephants.

Even more general was the museum's explanation of evolution, something Gagauzia surely can't claim much credit for. Or maybe they were trying to suggest that, after the fish and the first land mammals and the apes, the pinnacle of evolution was the Gagauz male. If any local really could get a pram down these streets, perhaps that'd be true.

By now, eight minutes in, I'd seen it all and mimed my desire for departure to Norman. He started to blather on, muttering something that involved the number two. I didn't know what he was talking about, and if he was tapping me up for some more cash he could sod off. I'd already paid £1.25 and I think we'd both got a fair deal at that price. In my Comrat I-Spy Book of Things To See, every box had now been ticked. In half a day of casual strolling, I was now fully qualified as a Comrat City Tour Guide.

After a final visit to Andy's Pizza, where once again the flies outnumbered the customers, I walked back to my hotel and retired to the bar area. Oh, how exciting! Sitting there was another tourist, an Australian called Kate. She was passing through town as part of a guided tour on its way next to Transnistria and then on to Ukraine's Chernobyl, a genre of travel now known as "disaster tourism". My journey fell into the same category, the biggest disaster being how shit my bike was.

Phil, the Irish tour leader, appeared and he asked about my trip. He said he'd like to talk more and would be back later but that he and Kate had "some work to do". He didn't say it as though it were in quotes, but they never returned and so after all their "work" perhaps they just fell asleep in each other's arms.

I re-entered my room, stepping over the puddles of molten lead and, with the internet still on the fritz, switched on the telly, more in hope than expectation. Bizarrely, I found my team, the improving Blackburn Rovers, playing a pre-season friendly against Everton, a game that wasn't even televised in Britain. Given how few fans Blackburn have, I'm guessing this wasn't a massive ratings grabber here in Moldova. But still, washed down with a nice glass of that Kvint brandy I'd liberated from Transnistria and a three-nil victory, it was a satisfactory end to my stay here in this fair wannabe nation.

If Comrat had been just another provincial Moldovan town, then I wouldn't have made this much effort to enjoy it. But it's not just another provincial town, or at least it might not be one day in the future. The Wannabe Bible gives Gagauzia a long-term success rate of 35%, only 10% behind Transnistria, and bear in mind Transnistria is already independent, sort of, and has been for nearly thirty years. Don't be too surprised if, some time in the next few decades, you hear about a weird little country that's just appeared on the eastern fringe of Europe, one that happens to be called Gagauzia.

So should you make the effort to come here? Even if I said yes, you almost certainly wouldn't, and I'm not going to say yes. There's almost nothing to do and nowhere to eat, the shitty hotels are overpriced and it's a long, long way from anywhere else. But if beach holidays and over-familiar city breaks have become boring, then come to Comrat and be bored here instead. Maybe the Moldovan Tourist Board could use that for their next campaign.

*

Today was my last in Moldova, but there was another wannabe to see, albeit briefly.

I got up early. Even at seven in the morning my room was boiling. Was it next to the laundry or something? The bathroom was even hotter. That might have been good news for the clothes I'd washed, but it was so humid everything was still soaked. In fact, they felt wetter now than immediately after washing. Was that even possible?

On the road by eight, under a sky that suggested violence, within minutes of setting off it drizzled a persistent pissiness. The lanes were quiet again, few cars, fewer trucks, absolutely zero cyclists.

Even if a biker passed through Moldova to reach one of its neighbours, they wouldn't come this way. I'd done an obscurity test by searching some of today's place names on the CrazyGuyOnABike website, home to 14,000 biking journals, and it returned only one match from thirteen or so years of data. It was no surprise then that people in the few villages I cycled through stared at me like I was a Klingon.

"What is this strange creature that comes amongst us? Should we worship it or stone it to death?"

I had heard tell of a mythical Golden Lenin and I took a sizeable detour to find it. Away from the hamlets the post-apocalyptic feel returned. Soviet art in the form of statues appeared at the side of the quiet lanes every few miles, a metallic couple waving rigidly, a milk-white farmer in traditional dress with his basket of goods and a baby goat nestling his leg, a young woman in a green tunic proudly displaying two bunches of grapes. It all felt very surreal.

And then a veritable metropolis, Ceadir-Lunga, appeared

on a distant hillside. Around these parts a town of 16,000 is a city. I approached and penetrated its dusty edges. By now, the rain had stopped, but the heavens remained angry. The overcast grey sky matched the architecture of this place. Ceadir-Lunga is twinned with the concept of shabbiness. (It isn't. It's twinned with Bursa, a Munich-sized city in Turkey, which doesn't make a lot of sense.)

The town seemed to consist of a single, busy, ugly main road. In contrast to this drab canvas, on a tall plinth stood a sparkling, incongruously golden Lenin, no longer in approachable Jeremy Corbyn mode, but neither was he scowling at the masses. In fact, if I'm being honest, he looked like a giant Oscar statuette who'd put on a few pounds. I think the gold was a mistake. There was more dignity in his working-class, worker's capped, low-level Corbyn incarnation back in Comrat than this taller, higher, gaudier showpiece.

The second objective of the day was more in line with the theme of this journey. It felt odd that Taraclia in the far south of Moldova, on the way to nowhere, should have any special claim to statehood. It only has a population of 12,000. This is like Ashby-de-la-Zouch wanting to go it alone.

On its edge, the town welcomes you like a city, with its name in large concrete letters, two flags – one for Moldova and the other Taraclia – with the message in Russian "The Bulgarian Centre of Moldova".

The official story is that the town was founded in 1813 by Bulgarian immigrants, although apparently people had already been living here much longer than that. Whatever the truth, its current ethnic make-up is 77% Bulgarian, which is a significant amount and one reason they don't want to stay stuck inside Moldova.

Recently, the locals demanded more autonomy from the Moldovan state as well as the possibility of adding Bulgarian as an official language to be taught in schools, a clear case of putting nationalism over usefulness to their children's education. Bear in mind these kids are raised speaking Moldovan, essentially Romanian, which is spoken nowhere but this distant part of Europe. To add English, Russian, Spanish, French, Chinese, almost any language would have made more sense than Bulgarian. But perhaps if we don't have much, we cling to the one thing we do have, a national identity. How else would soldiers ever be recruited?

There was a hill I needed to climb to take me into town. It wasn't steep, but it was enough to defeat my exhausted legs and broken gears. Over the last few weeks they'd been slowly failing. The easier two cogs refused to hold the chain, meaning I spent more time pushing. I could, of course, visit a cycle repair shop, but I'd decided I wouldn't waste another penny on this bike. I'd already forked out more on it on this trip than I'd originally paid for it back in 2002. When I reached the end, so would it.

The hill took me past fields full of livestock. At first all the creatures seemed wonderfully free-range, hardly a fence in sight. But then I realised each individual animal was tethered to the ground, permitting less freedom than any fence would have done. It was like granting a prisoner day release and then supergluing his feet to the prison car park.

I cycled into the centre. For a wannabe so desirous of autonomy there wasn't much to the place. And there were either lots of police around or just one car making a nuisance of itself.

As far as sights, Taraclia seemed weak even compared to Comrat. Its gold-domed, red-painted church was perhaps in better condition, and I definitely had time to examine it, trapped as I was beside a sheltered stone sarcophagus in its grounds as another storm poured water relentlessly from the sky.

And that was Taraclia. After half an hour the rain eased and I continued on my way, the dirty roads muddying everything I owned. At a junction, a man in a car beamed widely in my direction and waved so enthusiastically that I assumed his greeting couldn't be for me. It was performed with the vigour of someone seeing their long-lost brother. I looked around but couldn't see the target of his affection. As he passed he was still glancing towards me and so I gave him a wave. His face lit up, his smile filled with such ecstasy he may have had an orgasm. Goodbye Taraclia and your super-friendly folk!

Oh yes, I forgot to mention an important detail about this place. These demands for autonomy came after a visit to the area by – oh, call it coincidence if you like – the Russian ambassador to Moldova.

"Gagauzia has autonomy," you can imagine Farid Mukhametshin saying slyly to the local councillors. "Why not your good selves?"

Not insignificantly, 5% of the population are ethnic Russians and so, if anything did kick off, the motherland would have the perfect excuse to send the big guns in to protect them. And they'd do it. Just ask Ukraine. Speaking of which, that's where I'd return to next. I had a ferry to catch.

Chapter 13: Potholes and Portholes

Budjak and Odessa People's Republic

Entering Ukraine had been easier than last time. As I cycled towards today's destination, two teenagers herded a couple of hundred goats across the long, straight road. A rusty Lada overtook me, sped up and looked like he was going to take out as many animals as possible, only slamming his brakes on at the last minute. The driver's impatience and unnecessary brinkmanship motivated the lads to hurry up a bit.

It was hard to believe I was heading towards any sort of population centre. According to the map, the town was only a mile or so away on that hillside over there, but I could see no evidence of civilisation except the odd tower poking out through a forest. The few buildings I could see wouldn't have accommodated a football team, let alone the 16,000 people who supposedly lived here.

The "here" in question was yet another small but regionally important town you've probably never heard of, the capital of yet another wannabe country you've probably also never heard of. Why would you have? This bit of the world gets very little press. The town is Bolhrad and the country Budjak. If you're familiar with either, award yourself five points.

Unlike Gagauzia and the dot that was Taraclia, Budjak isn't small (unless you're American or Australian, in which case, sorry, it's tiny). It covers an area of 5,000 square miles and is the isolated lump of Ukraine that's sandwiched between southern Moldova and the Black Sea. Unless you're going to Odessa from the Romanian coast you've got absolutely no reason to go there and, as a result, hardly anyone does. And you've got to reach its eastern edge, over a hundred miles away from here, to find a town even as big as Bolhrad. It felt like the corner of Europe that everyone forgot.

As I approached, it became clear its buildings lay hidden beneath dense foliage. I'd never experienced an urban area so green. If you've ever seen photos of how Pripyat, the town devastated by the Chernobyl power station, is now being reclaimed by nature, you have some idea how Bolhrad looks today, minus the nuclear devastation, although given the state of its roads and pavements, that was open to question.

I found a hotel. On reception was a tiny, slim woman in her thirties. She spoke no English, but we both knew the procedure. A familiar exchange occurred.

"Komnata?" I said. This is "room" in Russian.

She nodded.

I raised a forefinger and then pointed at myself.

She smiled. Obviously, this pillock is travelling alone.

I raised the forefinger again, put my hands together and mimed a pillow for my head.

She nodded again. The pillock wants to stay for one night. She wrote down a number on a piece of paper. It was my turn to nod. Easy peasy. Transaction complete.

Now I'd left over-priced Moldova, hotel charges had tumbled again. Tonight my clean and comfortable basic room cost less than thirteen quid, and, unlike my "palace" in Comrat, it even had functioning air-conditioning too. Yes, because I'm worth it.

I wandered into town, noting that, if I could find nowhere else, right by the hotel was yet another pizzeria, a non-chain, provincial one, unlikely to present its menu in picture form. I'd be glad I'd learned the Cyrillic alphabet. At least I'd be able to have a stab at pronouncing the words I didn't understand.

All the streets were lined with trees, along the sides and down the middle of them too. There were so many you couldn't see how long the road stretched ahead. How far could it be to the centre of a 20,000 person town anyway? Well, further than you'd expect, because Bolhrad, it turned out, was a planned city, and it was planned to accommodate a lot more people than eventually moved in. At the time, I didn't know this. If I'd any idea how far it was to the centre, I probably wouldn't have bothered. But I did bother, and my endeavour was rewarded with a beer and a snack, sitting in the temporary sunshine of a tattered park. I was also treated to a statue of a mermaid and an erect dolphin. The dolphin was erect in more ways than one. As well as standing upright on its tail, someone had graffitied on to it a massive cock 'n' balls while simultaneously highlighting the prostrate mermaid's breasts. Thank you, Bankski.

Apart from cheap alcohol and pornographic aquatic creatures, Bolhrad didn't have much to offer. A brief search of the internet, however, presented one curious fact about the place, but without an explanation it merely led to more questions. Apparently, the Bolgrad Glacier in Antarctica was named after Bolhrad High School. It can't be normal to name lumps of ice after schools, can it? Perhaps Bolhgrad's educational establishment is special. That said, the next Antarctic glacier alphabetically is the Bolton Glacier, in honour of William B. Bolton, the inventor of the collodion emulsion process of dry-plate photography and so clearly the naming committee was casting around for anything. You should check the list. There's probably one named after you.

*

The Wannabe Bible suggests that, Catalonia and Székely Land aside, Budjak has at least as good a chance of achieving independence in the long-term as any of the wannabes I'd passed through on this trip up until the serious stuff started in Transnistria. And yet it isn't clear the people who live in this area even want independence. It may all be the work of a greater power.

The main driving force for separation is the Bessarabian People's Rada. Bessarabia is one of those places that older readers might have heard of but possibly didn't really know where it was, thrown off the correct geographical scent by the "arabia" bit of the name. In reality, Bessarabia approximately occupied both modern day Moldova and this here region of Budjak. According to the pro-Ukrainian website EuroMaidenPress.com, the Bessarabian People's Rada is a Kremlin separatist propaganda project, yet another attempt to destabilise Ukraine. The fear is this area will become a copy of Donetsk or Luhansk, an active war zone occupied by Russia.

But whatever the future for this region, it wasn't all going to kick off today. I had seventy miles to cycle to the next town of any size, Tatarbunary, but it'd be relatively easy. This area forms part of the Eurasian Steppe, the vast, flattish grasslands that stretch all the way from here, right across Russia and to

Mongolia in the east. And yes, that does mean it's pretty bloody tedious.

I cycled mile after mile without seeing any sign of human settlement, just tracts of grass disappearing into the distance. To break the monotony, a wedding party came past, a limo for the happy couple followed by loads of balloon-covered Ladas. Also keeping me on my toes were the dogs. At one point I was chased by a pack of three of the salivating buggers.

Towards the end of the day, the skies thickened up and storms moved in. Behind me and ahead were the blackest clouds I'd seen to date. A quick check of the map told me I still had ten miles to Tatarbunary. I pedalled like a cokehead to avoid the coming Armageddon and managed to reach the 11,000-strong town as lightning crackled in the distance.

I found another hotel in which no one spoke a word of English. However, where there's a will – I willed a bed, they a paying customer – there's a way. I was shown to my room by one of the Lullaby League, a tiny woman with an easy smile.

The Wiki page for Tatarbunary paints a particularly grim picture of the town. It tells of how running water is only available for four hours a day, how the Sasyk Lagoon – this is the Black Sea bay on which Tatarbunary sits – is so polluted that swimming is too dangerous and how cancer rates, especially for the young, are the highest in the whole of Ukraine. Paaaartay!

Even within a poor region of a poor country, the town felt forgotten about and shoddy. Everything looked unfinished, or perhaps these buildings had once been completed and were now on their way down again.

The storm finally provided a drenching and blew itself out to sea. As darkness descended, mad shouting kicked off on the street outside my hotel. Multiple engines were revved to screaming point. I opened the window to see what was going

233

on but immediately wished I hadn't. I suspect this was the first action these hinges had seen in years. It felt like the glass was about to fall out of its frame. In any case, the noise was coming from around the corner and I couldn't see anything, but someone sounded angry in an alcohol-fuelled sort of way. Perhaps this was just another Saturday night in a small, messed-up town in Ukraine.

*

On the way out of Tatarbunary the next morning, I passed the Sunday Market. At one end of it, a three-piece band dressed in army fatigues, one with a keyboard, played naff Costa del Sol hotel pop. They looked just like that Photoshopped picture in the Comrat Museum, Right Said Vlad. If I'd known the Ukrainian word for "autograph" I'd have stopped.

Compared to the rest of Ukraine, the roads so far in Budjak had been mostly free of holes, probably because they were so untroubled by traffic. As I moved farther east, the quality of the tarmac deteriorated, and apparently it was no one's job to clean the highways either. On a thoroughfare as wide as a dual carriageway, thick mud had been dragged on to it from unsurfaced side roads, resulting in four lanes being reduced to two. You can guess where I ended up whenever a car came past.

In places, the tarmac had also melted into weird and sometimes quite beautiful shapes. Since Moldova there'd been frequent signs telling lorries they weren't allowed on the highway if temperatures exceeded, say, 30°C, but the truckers paid no attention to this, presumably the reason why the tarmac was so badly deformed. This stretch would have made a serviceable motocross track.

Quasi-road-o carried on into Ukraine proper, but I was heading to Bilhorod-Dnistrovs'kyi, a town of 50,000 people on the Dniester estuary and so needed to turn off. I found myself on a Ukrainian Comedy Road. There were more potholed bits than not. Just as moon craters can have smaller, more recent craters within them, some of the larger potholes had deeper, internal potholes. The terrible surface easily quadrupled how far the traffic using this mess had to travel. Side by side, you could comfortably have fit six cars on this wide road. In the distance, a vehicle would appear, and by the time it'd reached me – it took quite a while as it repeatedly twisted and turned – it would have occupied every one of those six positions, from far left to far right and everything in between. It made a lot more sense to be here on a mountain bike.

Eventually, closer to Bilhorod, the surface improved, but it had been a rough old fifteen miles of lumpiness. As I cycled into town, a well-built, white-haired guy gave me a huge smile, stuck out his thumb and shouted "Hero!" to me. It's the same word in Russian but hardly appropriate. I mean, can you imagine Superman on a pushbike?

Wandering around, there seemed no focus to Bilhorod, another Ukrainian town of broken pavements and broken noses. Occasionally I'd see something to catch my eye. There was a scratty park with painted concrete blobs representing some type of alien creatures, and the entire side wall of a large building was covered in an old mosaic of a spaceman carrying a helmet labelled CCCP. In the town itself, it didn't get any better than this.

But it wasn't all neglect. A pack of eight street dogs wandered past. Most of them had ear tags and so at least someone was monitoring and caring for them. And old buildings were looked after too. Right on the coast was the town's main attraction, a well-preserved fortress dating from the thirteenth century.

Despite few people speaking English – no one at my hotel, nor the restaurant I later chose, spoke any – someone had still used it as the language of choice when it came to civil disobedience. On a wall near my hotel, an unhappy individual had scrawled "Fuck the Police!" although maybe safe in the knowledge that no one in town knew what it meant.

By Ukrainian standards, tonight's accommodation was pricey, a decadent £27, but for that I got a great room with a huge bed and a bathroom containing a deep corner bath, within which I soothed away several months of knee pain. However, this being Ukraine, there had to be something wrong with the place. That's how it works here. You're not allowed to open a hotel in Ukraine unless you tell the authorities exactly how you're going to screw it all up. Today, the Wi-Fi functioned well, but only if I sat outside, near the car park, on the bottom step of the iron staircase that led to my room. But by Ukrainian standards, that's no biggie. I'll take that over £79 in a nondescript British city's anonymous Premier Inn.

Having Wi-Fi was critical though because tonight I received an important e-mail. A week earlier, I'd requested permission to visit Georgia's breakaway region Abkhazia, another land, like Transnistria, supported by the Russians but with a more recent, bloodier history. If you're allowed to enter the "country", they send you a letter, a copy of which must be presented to the authorities upon arrival on one day and one day only. And now, as I logged in, the email was sitting there in my inbox, an invitation to visit a place the UK Foreign Office and US Department of State say you must never go. Gulp!

*

The route from Bilhorod to Odessa showed me a side of Ukraine I hadn't seen before, its Black Sea tourism. Everyone heading in that direction was crushed on to a single road on a narrow sand spit close to where the Dniester tumbles into the sea. Unfortunately, the sea views I'd been hoping for were blocked by the sort of low rent hotel development you might have expected in the dodgier bits of Torremolinos.

Dozens of people were sitting at the roadside offering cheap rooms to visitors, while grown men – in many cases, *over*grown men – wandered about the resorts in the snuggest of Speedos. The bright sunlight bounced off their ample forms, turning them a glisteningly clammy pork-pink.

Over time, the heat and dense traffic had badly twisted the tarmac around here, making it dangerous to cycle on as it frequently angled me into the passing vehicles. As Odessa grew ever nearer, the quantity of cars increased. When the only option became a three-lane highway with no hard shoulder, I got off and pushed.

In total, this was my sixth day in Ukraine and I'd yet to witness one of those comedy pissheads I'd seen on several occasions the last time I was here, but this was remedied within a few minutes of reaching Odessa's city centre. A drunk fella stumbled into a car, setting of its alarm. He looked around guiltily, shushed me with a wobbly forefinger on his lips and then crept away like a cartoon villain on exaggerated tiptoes.

Once installed in a hotel, I went to buy tickets for my boat ride to Georgia. The ferry company's Black Sea timetable is as fluid as the surface on which it operates. I'd been hoping to buy my passage for August 1st, the day after tomorrow. Fortunately for my tight schedule, the next departure had been brought forward a day. Less fortunately, it was completely full. Instead, I bought a ticket for the next sailing, on the 4th, although this date wasn't guaranteed and was only the shipping company's best guess at present. Ominously, the salesman said he'd e-mail me the day before departure to tell me when the boat would leave Odessa. I had visions of me as a wizened old man, phoning the office on a daily basis to be repeatedly told, "No, sir, but I'm sure it'll be arriving any month now."

The timing of this worried me. Although the journey across the Black Sea was scheduled to take two days, the company's website warned that, under adverse weather conditions, this could be extended to five. But it could be worse even than that. One online blogger told how a combination of such climatic misery and mechanical failure meant her crossing had taken a full week! And I had to be in Abkhazia, almost a hundred miles from my arrival point in Georgia, on September 9th or else I'd have to forget the whole thing. My schedule was as tight as a Botoxed smile.

I was going to be in Odessa for a lot longer than I'd anticipated. As a proper city of over a million people, there was a lot more to see and places to eat than, say, Comrat, but I didn't want to exhaust them too quickly. I returned to my room and made a plan of action.

For my first evening meal I chose Molodost, a Communist-era themed restaurant. I sat at a table in the street and ordered a beer while examining the menu. The drink arrived in a lidded jar alongside a tin opener. Is that really how beer used to be served in the USSR?

Keeping up the kitsch, the table mat was a recreation of an old Soviet newspaper. The most realistic nod to Communism came when I ordered my main course and was told it wasn't available.

In the end I chose a vague-sounding cutlet, whose mystery wasn't resolved even upon arrival. It could have been pork or chicken or a weird hybrid of the two. It was alright, but I wouldn't be going back for the full Russian restaurant experience, y'know, a teaspoon of polonium and a very short stay in hospital.

I will now attempt to summarize five days of Odessan fun in a series of pithy vignettes, otherwise we'll be here for longer than this period warrants. Not only that, but I'll make it appear as if all these events happened on one over-planned day.

The main waterfront in Odessa is rather odd. From a pleasant square tumble the Potemkin Steps, an impressive and elegant staircase of 192 ledges that bring you to a truly hideous seaport. There's nothing at all to redeem it, not the multiple rusting railway lines, the dozens of hulking cranes nor the refinery. It's a mess. I didn't hang around for long.

Besides, I had a job to do. I needed to print out my letter of invitation for Abkhazia, the one I had to present at the border checkpoint. The hotel didn't have a printer and so I located an internet café, a business concept that has all but disappeared in most places but not here in Odessa. The one I found today was stuffed full of young blokes playing computer games.

Organising the print-out wasn't as straightforward as I'd imagined. I figured I'd connect wirelessly from my tablet to the café's printer and send the document on its way, but the café had neither a wireless printer nor Wi-Fi of any kind. This is Ukraine.

"Yeah, we've been meaning to get it for some time," said the young blond lad on the dingy joint's main desk.

In the end, via Bluetooth to his personal mobile I had to send the document, which he then emailed to the café's e-mail address from outside on the street because the local phone service couldn't penetrate the café's walls. He opened up the file on his computer and gave it a read. I watched his face as his eyes flicked from line to line. I could see the exact moment they reached the word 'Abkhazia'. They expanded in size considerably. He leaned back and looked at me.

"So you're a big man?" he said.

No, I'm *really* not.

"Nah, just interested in seeing the place."

I suppose this transaction could have gone spectacularly badly. After all, the same Russians that are screwing over

Ukraine – and Odessa hasn't been immune to this – are propping up the regime in Abkhazia. By visiting that breakaway region I could have been seen as colluding with the enemy.

I smiled, and then he smiled – it was all going to be alright – and then he printed out the three copies I'd asked for.

One thing I noticed when walking around Odessa was the difference in working habits compared to Britain. As bored as till-based shop assistants are in the UK, they aren't allowed to show it. This wasn't the case here. In one supermarket, the girl on the checkout was so utterly sick of her job she rested her head on her hand and it nearly touched the counter. She may as well have been asleep.

And health and safety is treated differently here too. Actually, it just seems to be ignored. I can't imagine the quantity of scaffolding and risk assessments that'd be required if working on the outside of a tall building in Britain. Here, while repainting the opera house, the lone retoucher, unharnessed and thirty metres in the air, sat on a narrow wooden plank, suspended from the balcony above by two thin pieces of rope. I suppose the risk assessment was, "Yep, it's risky but so what? I need the money, so let's do it."

As I've said before I like markets for getting the measure of a place. The one I saw in Odessa was ridiculously large, about the size of two football pitches. It didn't limit itself to Ukrainian goods. There were Georgian *khachapuri* and *churchkhela* – two snacks we'll meet again later – and a million spices their sellers would mix into a combo for you, depending on what you wanted to use them for. There were piles of walnuts, every type of fruit and vegetable and, more worryingly, mounds of unrefrigerated seafood, marinated cockles in a deep salad bowl just sitting around, putrefying. In this heat, how long would it be before these fishy lumps of gristle became poisonous?

This market also proved itself to be one of the main sources of all those banal English-language t-shirts I'd been seeing everywhere I went. I hunted high and low and, amongst thousands, couldn't find a single garment with its message in Cyrilic. English is cool, apparently, whatever shite it says.

The place teemed with life, both conscious and not so much. Obviously, there were millions of shoppers, but two blokes were passed out in a corner, one snoring like a hog. An occasional woman begged. Other women, equally poor but with more gumption, sat in front of a single pot of walnuts, hoping desperately for a sale.

I felt a need for culture and hunted out a gallery. The art was mostly rural scenes, painted in the mid-1800s. What was telling was that, despite depicting the basic nature of country life back in the nineteenth century, almost any one of those pictures could have been knocked up from the current reality in today's Moldova.

In every room of the gallery sat a stern-faced middle-aged woman who scowled at each visitor as we entered. One of them carried out her duties in such an overblown way I couldn't help myself from bursting out laughing at her ridiculousness. I'm not sure that's the reaction she was after.

Not all the old ladies in Odessa were so unfriendly. Outside the gallery, I sat on a bench for a minute. I was joined by a sweet woman in her eighties with an unruly mop of long, white hair.

"Do you speak English?" she asked.

She was very excited to hear where I was from. She'd been an English teacher during the country's old USSR days and had worked as far away as Vladivostok. Now she had to get more creative to practise her language skills.

"I sometimes go to the medical academy," she said. "There are lots of people there. I saw a white face, then a little yellow face, then a brown face. And he was Indian," she said, giving a small whoop. "I speak English to them all!"

"You know this gallery?" I asked.

She smiled.

"This is *my* gallery," she replied. "I've been inside hundreds of times." Then she looked around. "Who are you with?"

"No one. I cycled here alone from Spain."

"When I was fifteen," she started, "I went cycling with a big group of girls."

"Fun?" I asked.

"No, it was awful," she smiled. "Just awful."

I laughed, and she laughed, and then her face became more serious.

"My mind is going," she said. "Sometimes I can't remember where I left my stick. Is it at home or where I went for a walk? I don't know."

Her mental abilities may have been fading but not her physicality. She danced around while telling her story. Perhaps her stick wasn't always necessary. And then she breathed out a massive sigh.

"It's nice to look back on life and think of all the things I've done," she said.

"Happy memories?"

"Happy, yes. And some not so happy."

She told me she got married at twenty-two. I wondered if the reason she was out here talking to strangers was because her husband wasn't around any more. I didn't want to drag up any of those less than happy memories by prying. She started to tell some other people sitting on the next bench that I was English and fell into a deeper chat with them.

"I have to go," I said.

"Where to?" she asked.

"The Trade Unions building."

She looked wistful.

"Mmm, some not so happy."

As well as being the launching point for exploration of broken Europe farther east, Odessa has its own entry in my list of wannabe countries, although it qualifies more through a technicality. In the centre of town is a large, neoclassical, five-storey building that was once home to Trade Unions House. In 2014, protests between pro- and anti-Russian supporters flared up here, quite literally. The building was torched, resulting in the deaths of forty-eight people with over two hundred others injured.

At the same time, the Odessa People's Republic was proclaimed by one internet site, although local pro-Russian groups later refused to take responsibility for this. Once again, it was believed this announcement had been made by forces closer to Moscow in order to destabilise this city of strategic and logistical importance.

Today, all evidence of recent fire damage has been removed. Tributes to the deceased – photos, drawings and poems – covered the wall at the front of the building and tiny shrines dotted the grounds. But such memorials were not needed to jog the national memory, not when soldiers and civilians still die on a near daily basis in the east of the country.

These five days I'm cramming into one became six. I received an email from the ferry company to tell me the boat would now leave not on the 4th, but the 5th. This was pushing my schedule to breaking point.

But in this six-compressed-into-one day I didn't go hungry. For my evening meal I started with King's Ear Soup, which contained less auditory organ meat and more prawns, salmon and zander. I followed this with Ukrainian salad – that's potato, herring, spring onion, croutons and mayonnaise – and then meat-stuffed *vareniki* dumplings. Following these came fried potato pancakes with bacon, mushroom and sour cream called *draniki*. And then chicken and roast vegetables in a spicy tomato sauce, and fried potatoes with onion and bacon on the side. Oh yeah, and a pizza.

I was understandably gorged but content, for tomorrow I had a ferry to catch.

*

All you need to know about the Black Sea journey is that my time aboard was a lot like how I assume prison to be: bunks, confined spaces, three meals a day and no exercise with a bunch of blokes who look like they'd lost a lot of fights. But I made some new friends, among them Americans, Germans and Japanese. It was a lot more fun than I'd imagined.

During our first lunchtime, one of the Germans made a joke.

"This ferry would be an easy target for a Russian destroyer," he chuckled.

His timing was immaculate. Bang! And all the lights went out. We looked at each other, initially concerned. Then we laughed nervously before just sitting there quietly, waiting for something else to happen. It didn't. The engines had stopped, and they stayed stopped for the next four hours as we drifted ever closer towards Crimea. That would've been an unplanned visit to a "new country" – in reality, an annexed country – that could only have ended badly.

The engines were eventually fixed and we disembarked in Batumi, Georgia's jazzy Black Sea resort, on the evening of September 7th. It still wasn't a given I'd reach Abkhazia in time, but I wasn't even officially in Georgia yet. There was passport control to deal with.

Unfortunately, the foot passenger route through customs had a non-bike-friendly turnstile. The border guard responsible for this section told me to go around the building, to where the cars would go. And when I did that, the official there said I had to go through as a foot passenger. I seemed to be locked in an eternal passport purgatory.

"I was told to come this way," I somehow mimed.

After a quick consultation with one of his mates, he decided that, whoever I was, whatever it was I wanted, I wasn't worth the trouble and so he let me pass into Georgia utterly and gloriously unchecked.

If you want to smuggle drugs, do so on a bicycle.

Chapter 14: Once More Unto the Beach

Adjara, Samegrelo and Abkhazia

More than anywhere on this ride, I'd been looking forward to Georgia. In recent months I'd met a handful of people who'd raved about its beauty, its hospitality and its food. A friend of mine, John, a man blessed with a life of travel and cursed with a love of Blackburn Rovers, has written *Lonely Planet* guidebooks for countries on three continents, and Georgia is one of his favourites. That's some recommendation.

In the Georgian language, if you transliterate from its gorgeously squiggly script, Georgia is *Sakartvelo*, the only country in the world to contain the word "bicycle" in its name, albeit in French. Would it therefore be a cyclist's paradise perhaps? Er, no, it wouldn't. Its drivers are absolutely nuts.

The traffic in Batumi was manic. Its bike lanes were uncyclable, both in terrible condition and covered in people entirely unaware of their existence. Instead, for my own protection, I cycled aggressively in the road, positioning myself centrally, like a car, to make sure I could be seen. Given how many accidents I witnessed between fully visible vehicles, this might not have been the safest strategy.

Despite its bicycle-unfriendliness, I liked the vibe of Batumi from the off. Whenever you travel and see a foreign word on a shop front or billboard, it says something to you even if you can't translate it, and its meaning is different for everyone. When I see a Russian word, or one in any other Cyrillic language, its backward Rs and Ns send icy blasts of Cold War repression through my brain. When I see anything written in Greek, I'm transported back to school and its maths and physics lessons. For me, the Georgian alphabet had no preconceived connotations. Its weird curls and loops just screamed, "I'm freakin' strange!" Adding this linguistic exoticism to the town's abundance of neon and dark, often seedy-looking corners, I felt like I'd arrived on the set of *Blade Runner*.

Because of the ferry delays, I'd need to leave Batumi first thing in the morning if I wanted to have a hope of getting to Abkhazia on time. This was a huge shame. This town demanded at least a day's exploration that it wasn't going to get. I had tonight and tonight only.

Lonely Planet John had told me about one of his Batumi-based friends, the delightful Sophia, who owned a B&B, a few rooms around a courtyard that housed her multi-generational family. Sophia was pretty, petite and in her thirties with a soothingly calm voice and a fragile smile. She was instantly loveable.

As well as shelter I needed food. I found a restaurant and asked the waitress for a recommendation.

"I'm glad you speak English," she said with a grin.

"Why's that?"

"Most visitors are Russian. I don't like to speak Russian."

Whether or not this was merely a personal view on the language, Georgians have good reason to dislike Russia. For a start, there's the problem with Abkhazia, which we'll see soon enough. But in 2008, its northern neighbour also invaded Georgia's South Ossetia, which it continues to occupy. Worryingly for Georgia, its territory lies little more than thirty miles from Tbilisi, the country's capital.

If there's one food that could claim to be Georgia's

national dish – like pizza in Italy or fish 'n' chips in Britain – it's *khachapuri*. Every part of Georgia has its own take on this cheesy bread, but the most famous version is from Adjara, the region surrounding Batumi. Its pizza-like dough is shaped into a boat, filled with local cheese and then baked. Towards the end of the cooking process, a raw egg and a few sticks of butter are inserted into the cheese. The baking continues until the butter has melted and the egg's albumen has turned white but not yet solidified. Once served, you rip bits of bread from the hull of the boat, using the first piece to mix up the cheesy, buttery, egg-yolk mixture, and then dip and devour unctuous mouthfuls until the whole thing has disappeared. It's heavenly.

I quickly polished off my khachapuri. My waitress had also recommended *khinkali*, Georgia's take on ravioli or Polish pierogi but more substantial and better than both. There's a knack to eating khinkali. If you simply attack them with a knife and fork, you'll miss out. Each one is basically a little sack of tasty stew, a soft pastry bag filled, twisted and sealed. You hold the dumpling by its top knot and, approaching from the side, take a nibble, slurping out the flavourful broth. Only then is it safe to eat the rest. They're usually stuffed with minced meat and spices. Today my khinkali had a wonderful blast of fresh coriander. Munch down what remains of the dumpling and discard the top knot, or eat it and look like a tourist.

Georgian restaurants are slowly infecting the countries that surround this weird land. It can only be a matter of time before every British high street has one. And then, a few years down the line, you'll see an advertisement for a McKhachapuri and know that all is lost.

I also needed something to wash down the food. I'd heard lots of good things about wine from here. After all, this was supposedly the country that invented it. Grape-decorated stone jars have been found dating from 6,000 years ago. I opted for a dry white, which tasted to my jaded palate more like Spanish sherry. To be honest, fine wine is wasted on me. Since our £1-a-day cycling adventure a few years ago, I can quite comfortably manage the stuff in Spain that comes in tetrapaks.

Batumi is a tourist resort and, as a result, more expensive than most places in Georgia. Still, the financial damage inflicted by the meal was small. Georgia was going to be another country easy on the pocket.

*

As already mentioned, Batumi is in Adjara, sometimes also known as Adzharia. For a while after Georgia shook itself free of the USSR, this region acted more or less independently of Tbilisi, controlled by one man, an authoritarian gangster called Aslan Abashidze. While he managed to keep Adjara safe within an unstable Georgia and increased its prosperity, as well as his own, his reign couldn't last forever if Georgia was ever going to re-establish itself as a real country on the world stage. The Rose Revolution that brought reformer Mikheil Saakashvili to the fore was the catalyst for change. That said, the Wannabe Bible still believes Adjara stands a better chance than most of going its own way.

Today I'd cycle out of Adjara and into another region with a small possibility of existing on its own, at least according to the Wannabe Bible, and that was Samegrelo. If both Samegrelo *and* Adjara gained independence, Georgia would find itself in a particular pickle, freshly land-locked and surrounded by unstable nations on all sides. It couldn't even turn southwards and away from Russia. There lie Armenia and Azerbaijan, still at war with each other.

But before then I had to escape Batumi and my homely B&B. The weather was misbehaving, giving this corner of Georgia a solid liquid thrashing. I really didn't want to cycle a hundred miles in torrential rain.

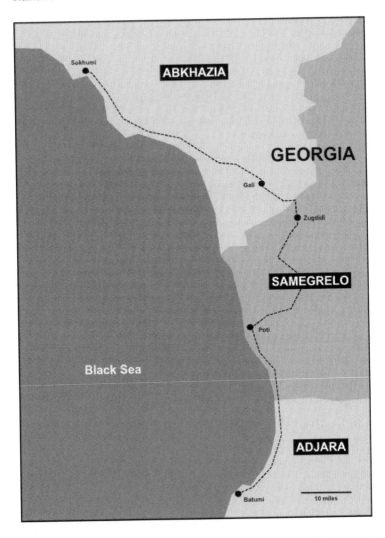

I checked the Abkhazian government website and considered applying for another visa for a later date, but the application form was now in a different format, one that involved downloading a fill-in-able document whose fields were simultaneously uneditable. Maybe this was a temporary glitch or perhaps the problem was at my end. Either way, it would be another hold-up. No matter how soggy I'd get, I had to go for it today.

I carried my bags downstairs, thanked Sophia and turned towards the exit.

"You'll have a little breakfast?" she asked in her elfin voice.

I looked to the skies. I was itching to get going, but not in this weather.

"Yeah, alright," I smiled, thankful for the excuse to wait it out a bit.

"Sit down," she said gently.

The breakfast could never have been accurately described as "little". It started off sensibly with some sliced apricots and plums. Then a basket of fresh bread arrived, along with two fried eggs, a plate of tomatoes, cucumber and cheese, another plate containing four pancakes, two stuffed with coriander-spiced mince and two with cheese. And some butter, jam and honey. And a coffee.

Despite starting the day hungry, I was really struggling to get the whole lot down, delicious though it was. I decided to make one final push to finish the rest of it off when five more pancakes arrived, this time thick, sweet ones. There was a creaking noise and my stomach ruptured.

As the breakfast had taken quite a while to work through, I'd given the weather time to sort itself out. It was still raining, but barely. I thanked Sophia profusely and headed on my way. If you ever find yourself in Batumi, go and stay at Gulnasi's Guesthouse. Especially if your name is Mr Creosote.

I've been to several other places on this planet where the driving was haphazard, but whatever system was used it always seemed to work. The idiots didn't keep crashing into each other. This wasn't the case in Georgia. Traffic accidents happened all the time. It was like a demolition derby conducted on a national scale. Cycling out of Batumi, I heard the telltale squeal of brakes followed by a metallic crash and the tinkle of broken glass. Looking around, a shiny BMW's value had been substantially reduced.

And it was no wonder they hit each other so often. Side mirrors were merely for decoration. Cars, taxis and minibuses would stop without warning, or turn without indicating, or indicate without turning, or simply block the street entirely. More inexplicably, some vehicles would crawl down the road, one wheel on the verge, at five miles an hour, for miles and miles on end. It was like the whole country had chosen this morning to start learning to drive, but only after all the instructors had been shot.

A few miles out of Batumi, under improving skies, I experienced my first Soviet tunnel, a style flawed on so many levels that almost any other design would have been better. Just allow yourself a couple of minutes to consider what a good tunnel would be like. Personally, I think a minimum would be something well-lit, with a decent surface and a safe walkway for pedestrians, if walkers were going to be catered for at all. Of course, the Soviets would have considered this the sort of tunnel that gaylords would prefer, and, in a famously homophobic nation, something more macho and likely to kill you was required.

On the issue of lighting, today's first tunnel had one five watt bulb every fifty metres. For most cars with their bright headlamps, and for me with my head torch, I could live with this. There was also a pedestrian walkway. Before I entered the tunnel I was in two minds. Should I try cycling through or push my bicycle down the walkway? The ideal solution would have let me decide once I was inside and seen how ferocious the traffic was. But not here. The walkway was a metre and a half above the road, certainly too high to throw a heavily-laden bike as a monster juggernaut bore down on me. Since I'd no way to switch from cyclist to pedestrian mid-tunnel, I opted for what I thought was the safer option of walking. But it wasn't really that much safer, what with the walkway being very narrow, without any sort of railing to prevent you falling blindly into the road – remember, most pedestrians wouldn't have lights – and with a flooring that consisted of broken concrete blocks that had in some places fallen apart entirely, leaving behind ankle-breaking voids. This tunnel made me feel like *Manic Miner*, permanently having to keep moving as the platform dissolved beneath my feet. In short, it was a miserable half-mile push.

And then came another tunnel, and one with an additional horror. This inky entrance to Hades was guarded by a couple of ferocious dogs, like a two-headed Cerberus, but, y'know, also with two bodies. They started to snarl viciously at me, saliva dripping from their fangs, at which point a man climbed out of a nearby car and chucked some rocks at them until they stopped. The inside of this tunnel was exactly the same as the other, only worse because it was longer.

Out the other side of Hell, I was glad to get moving again, but I needed some water. I rolled up to a truck stop and went inside its dark interior. A couple of women stood behind a makeshift counter, selling nothing to no one. I saw a bottle of water in a display cabinet and pointed to it. One woman looked to the other and then to me.

"No," she said.

Why the hell not? Perhaps she'd misunderstood what I wanted. I asked for water in Russian. She shook her head. Maybe it was the last one they had, a display model, and not for sale. Thinking on my feet, I went back to my bike, removed its water bottle, returned to the women and mimed filling it up. Ah, that was better. She pointed me to an outside tap. I'd forgotten to check beforehand if mains water in Georgia was potable, but it looked like it'd have to be. I filled my plastic bottle and left the building, but not before catching a glimpse of their storeroom, one piled high with hundreds of bottles of water.

At the next place I stopped, I was approached by a local, one who looked like he'd gone to a backstreet doctor for a cheap transplant and inadvertently been the recipient of George Best's discarded liver. His face was yellower than Homer Simpson's. My new friend said how he'd like to go swimming with me. I didn't know if this was a come on or if he just wanted to drown me to access my mostly functioning organs. In any case, no thanks, fella, I had a war zone to see instead.

I continued on my way. People walked along the roadside and frequently waved and cheered at me, whereas cows wandered into the road and received a reverence from drivers I'd only seen before in India.

After Poti, the home of Georgia's other ferry terminal, I took a dodgy shortcut. The road was unfinished for the most part and full of mud-filled potholes. My bike's gears were making a painful grinding sound, which wasn't helped by the quantity of mud and stones they had to deal with. It sounded like something was soon to expire.

Low houses with gardens full of chickens and beehives lined the track. And it wasn't just cows on the road here. Goats and hairy pigs were everywhere too. Many of the porkers had an uncomfortable-looking, triangular wooden contraption fastened around their necks that looked like they'd run at speed head-first into a fence and then accidentally removed part of it as they extricated themselves.

I eventually reached Zugdidi, a town of 43,000 and the capital of wannabe Samegrelo. After installing myself in a cheap hotel, I popped to the local bike shop to look for some gear-soothing oil, but apparently lubrication wasn't high on the Georgian cyclist's wish list. Instead, a supermarket provided a bottle of the thickest vegetable oil I could find. It was better than nothing. I was just hoping no one would throw an egg at me tomorrow or else my entire chainset would be covered in mayonnaise.

The calories expended on today's one hundred mile ride needed to be replaced. I settled down for beer and grub in one of Zugdidi's more upmarket restaurants, one with an interesting approach to musical entertainment. Piped music would play for a track or two – Sade was popular – and then a live two-piece band would chime in with a song of their own to absolutely no response from the almost full room. Still, it's showbiz, innit?

Over in the corner a table of twenty were indulging in a *supra*, a traditional Georgian feast involving lots of food and even more toasts. You aren't allowed to drink unless it's to someone's health or to the nation or to honour the speaker's favourite goat or something. No wonder Georgia has such a nationalistic streak when you have to praise the country's glories every time you want a slurp of wine.

Luckily, I had no such alcoholic restriction. The beer flowed and accompanied my starter, *badridzhani nigvsit*, aubergine rolls stuffed with walnut paste. Georgians are a bit mental about their walnuts. They put them on everything. My main course was *shkmeruli*, chicken in an extremely strong garlic sauce. This choice wasn't accidental. Tomorrow I expected to be interrogated by Russians. Hopefully, my terrible breath would make this process as brief as possible.

*

At seven o'clock the machine gun rattle of rain against my window jolted me awake. I looked outside. Although I could just about make out the ground three storeys below, the scene was more akin to that from the porthole of a mid-Atlantic trawler during the perfect storm. The question wasn't whether I *should* go out in this, but whether I *could*.

I'd booked breakfast and so wearily prised myself from my bed and went downstairs to refuel, even if it looked as though I was going to be spending the day stuck inside this cheap hotel while my Abkhazian letter of invitation went unused.

The breakfast was wearier than I was, two tiny hot dog sausages, a hard-boiled egg and a husk of dry bread. At least there was a sachet of pâté to have after the sausages, or so I thought. It turned out to be mustard made from the insides of Vesuvius. A mere knife-end's worth had me gasping for breath. It didn't really matter. The bread was too dry to eat anyway.

I returned to my room and continued to watch the weather through my window. Eight o'clock, half eight, nine o'clock, the elements tore into the scene outside. People dashed from one building to another, umbrellas ripped from hands or turned inside out. And then suddenly, at nine o'clock, the Georgian Rain God had a moment of reflection.

"Well done, fella," he seemed to say. "You've come this far, despite what me and my international mates have thrown at you. Have this one on me."

The rain stopped and peace returned to Zugdidi. Huzzah, I was going to Abkhazia after all!

I checked out of the hotel and carried my belongings to the street below. Ah, the oil! I loaded my chainset and cassette with vegetable lubrication and set off. That grinding, squeaking whine was silenced immediately.

The border was about five miles from the centre of Zugdidi, the roads becoming steadily quieter and less trafficked as I got nearer. Cars are not allowed to cross into Abkhazia here, or anywhere it connects to Georgia. Only the occasional taxi passed me by.

Near the border was a statue of a revolver with a knotted barrel. I wasn't sure whether this was meant to be a symbol of peace or a gibe at the opposition's badly-maintained military hardware.

The sun stayed well-hidden, the green-grey hills giving few hints of the trouble this region had seen in recent decades. In the distance, a huge Abkhazian flag on an over-sized pole waved mockingly to the Georgians on this side of the border.

As far as the Georgians are concerned this isn't a border at all. How could it be? After all, Abkhazia is still a part of Georgia, one that's illegally occupied by Russia under the pretext of supporting Abkhazian independence. No one believes for a second Russia cares about the Abkhaz cause. It's just another way to keep your neighbours unstable and, more importantly, out of NATO.

I rolled up to an area of undefined purpose. Lots of cars were parked up and people milled about, mostly old women carrying huge plastic bags. Eyes turned to me as I cycled into the action. One bloke gave me a cheer, but it sounded more sarcastic than celebratory. Everything felt a little weird, but I put that down to knowing too much about this place already rather than any vibe I was picking up from the crowd.

I knew what I was expected to do. Although there was no official border here, I had to report to the window of the Georgian police booth. Five black-uniformed men were sitting inside, chatting to each other but looking bored. It wasn't clear what four of them were supposed to be doing, as there was only one computer between them all. The black-haired man in charge held out a hand and gave a flick of his fingers to suggest he wanted something from me. I gave him my passport. While he examined it, I looked at the ground. A mangy dog nibbled one of its own paws in front of the office.

"Where are you from?" he asked.

"England," I replied. I don't like to give this response, despite its truth, because I should really say the United Kingdom, but whenever I've answered like that in the past I've been met with a blank stare.

He looked at my passport again, sniffed loudly and closed it, placing it beside the computer. Then he went back to chatting with his mates. This was an important part of the procedure, the bit when travellers wait pointlessly because they've committed the perceived crime of wanting to visit Abkhazia and because the Georgian official is a complete dick who likes to exercise the full thrust of his limited power. It makes his little willy tingle.

Periodically, another official – non-uniformed, wearing a pressed yellow shirt and dark trousers – would climb out of his BMW parked beside the office to oversee events for a minute or two before returning to his vehicle, presumably for another snooze. At one point, he merely opened the driver's door and shouted something across to the office. I thought perhaps this was the signal to let me through, since my captor picked up my passport and seemed about to hand it back to me. Instead, he smiled a creepy grimace and put it down again. S'alright, I've got all day. I looked behind me, genuinely interested in the comings and goings of the people around me. And I suspect this was the reason he then handed back my passport. There was no point keeping me there if I was enjoying myself.

This delay had been expected. I'd only waited needlessly for twenty minutes. I've heard tales of travellers being forced to hang around for four or more hours. Sometimes the Georgians keep them there just long enough for the Russian side's lunch hour to start, making them wait even longer to get through. If Georgia believes itself to hold the moral high ground in this conflict, these arseholes aren't doing it any favours.

I continued towards the border. I passed a jeep flying the EU flag. Its bonnet contained the letters EUMM, the EU Monitoring Mission, an unarmed peacekeeping force stationed here. Later, while cycling through the non-occupied part of Georgia, I'd meet Thomas, a German who'd worked for the EUMM a few years earlier. He was amazed with my story of Abkhazia because, despite his official capacity, he'd never visited the place. His role had been to handle refugees coming from the breakaway territory, interview people crossing the border and maintain records of his findings, which were then submitted to Brussels.

"But nothing was ever done," he complained. "Or at least it seemed that way."

"What *could* be done?"

He shook his head.

"I don't know. No one knows."

"Why didn't you ever visit Abkhazia?" I asked.

He looked pensive.

"It's complicated," he replied.

I was about to find out if this was still true.

The Enguri river separates Abkhazia from the rest of Georgia, and an 870-metre bridge crosses it. It's the only way to enter Abkhazia from this eastern side. I was the only one on a bicycle. Everyone else trudged wearily, loaded with bags. The bridge ended and trees crowded in, making the track feel more claustrophobic. I was now getting to the meat of this crossing. Soldiers wandered around. Barbed wire lined the roadside. Military roadblocks prevented vehicles from trying their luck and crashing through. I felt like I was playing *Call of Duty*, albeit woefully ill-armed, hoping to take out any potential assailant with a sharpened bicycle pump.

I approached the Russian – I beg your pardon – the *Abkhazian* border office. Standing outside was a guard, his red, rheumy eyes suggesting the previous evening had been drowned in vodka. I could hear someone speaking English in a European but non-Russian accent. A fifty-something woman was talking to an old local lady and asking her how to say "thanks" in Abkhaz. The old lady's reply was an eight syllable nightmare despite the fact that Google tells me the answer is simply "*Yitabup*". Maybe she was having a laugh with the stupid outlander.

"You speak English very well," the first woman said.

"I was an English teacher," the Abkhaz lady replied.

"Me too!"

English teachers of the world unite!

It turned out the entire group before me in the queue to pass into Abkhazia were teachers, Portuguese ones. The English teacher was with a male philosopher and a female mathematician. Their presence made this border crossing appear as safe as my research had suggested. If the purpose of this book had been to make myself seem hard and dangerous, I'd have left them out of it. It would have just been me, the steely adventurer, facing the evil Russians alone! The truth is I'm about as hard and dangerous as Christopher Biggins.

You would, however, have some reason to think what I'm doing is reckless. The UK Foreign and Commonwealth Office advises "against all travel to the breakaway regions of South Ossetia and Abkhazia, and against all but essential travel to areas near the Administrative Boundary Lines with Abkhazia and South Ossetia."

And the US Department of State warns you off with: "Russian troops and border guards occupy both South Ossetia and Abkhazia...Entering the occupied territories will likely result in your arrest, imprisonment, and/or a fine. Violent attacks, criminal incidents, and kidnappings occur in the region. Land mines pose a danger to travellers near the boundary lines of both territories."

Scary stuff, but not in reality. That said, a Georgian man was shot dead here in 2016, but, according to Abkhaz officials, he was hardly following the rules, and alcohol played a large part. The man had arrived without any documentation and then drunkenly threatened a border guard with violence when he wouldn't let him through. The guard raised his gun and fired off a warning, which caused the Georgian man to attack him, and so the guard shot him. However, maybe this case isn't quite so clear cut. After all, the victim was shot six times, including once in the face when he was already on the ground. Oh, and the Abkhaz border guard then legged it from the scene. A court in Zugdidi sentenced the guard to twelve years' imprisonment, but he still walks free somewhere in Abkhazia. This story is no reason not to visit though. If you're going to avoid everywhere in the world someone has been wrongfully shot by the authorities, London would be completely off-limits, as would almost every city in the US.

I handed over my passport and my letter of invitation to a uniformed man sitting in a small wooden hut.

"Now we wait," said the Portuguese woman.

It didn't take long. They were certainly more efficient than the Georgians. With our passports returned we had to walk down a narrow tarmac path with razor-wire fences on either side. Then came a bag search. Absolutely everything was going to be opened and rummaged through. The teachers had their bags checked first and proceeded to the next hurdle while I took my turn.

The person in charge of this section was a young Russian woman with a long, blonde plait who spoke excellent English.

"Where have you cycled from?" she asked breezily.

"The south of Spain."

She looked blankly at me.

"Where?"

"The south of Spain."

The blankness became confusion.

"What? Like Spain, Spain?

Was there another kind of Spain?

"Yes."

She shook her head and smiled. A fellow guard walked past, playing with his phone. She said something to him in Russian while nodding in my direction and they both laughed. I don't mind if you think I'm mental, just don't shoot me in the face.

She went through each bag in turn, removing clothes and tools and sleeping bags and tents and electronics. I saved the pannier containing the carrier bag full of pills until the end.

"What's in that one?" she asked.

"Just medication," I replied, opening the bag. "I have high blood pressure."

She looked inside, but apparently carrying hundreds of drugs was no cause for concern.

"OK, thank you," she finally said.

The documents needed another check, and then I passed through customs, which consisted of a fat bloke smoking a cigarette, who waved me through without bothering to look up.

I'd made it!

The teachers were hanging around the car park on the Abkhazian side of the border, negotiating a taxi at the same time as trying to tell the driver where I'd cycled from.

"Spain?" they said.

Nothing.

"Bullfighting?"

Nope.

They mimed an angry bull and snorted.

"España!" the taxi driver finally said, smiling in my

direction and giving me a thumbs up.

I trundled into Abkhazia, not knowing whether to feel excited or creeped out. This part of the country had seen some fierce fighting. The trouble had come in two waves, once when the USSR fell apart in the early nineties and then again in 2008 when Russia threw its full weight at Georgia, both here and in South Ossetia. The Abkhazian wars had seen around 5,000 soldiers killed, shared fairly equally between both sides, but up to 30,000 civilians murdered, almost exclusively here, Georgians butchered by Abkhazians in a dreadfully efficient act of ethnic cleansing. I decided to feel creeped out, at least for a while.

For a few miles, there was nothing but lush, dense forest, the sort of place where anything could be hiding, a mutant grizzly or a nutter with an AK-47. The recent heavy weather and Abkhazia's subtropical climate made it feel like I was cycling through the Amazon. I passed a few buildings, broken and now merging back into the woods from which they'd once stood out, but at least the tarmac was pristine. There is very little traffic on this remote end of Abkhazia's one main road.

After about twelve miles I came to the first town, Gali. Even the websites that tell you Abkhazia is safe enough warn you about this place and how lawless it is, especially after dark. I didn't see many people as I cycled through, but some of the men I passed gave me a friendly smile or a wave. Without reading about it, I'd never have known it was dangerous, if indeed that's still the case.

As far as friendliness went, the women were a different story, and it made me consider all the greetings I'd received, or not, throughout Europe on all the trips I'd ever done. Here, I passed a group of four women, staring at me from a fruit stall at the edge of town. I waved but got nothing back. Women, especially women on a lonely road, have good reason to be wary of men. Some blokes would see a friendly smile or wave from a woman – any woman – as a come on. Why even risk it?

A car eventually passed me. It had an Abkhazian number plate but one of those old 'D' stickers, indicating a car from Deutschland. I wondered what its story was and the convoluted route it'd taken to get to Abkhazia. Was it here with the blessing of its previous owner or had it simply disappeared from Frankfurt one night? Now that Albania was no longer the stolen car capital of Europe, they had to go somewhere.

The forty odd miles between Gali and the Abkhaz capital, Sokhumi, only had the occasional house. The first thirty miles from the border saw the most dilapidated ones. For every home still standing and inhabited there was at least one more bullet-riddled or smashed to pieces and left to rot. Some of the older derelicts had once been grand, a few looking like former colonial mansions. These were being slowly reclaimed by the forest, dense foliage obscuring what man had created, as though Mother Nature was ashamed of the destructive species She had unleashed upon the world. One day, humankind would destroy itself. The landmines would rot away, rivers would eventually unpoison themselves and peace would return to Earth, until the next "intelligent" species evolved to mess it up again.

To break up the monotony of this long flat road, occasional bits of street furniture appeared. Two large flags flew side-by-side, one Abkhaz and one Russian, partners in a very unequal partnership. Every now and again, a huge billboard, in the green and red of Abkhaz's national colours, would show the faces of those brave heroes who'd died for this bit of land, y'know, the one that looks exactly like that bit on the other side of the border.

Strangely, the lack of cars caused a problem for some

drivers. The cattle that happily cohabited the byways of Georgia were used to having Abkhazia's entirely to themselves. I passed the occasional cow standing on the road asleep. Because they'd possibly never seen a bicycle before they were terrified of me, but they were definitely King of the Road in every other respect.

One driver had a solution to the cow problem. He drove at top speed towards a herd meandering across the tarmac. At the last minute he slammed on, skidded a little and came to a standstill, but not before giving a gentle but car-sized nudge to one bovine beast. It got the message and moved out of his way.

There were also a lot of stray dogs on this stretch of road, but unlike those in Romania they were far too malnourished to give chase. When money's short and food is scarce, leftovers are scarcer still, and bins don't serve up the same scavenging and energy-providing possibilities.

As I neared Sokhumi, the traffic increased and the quality of the roads deteriorated. Once inside the capital, the tarmac was as broken as anywhere in the former Soviet Union. The pavements were particularly rough, with tree roots bursting through the earth and cracking the flags, turning every stroll around town into an assault course. I guess if you're wheelchair-bound in Abkhazia, you're also house-bound.

I was wary of where I was staying tonight. While Booking.com allows you to make reservations for Abkhazia, the internet doesn't provide a lot of the local information you'd usually take for granted. And my hotel didn't appear at all on my map app. There was one with the same name in a town called Gagra, fifty miles away. Maybe I'd booked into that one instead, which would have been no use whatsoever.

I found the street my hotel was supposed to be on and cycled down it. Although the road was wide, the buildings around here were broken and squalid, true of most of the places in downtown Sokhumi. And then I came to a gleaming white building, standing all by itself. Its edges were sharp, not crumbly like those around it. Its metallic bits shone brightly. This was the Assir Hotel, my hotel, a complete anomaly in Sokhumi. The reason it wasn't on the app was because it was so new.

I'd read that some visitors to Abkhazia have been made less than welcome, some even receiving death threats from the locals. That said, from what I could gather, this venom was aimed at a party of the heavily-pierced, including men, and when travelling it really doesn't help your case even to hint at what could be perceived as sexual degeneracy to the owner of a small-town mind. You can crow all you like about your human right to dress the way you want, but if I were you, Trevor, I'd remove that nose-ring before coming to Abkhazia, lest you receive an additional piercing, one administered by an ignorant local with a steak knife.

But you shouldn't believe everything you read on the internet. I was welcomed into the Assir like a long lost son. The inside of the hotel was as lovely and unSokhumian as the outside. Iana, the bubbly receptionist, spoke very good English. In reality, it was just like any hotel anywhere else in the world, except perhaps all the places I'd been in the former USSR, and it only surprised me because I wasn't expecting it. And all for the price of an English campsite.

It had been a long day's ride after a *very* long day's ride. I'd cycled about 170 miles over the last thirty-six hours and my legs were painfully aware of this. I headed out to have a look at the town but, given the creaking nature of my knee joints, decided to limit the breadth of my explorations.

I aimed for the seafront. Sokhumi had, once upon a time, been one of Georgia's premium resorts, a backdrop of four thousand metre-plus mountains sitting on the balmy Black Sea. It had been particularly popular with Russians, only ninety miles from Sochi, the location of the 2014 Winter Olympics.

While numbers were vastly reduced, the tourists these days were *exclusively* Russian. Abkhazians couldn't afford a holiday and no Georgian would dream of coming here, lest they be considered a traitor. But if this place once had any grandeur, and it apparently did, it was long gone. The seafront consisted of a long promenade with a derelict ferry terminal at one end and, in the far distance, what looked like an industrial but unvisited port. From sea wall to water's edge, the grey beach was narrow, but well-stocked with humans, even on an overcast day like today. Weird metal structures littered the sand, giving no clue as to their previous purpose. The promenade played host to a few souvenir and snack stands, although business seemed to be slight. Even with the number of bodies on the beach, it had a strange, out-of-season feel, despite today being the very height of summer. I think this was as good as it got nowadays.

I have blond-brown hair – not particularly unRussian – but there must have been something about my appearance that screamed "NON-LOCAL!" given the number of stares I was receiving, but none of their gazes came across as aggressive and certainly no one suggested the end of my life was imminent.

I couldn't be arsed to go hunting for restaurant-based food tonight. Besides, my short trawl of the streets hadn't turned up anywhere obvious to eat near the hotel. I returned to my room via a very unsuper supermarket. The tiny shop hardly sold anything that could be made into a meal and, even if it had, its aisles were so narrow – more like fissures really – and so full of people that shopping was near impossible. I escaped with a packet of *Pringles* – they'd been hiding beside the till – and a bottle of *chacha* from behind the counter. Chacha is a strong Georgian spirit rather than two-thirds of a dance, although if you drink enough of it...

*

I only had one full day in Sokhumi, and the first task at hand was to get my visa. The letter of invitation had allowed me into the place. The visa would let me out again afterwards.

I located the Ministry of Foreign Affairs, one of the few other intact buildings in the town, and found the visa office. Just because I'd arrived during their advertised opening hours didn't mean they were prepared for business.

"Come back in half an hour," an official said. "Today's visas haven't arrived yet."

When I returned an hour later, eight people were waiting. I took my place at the back of the room and expected to be there for a while before my turn. The visa office door opened and the head of the man I'd spoken to earlier appeared. He saw me, pointed in my direction and told me to come in, much to the visible, and in one case audible, annoyance of everyone who'd just seen me arrive.

I went into the tiny office. A different man took my passport and entered my details into a computer, and then I had to pay with plastic. They didn't accept cash. Did I really want to be handing over such valuable personal information to a rogue nation? They might nip to Amazon.com and buy a load of military hardware with it. Rather than my usual debit card, I gave an old credit card instead, one I hadn't used for several years. I'd know who was responsible if my next statement included transactions for bazookas and aircraft carriers.

With my Abkhazian visa tucked loosely into my passport – they don't stick it inside like real countries – I left the building to look for the calories I didn't have yesterday. Although Abkhazians use many of the same names for food as Georgians, these words are rendered in Cyrillic rather than the Georgian script. For the sake of its visitors, Georgia occasionally offers up an English translation. But Brits, Americans and Australians don't come here. Abkhazia has no reason to provide such linguistic niceties. This being the case, I now had to transliterate menus from Cyrillic to form a possibly Georgian word that I almost certainly didn't know in the first place. It was because of this technique that my lunch ended up being another khachapuri, so overjoyed was I when I managed to fashion a word I actually understood.

I then wandered around the still unexplored parts of town. I saw the gutted, eleven-storey parliament building, scene of some of the fiercest fighting. I also had a look at both Liberty Square and Freedom Square, scrubby places named without a tad of irony. It's a strange sort of freedom that leaves your economy in tatters, provides you with an unusable passport and relies entirely upon the Russians to prop you up.

It was time, as it always is in odd places, to see the central market. To get there, I clambered over mounds of rubble and waded through muddy puddles. The market itself started off nicely chaotic, with stands selling pointless trinkets and clothes whose slogans were once again all in English. This would be like visiting a market in Doncaster and finding all the shirts printed in Sanskrit.

Then I went upstairs, into the more interesting food section. An older woman on an overstuffed stall hawking walnuts and home-made wine amongst other things called out to me. I smiled at her but kept walking. I passed several other stands selling identical items behind which stood identical women. Whoever had designed this level had done a lot of cut 'n' pasting.

Then I came to a pungent meat section, large chunks of animal hanging on hooks in an unrefrigerated corner. Online advice says uncooled meat stays edible for only two hours.

Russians are obviously harder than that.

I wanted to buy something and so, in order to reward her capitalistic spirit and forward-thinking marketeering, I returned to the first woman who'd drawn my attention. Showing interest in her wine, she offered me a plastic capful as a taste. Yes, sweet and heady, rich and full-bodied. I nodded approval. She decanted it from a five-litre keg into an old 1.5 litre Coke bottle. EU safety standards didn't apply here.

I also bought a couple of *churchkhela* from her. Sometimes known as Georgian Snickers, these are nuts, usually walnuts, threaded on to a string, repeatedly dipped into thickened grape juice and then dried. After several dips, the nuts have a thick, chewy coating in colours ranging from reds to yellows to greens. They are a very portable, highly calorific, high-protein morsel, the perfect cycling snack.

The old woman's stall looked wonderful, with its colourful spices and bottles containing various liquids of every hue. I mimed to her that I'd like to take a photo, but she shyly refused. She couldn't risk it. She was probably still signing on.

The market had more to offer. I strolled down some stairs and my nose told me I was in live animal central. Three musky piglets squealed raucously, trapped in a tiny cage. Other jails confined chickens and rabbits and quails. As a typically hypocritical lover of both meat *and* animals, it wasn't a pleasant place to hang around.

There were few other sights to see in the capital. I spent the rest of the day just wandering. Sokhumi looked to be dying a slow death. From the outside, some of its tower blocks were especially grim, with their abundant mould and crumbliness. What the hell were they like inside?

The town was liberally scattered with war monuments, their recent victory being just about the only positive they could cling to. If instead they'd cooperated with Georgia then, yes, they wouldn't be able to fool themselves that they were an independent nation, but things would be a lot better on both sides of the border. The previous owners of those destroyed houses on the way here wouldn't have had to flee for their lives as refugees within their own country or been murdered for not doing so. It seemed a grim reality that the further east I went, and as each of this ride's independent movements became something more tangible, the worse life became. Independence clearly isn't all that.

Visiting Sokhumi was a confused experience, its recent turbulent history making it extremely interesting but, at the same time, tediously grim. It's not a place you leave feeling refreshed and uplifted.

Back in my room, I looked at my alcoholic haul. I had almost all of yesterday's chacha left – at 52%, despite a grappa-like taste, it made for slow consumption – as well as all of today's litre and a half of red wine. Now that I could sample it by the glassful, the vino had a weird, beetroot flavour, but I was still taking both drinks with me. I wondered what the alcohol allowance was at the Abkhazian-Georgian border. Most of the guards were carrying a couple of bottles of vodka across *every day*, albeit safely within their veins.

*

The ride back to the border and to relative normality was mostly uneventful and conducted in the first bright sunshine of my time in Georgia. The clear skies enabled me to see just what a beautiful land this was, layers of mountains disappearing into the distance.

Around the halfway mark, I was stopped by the police. Remove from your mind any thoughts of terrifying Russian anti-riot thugs. These two were more like Laurel and Hardy. The older guy was obese and lucky to reach five foot, the youngster tall, gaunt and with typical teenage skin. I don't know what they stopped me for, and I don't think they knew either, probably just to kill some time on an otherwise dull day on a driverless road. Whatever they wanted couldn't have been important because when they realised we had no language in common – to be honest, I wouldn't have let them know even if we had – I was on my way again.

A few miles from Gali, I stopped at a shop for water. I tried the door but it was locked, presumably for lunchtime. A youthful scream was emitted from the store's attached garden. The shopkeeper's twelve-year-old son was summoning his mother. Quick, mum! We've got a customer, fer-Christ-sakes! Times were tough and lunch could wait.

She opened up, I went inside and bought what I needed. The young lad followed me out of the shop and looked at my bike. The expression on his face was the one yours would have if someone showed you their brand new alien spacecraft. He picked up my stupid helmet and his jaw dropped.

"Oh-ma-gaaaaaaaaaaaaarrrrr!" he roared, his eyes flicking from me to the orange-pink monstrosity in wonder, like he was holding the world's largest diamond or the severed head of an important royal. Then he noticed my front light. I switched it on, its weak beam barely visible in today's bright daylight. "Oh-ma-gaaaaaaaaaaaaarrrrr!" We went around my bike's features one by one. I was treated to an "Oh-ma-gaaaaaaaaaaaaarrrrr!" at every fixture and fitting. God knows what he'd be like if he ever saw something genuinely impressive. I think he'd probably pop.

A little later I saw the perfect metaphor for Abkhazia. On the tallest flagpole I'd ever seen, a seriously tattered national flag blew in the breeze. Here she was, Abkhazia, ostensibly independent, but supported in such a way that no one could come and help fix her obvious problems, at the mercy of forces outside her control.

After today's sixty miles, the border finally, thankfully, reappeared. The long queue of people I'd seen entering Georgia a couple of mornings ago had evaporated by this time of day, early afternoon. There was no bag check. The Russians processed me within seconds and even the Georgians couldn't be arsed to delay me. I was through the entire barbed wire mess in less than five minutes.

I cycled away from the border, smiling. My belief that a visit to this war-ravaged corner of Europe would be safe had been justified. I went back to my previous hotel in Zugdidi. Despite not recognizing any of the staff, which consisted entirely of elderly gentlemen, I was greeted like a returning hero. As well as the gateway to Abkhazia, Zugdidi is also the launching point for Ushguli, at 2,100 metres one of the highest villages in Europe. It would be more usual for a cyclist – a fit, young cyclist on a decent bike, that is – to want to head in that direction. And, yes, if I'd managed to get all the way to Ushguli and back in the time I'd been gone, I would probably deserve to be fêted. On the other hand, if they'd known I'd visited treacherous Abkhazia, they might have thrown me out of the hotel.

Knackered, I crawled into my room. I realised I'd been running on adrenaline these last few days. The frisson of being somewhere I shouldn't be had kept my energy levels fizzing. Now it was all over, I crashed. I was too tired to shower and too filthy to lie on the bed. I took a towel from the bathroom, used it as a pillow and fell asleep on the room's wooden floor.

Looking back on my stay in Abkhazia, I have mixed feelings. It was at times surreal, mundane, horrifying, beautiful and depressing, but always illuminating. To have travelled around all these wannabe independent bits of Europe without seeing one that had taken the experiment to its logical conclusion wouldn't have told me much. As someone for whom freedom has always been of paramount importance, I was beginning to see how independence could just as easily be a curse.

There's now only one independence story left to tell, one whose violence is bloodier even than the civilian-massacring one here in Abkhazia. It's more recent too. In fact, it's still ongoing. But it will take me a while yet to reach it. Please bear with me as I take you on a little tour of Georgia and Armenia to get there.

Chapter 15: Georgia on My Mind

I'd planned a lazy day in Zugdidi to recuperate from the last few day's heavy mileage and unavoidable wild imaginings. The Rain Gods also thought this an excellent idea. They provided a day so unappealing I didn't even consider leaving my room until mid-afternoon. The quantity of rain made Wales look like the Sahara.

For hours I wallowed, only disturbed around lunchtime by a knock on my door. I opened it to see one of the hotel staff.

"Good day!" he said in Russian.

"*Dobri den!*" I replied.

Then he just stood there, staring at me. I smiled. He smiled. I smiled some more. I didn't have the Russian to take this nascent friendship to the next level. A full fifteen seconds passed as we stared at each other wordlessly. Then he nodded, spun around sharply and marched away. Perhaps he'd just read *Running A Hotel For Dummies* and had misinterpreted the advice on greeting your guests.

The weather eased and so I went out, finding food in the tiniest of restaurants. It only had two picnic-style benches and a woman was asleep on one of them. I approached the counter. Without having to ask, I was offered something already prepared, covered in a tea towel. Whatever it was looked interestingly deep-fried. I was starving. Bring it on, and anything else you have!

"And a beer," I said in Russian.

"No beer," she laughed. "*Kompot?*"

"*Da,*" I accepted begrudgingly. I didn't really want the over-sweetened fruit drink, but it'd do.

I sat at the restaurant's one free picnic bench. Almost

immediately two meat patties arrived, along with mashed potato and a spicy tomato sauce. Everything tasted alright but had the warmth of something freshly made about an hour ago. As if to emphasise the first dish's tepidity, it was then accompanied by a plateful of sesame seed-covered ratatouille with the temperature of a mid-afternoon barbecue on Mercury.

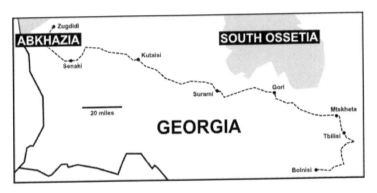

Then the deep-fried things I'd originally selected turned up. Would they be stuffed with meat or cheese or something more exotic? No, they wouldn't. They wouldn't be stuffed with anything at all. They were just fist-sized lumps of dough, deep-fried. This sort of behaviour wouldn't have been acceptable even in Scotland. Drier than sawdust, I couldn't have eaten them if I'd wanted to. I'd have needed the saliva-manufacturing skills of a bloodhound. Georgian food wasn't the uniformly excellent stuff the internet had suggested.

I shuffled back to my room as it started to rain again. As planned, I'd expended very few calories today. Hopefully, this would pay dividends as I carried on my way tomorrow, but for now I'd just get some more sleep. Ah, peaceful uninterrupted sleep.

I was woken up around two in the morning, jolted

conscious by the noise. Either someone was having really good sex in the next room or I was witness to a murder.

*

This morning I headed east in the direction of the far-off capital, Tbilisi. Despite my day off, I still felt weary, like my body was closing down in preparation for some stupid illness. Feeling like this, I could've done without the silly sod I met halfway to today's destination. A mountain biker in his early twenties was pootling along in front of me. I tried to overtake him but he suddenly sped up. I eased off, slipping back behind him, and so he slowed right down. I didn't need this.

Up on the hill beside the road was an old monastery. I'd let the daft bugger disappear into the distance while I took a photo or two. But he didn't. He circled back towards me and stopped on the opposite side of the road. This was very odd behaviour. It didn't help that he looked Middle Eastern and it'd only been a few days since a couple of American cyclists had been killed in Tajikistan by an ISIS bellend.

I continued on my way with him in front again. He rode with one hand, swerving all over the road and then tried it with no hands and nearly fell off, the pillock. He slowed right down. This was my chance. I pedalled like a mad thing and overtook him, thrashing the bike until I thought I'd put enough distance between us. Relaxing back into a steady pace, he eventually caught me again, smiling as he passed, and then turned off into a side road, having proven to us both that, yes, he could indeed cycle faster than someone fully loaded and twice his age. Well done, knobbie! (But thanks for not blowing me up or cutting off my head.)

I arrived in Senaki, a bustling and yet instantly forgettable medium-sized town and looked for a place to stay. I found somewhere advertised as a motel but in reality it was a walled compound of small bungalows, about ten of them.

The whole place was exceedingly tatty. There was no obvious reception, but a tiny old woman dressed entirely in black shuffled out to meet me. Realising our lack of linguistic harmony, she phoned someone who spoke English.

"And how much is it?" I finally asked the man on the phone.

"Where are you from?" he replied.

Obviously, nationality made a difference. I suspect it would have cost a lot more if I were Russian.

The old woman took me towards one of the bungalows and opened its front door. Its first room contained nothing but a manky bare mattress on an old metal bed frame. Mmm, this wasn't good. But she kept on walking into another room, one with a made-up bed covered in crisp (rather than crispy) white sheets. And the Wi-Fi worked. So what if the front door didn't lock?

She left and I crashed out. Today's ride had only been a piddling thirty miles, but I was pooped. Was there something wrong with me or was this just cumulative fatigue after 5,500 miles in four and a bit months?

After a rest I cycled back into town to look for food. Options were limited, but then I found a sort of shop-restaurant combo.

"Khachapuri?" I asked. I'd really fallen in love with this Georgian cheesy bread.

"Yes," the waitress replied. "And do you want fish?"

I wasn't sure. I mean, fish and cheesy bread aren't natural bedfellows, are they? She took me to the kitchen and showed me a fridge full of dried herring. Now I *was* sure, sure that I didn't want fish. She opened a second cooler. It contained a shelf loaded with thick greyish sausages.

"Can I have one of those?" I asked.

She looked doubtful, took one out of the fridge and smelled it. Maybe the jury was out and so she had me sniff it too. With no other obvious option I decided to take my chance.

The food arrived. Today's khachapuri wasn't the boat-shaped style I'd had twice before but one where the cheese is baked inside the bread. It was tasty but not as great as the others, but it was a damn sight better than the rest of the meal. The sausage was unfortunately reminiscent of *andouillette*, that intestine and colon monstrosity I'd suffered back in France on my Capitals of Europe tour. Today's was comfortably the second worst sausage I'd ever eaten, full of chewy organ meat and other mystery items.

On the table next to mine was a group of Georgian men. One of them gave me a thumbs-up when I ordered a third pint with my meal. I needed liquid to get the lungs and spleen down, but he didn't know that. I guess being a massive pisshead makes you a real man in Georgia.

*

Despite much improved weather and a shortish day with few hills, I reached Kutaisi, Georgia's third largest city and historic capital, feeling drained. I needed to stop, and soon. As a temporary solution I gave myself another day off the bike.

Hotels in Georgia are often not as they are elsewhere. This was particularly true of tonight's resting place. I chose the White House Hotel, a rather grand title for what was in effect a spare bedroom in someone's home. I was shown around the property by a rotund twelve-year-old before the rest of his family got involved. The room smelt of dust and its bed creaked like a medieval instrument of torture. I was also sharing the bathroom facilities with the whole family. Still, for all its shortcomings, it cost less than a fiver, the cheapest room I'd found anywhere and cheaper than 90% of European campsites too. I'm a sucker for a bargain.

In a country that, on the internet at least, shouts loudly

about the quality of its cuisine, elements of my last two meals had been borderline inedible. I was hoping Kutaisi could turn this around. I headed out to look for an authentic Georgian restaurant, preferably with an English menu to take the guesswork out of the selection process.

"Are you looking for an authentic Georgia restaurant?" asked a young woman on a street corner.

"Yes, I am," I replied too enthusiastically. It was as though she were psychic.

Into my hands she thrust a menu, an English one. Normally I'd steer well clear of any restaurant employing hawkers, but she was selling exactly what I wanted to buy and seemed wonderfully and nervously non-salesperson-like. It could've been the best sales technique ever.

She walked me around the corner to her restaurant and I took my place at a table. I ordered *kharcho*, plus a pile of skewers of the juiciest barbecued pork and, predictably, another khachapuri. Kharcho is an exceedingly tasty paprika-loaded beef stew containing sour cherries and ground walnut, like a more complex goulash. It was all fantastic. Maybe Georgian food was worth shouting about after all.

I wanted to explore the city but a creeping sickness suggested I take it easy for a bit. It wasn't just how weary I felt. Since arriving in Georgia, my stomach and all systems south had been misbehaving. I still had another six hundred miles to go. I needed to take better care of myself. Over the next couple of weeks, I wanted to get to the end of this ride, not the end of my life.

I headed back to my room. It became clear there was more to this place than met the eye. It sounded like there were rodents or at least giant bugs running around inside the walls. And the building's electrics were eccentric. I needed the bathroom but couldn't work out how to switch its light on. It was like an escape room. Neither of the two switches seemed to do anything. Eventually I figured out I had to turn on both at the same time.

Leaving the bathroom a few minutes later, I came face-to-face with an otherwise unknown family member, a lump the size of Gibraltar, stripped to the waist and with so much back hair that I could have knitted a football team a set of matching cardigans. I gave him a friendly nod. He didn't react. He was probably just thinking what a tasty snack I'd make. I skulked back to my room, remembering to say goodnight to the wall rats.

*

I awoke after a night of weird, sweaty dreams and multiple bathroom visits. Today's itinerary would have to consist of short hops, very much café-to-café-based.

My first stop was the market, but it wasn't a patch on Sokhumi's, despite this city having twice its population. And after a look at its very unroyal-looking royal district, I popped up the town's hill to find its funfair. A fairly steep climb led to the discovery of a few forlorn rides that weren't even running and a bunch of old, bored men sitting around in silence. It was senseless pushing myself to see this sort of rubbish and so I retreated for a while.

After a short snooze I returned to finish off Kutaisi's dwindling list of sights. Next up was its Museum of Military Glory, which is rather an optimistically blinkered name for a country with 20% of its land occupied by other nations. Perhaps its staff felt this too. I entered to find them, three old women, sitting in the dark on uncomfortable wooden chairs. Apparently the museum was closed, although the official timetable said they still had another hour and a quarter to go. Maybe they were knocking 20% off the museum's opening hours to account for the reduced glory.

I considered my options for the ride. Perhaps I should end in Tbilisi and finish the rest of the journey by minibus or train. After all, the trek from Tbilisi to my end point was four hundred miles, but it also included two Everests of ascent. In my current state, I seriously doubted I could manage it. I'd heard tell of a succession of Armenian hills with twenty-five-mile climbs. Even if my body held out, my misbehaving gears suggested I wasn't looking at a long, miserable bike ride but rather a long, even more miserable walk.

I had a decision to make.

*

Another night of strange dreams and liquefied innards followed. At ten o'clock I had a second crack at the War Museum. The same three women were still sitting there in the dark. Had they even been home last night? I pulled out my wallet, but they waved away all thoughts of remuneration. And they even switched on the lights for me.

To be honest I'm not sure I learned very much. Apart from the heading captions, everything was in Georgian or Russian. Most of photos were from World War Two with only a single panel about Abkhazia and South Ossetia, the conflicts I was interested in.

"Georgia lost twenty per cent," the guide said, looking sadly at a photo of Abkhazia. I very nearly mentioned I'd visited the place. "We Georgians don't go there." Yep, that's right, keep it buttoned.

*

Things were getting worse, the roads, the traffic and, in particular, the way I felt. It was silly really to cycle fifty miles and sweat my way up 1,700 metres of ascent on a day as hot as this one. If my failing body didn't finish me off, then the cars overtaking the overtaking cars on this vergeless country lane would. I tried to eat as much as possible to fend off the light-headedness, but it wasn't enough. I needed more. On a steep, endless climb, I thought I saw a café up ahead. When I finally approached the building, it looked more like a hovel, and I wondered if my imagining of refreshment had just been wishful thinking. I walked up to the porch and saw an old couple, the woman peeling hundreds of cloves of garlic. Her old fella pitched in by drinking beer.

"Do you have any tea?" I asked in perfect Russian. Well, what I actually said was the Russian word for "tea" in a slightly inquisitive tone, but let's not split hairs.

They *did* have tea. So perhaps it *was* a café. Or they were just a very accommodating old couple. I sat down at a table. The old bloke started to mime.

"Do you want something non-specific to eat?" his actions seemed to suggest.

"*Da.*" I couldn't remember the word for "please".

After an unfeasibly short time, a cheese-stuffed khachapuri arrived, one of the best I'd had so far, full of dairy gooeyness.

I somehow managed to ask the old dude how far it was to Surami, today's destination, and he somehow managed to tell me there was another tunnel between here and there. Fantastic.

Shortly after I left the café, I met Paul, a cyclist from Scarborough.

"Have you ever seen driving as fuckin' terrible as this?" were his first words.

I hadn't. No one has. Well, maybe James Dean.

Let me try to give you a British equivalent of what the standard of Georgian driving is like. Imagine if the UK were populated by no one but 1) fifty million horny teenage male virgins who'd never had a driving lesson, and 2) one utter gorgeous, smoking hot eighteen-year-old girl. Now, give each lad twenty minutes to neck ten pints of Special Brew and then get him to race from Inverness to London – not on the motorways, mind – and whoever wins gets to lose his cherry to the hot girl. As a bonus, participants get a thousand pounds for every other car they force off the tarmac. Unfiltered testosterone, rage and a complete inability to drive make Georgia a place where no one is safe on the road.

Through another awful tunnel, a nice descent into the village of Surami was ruined by more suicidal drivers. At least the nutters were slowed down at one point as the police cleared away the aftermath of yet another accident.

Between here and Tbilisi, the traffic would only get worse. An idea was forming in my head, one that involved giving up really quite soon. Tomorrow, in fact, in Gori, the birthplace of Stalin. This shitty bike had oppressed me on this journey. What better place to end its days than in the home of the world's greatest oppressor?

Before then though was tonight's village, and Surami was an odd fish. It started off feeling a bit Ethiopian. I'd accessed it from the main highway by a series of dirt tracks that wound around tumbledown wooden shacks. I couldn't believe there'd be any sort of hotel in a place like this. The main road through town, however, was asphalted, and today the village seemed to be in the middle of a little party.

I found a place to stay – it was another one that felt like I was living in someone's house – and went for a walk. There were no actual sights in the centre of town, but everyone was in a good mood. Perhaps this was down to the price of beer. I sat down for a little drinky and paid just £1.12. For two pints!

Horse-drawn carriages kept trundling past. Maybe this was just the way that locals got around the place, but in each case its occupants were smartly dressed families and Georgian folk music blared from each carriage's tiny speakers at ear-bleeding volumes.

As I drank my beer, a car drove past. In its back window was a puppet that leant out and waved at passers-by. And there was a little road train carrying mums and kids on it. If today wasn't their annual fiesta, this was the most fun village

284

in the world.

I used my roadside position to perform an experiment. Of the next ten cars that passed, I'd count how many had more than superficial accident damage and therefore determine the national average. This was flawed methodology, I know, but the results would surely tell us all something. The answer was seven, and, given the standard of driving, I was surprised it was so low. That said, three of them were utter wrecks and looked like they were limping to the knacker's yard. If you ever consider driving to Georgia, come in someone else's car.

*

Most of today was spent on the motorway, the nicest, calmest road Georgia had to offer. Its central barrier meant drivers couldn't slam their cars so easily into those coming in the opposite direction. Because of this lack of adrenaline-filled adventure, most drivers avoided it. The scrappy main road running parallel was heaving with traffic, whereas the motorway was almost empty. This was the closest thing Georgia had to a cycle path.

Despite my route being mostly motorway, the scenery was still attractive. Unlike similar British roads, often high-sided to generate maximum tedium and sleepiness, here I could see all around, gentle hills ahead and purple-grey mountains disappearing off to my right. No one was falling asleep with boredom here.

I was on the outskirts of Gori, the end of my ride. On its edge I passed through the suburb of Kombinati. Here were dozens of huge, concrete apartment blocks that looked condemned and mouldy but still fully occupied. The end flats had balconies, many of which were lopsided and partially collapsed. They could have fallen at any minute and taken out all those below.

Someone had rebuilt one apartment's terrace with bricks.

But what was weird about it? That was it! They hadn't used any mortar. Maybe the weight alone would hold it all in position, even during one of the earthquakes to which this region is particularly prone. Let's hope so for the sake of anyone walking on the pavement beneath.

As I stopped to take it this weird urban landscape, a passing car added a touch of comedy. It carried a large sheet of plastic on its roof. And I mean *really* large. It was twice the length of the car and dipped down at the front and back, obscuring the driver's view in both directions. I saw it and smiled to myself. Through his open window, the driver clocked me and gave a big grin in return. Just another day in Georgia.

I rolled into Gori, this ride's final destination. This was it. The end. I could stop now. Right this minute in fact. Mmm, none of this had the euphoric end-of-tour feel I was used to.

Maybe I could manage a bit farther. Yes, Tbilisi – a capital! – would make a much more suitable, more climactic terminus. Besides, I'd been feeling a little better today. The bike was still a useless lump though.

While looking for somewhere to stay on the uneven streets of Gori, I was approached by Stefan, a young fella from Dresden. He was also cycle-touring, though his machine was currently at his selected guest house.

"Is the place any good?" I asked.

It was. My room wasn't very big and the facilities were shared, but they included a fully equipped kitchen and even a bloody piano! And all for less than ten quid a night.

We popped out for an afternoon drink and bumped into Andreas, an Austrian I'd cycled past earlier today. Stefan pointed him in the direction of the guest house as well. He should have been on commission.

Remember when I was in Abkhazia and said I'd later meet an EU Mission Monitor? Well, this was Thomas. As I sat sipping a beer with Stefan and Andreas, he turned up, sat down and joined in with his fellow German speakers. Thomas lived here in Gori with his Georgian wife. By the way, that's Georgian as in "from Georgia", not "from the Georgian era", otherwise she'd be about 250 years old.

Given his previous role, I brought up the subject of South Ossetia, Georgia's second breakaway region, which really wasn't very far from here. Ossetia was one wannabe country I wasn't allowed to visit. Visas are only issued under exceptional circumstances, and you can't enter from Georgia, only via Russia. This meant I'd also have needed an expensive Russian double-entry visa. And the only way to access South Ossetia from Russia is through a massive tunnel and I'd already had my fill of those.

There had been news stories recently that, under cover of darkness, the Russians were moving the current South Ossetian border fence further into Georgian territory. They were invading the country by stealth. The new boundary was already just a few miles from the main road that connects Tbilisi to its Black Sea ports.

"Yes," said Thomas. "It's shitty, shitty, shitty."

In 2008, there was a war between Georgia and South Ossetia. Or in reality between Georgia and Russia, because Russia bombed several places in non-Ossetian Georgia, including Gori and most of the other sizeable towns in the country. The official line was that Georgia had struck the first blow but I've heard a more compelling account that Georgia didn't make a move until Russian forces were already on the way through that huge tunnel into South Ossetia. Whatever the truth, South Ossetia is still propped up by Russia and Georgia is missing a large chunk of its sovereign territory.

"The South Ossetians were very cruel," said Thomas. "They cut off the forefingers of any men they caught so he could never fire a gun again."

But that wasn't all.

"There's a video of them online with a prisoner of war," he said. "They told him to trample on the Georgian flag. When he refused, they covered him in petrol and set him on fire."

Dark tales existed on both sides of the fence. The Georgians were accused of equal atrocities by the South Ossetians. There are no such things as monsters, except in war, and on all sides.

We were sitting within view of Gori's number one tourist attraction and the main reason anyone stops here at all, its Stalin Museum.

Thomas, who'd lived here for years, looked across at the building and sneered.

"I've never been inside," he said.

I, on the other hand, wasn't passing up such an opportunity. It wasn't as though my entry fee was going into the mass murderer's pocket. I don't know if I was really expecting a sort of Gulagland festival of grisly honesty, especially given that Stalin was the most famous son of the town, but I wasn't ready for such a historic whitewash. As one reviewer said, it was like having a Hitler museum and missing out the bit about the Second World War.

My favourite part of the entire experience was the gift shop. Who would buy a Stalin t-shirt? I was very tempted by the kitsch of the Stalin coasters, but for ten quid they really weren't worth the joke.

Stefan, Andreas and I spent the evening around the guest house's communal table with beer and a couple of young backpacking women who turned up late.

"I was in the mountains in the north-east of Georgia," Stefan said. "I was hitching and got picked up by two guys. They took me to a birthday party." He laughed to himself. "The house was very basic."

"How basic?" someone asked him.

"No electricity or water. But we didn't need water. Everyone drank tumblers of wine or vodka after each toast. Lots and lots of toasts. We were all still drunk the next day when we continued on our journey."

"Even the driver?"

"Especially the driver. Then halfway down the mountain we came to a roadside shrine, his uncle's shrine. We all drank more vodka to honour his uncle and got back in the car."

This was Georgia's alcohol-fuelled circle of death. Drink, drive, die and then have everyone else drink to your memory, before a bit more driving and dying.

Two images stuck with me from my day in Gori.

The first was a man well into his fifties, if not beyond, missing both legs, and operating the only sort of wheelchair that could handle these collapsed streets. Its tyres were huge, like those of a small motorbike, and its heavy metal frame was propelled with great effort using a clunky hand pedal. On an already sticky day, the old fella turned the mechanism repeatedly and edged his contraption forward just a few inches at a time. It was frustrating to watch him navigate the bumpy pavements, but at least he was mobile. If you lived in Georgia and struggled to walk, you couldn't expect the state to provide smooth surfaces and ramps like they do elsewhere. Here you had to acquire a self-powered all terrain vehicle or otherwise stay indoors.

The second arresting image came from a street mural painted on to a bullet-riddled wall. It showed an outline of an intact Georgia being bombed by a plane. Beneath it all was the slogan "The Price of Independence". That single artwork encapsulated my entire ride.

*

I was heading to Mtskheta. Despite only 8,000 inhabitants, it is one of Georgia's oldest cities and just fifteen miles from Tbilisi. The scenery distracted me from the fierce headwind. I felt like I was in Scotland or the north of England, bleak, bare moorland on one side of the road with more dramatic crags on the other.

It was here I came closest to South Ossetia and the section of the border the Russians were surreptitiously moving outwards. Nearby, I passed an IDP village – one for Internally Displaced Persons – refugees within their own country. Non-Abkhazians and non-Ossetians who'd been living in the pre-breakaway republics left behind everything when their erstwhile neighbours turned ugly. And now South Ossetia was creeping up on them again from just over that hill.

The IDP village looked a depressing place, miles from any other sizeable settlement, consisting of rows of cheaply-built beige bungalows with corrugated iron roofs. The village lacked any sort of amenities or an obvious way for its residents to generate an income. Living here, or more accurately *existing* here, seemed like a form of stasis. But at least they were safe. For now.

In Mtskheta I found a hotel with a lovely terrace out over the Mtkvari river that winds through this small town. On the opposite bank stood low green hills, very walkable in a Lake District sort of way. When darkness fell, an illuminated monastery glowed from a distant hilltop. It was a enchanting corner of the world. Unfortunately, prettiness is clearly no safeguard against terror.

*

Today would be the real end of my ride, as I triumphantly cycled my clunky beast the final thirty miles into Georgia's capital. As expected, the traffic on Tbilisi's edges was manic. After ten death-defying minutes on a dual carriageway that offered the only route into town, I sought out the quieter backstreets, although in Tbilisi the word "quieter" doesn't mean the same as it does anywhere else.

Coming into the city from this direction gave me a chance

to see one of Tbilisi's less central landmarks, the Chronicle of Georgia monument. Although it's sometimes called Georgia's Stonehenge, it is orders of magnitude more impressive than that pile of undecorated rocks in Wiltshire. Sixteen thirty-five-metre-tall black monoliths stand atop a hill overlooking Tbilisi's lake and are exquisitely carved with stories about Christ's life and local heroes. Walking within its soaring structure was a humbling experience.

On countrified roads, I cycled the northern edge of the city, its urban sprawl filling the valley below. At first glance it wasn't a very attractive place, seedy-looking apartment buildings stretching for miles. The road turned towards the centre and dropped me into the chaos of Station Square, near the city's main train station. Everything seemed a bit mad. Some argue Georgia is in Asia rather than Europe. With the number of people wandering around today it certainly felt like India or China.

I'd decided to spend a few days here. A city the size of Tbilisi deserved a more thorough exploration than the nondescript places on the way here. I sat in my room and thought about what to do next.

There was only one more wannabe left for me to see, one for whom independence was an ongoing daily battle. I wanted to get there on or before a very special day in their calendar. By listening to my body over the last week and slowing down, there was now no way I could've biked there via the route I'd originally planned, even if I'd wanted to. And I *really* didn't. I wanted nothing more than to stop cycling. Besides, the bike was in no state to tackle the huge hills between here and there.

I formed a new plan. I'd ditch the bicycle here and take the slow train to Armenia's capital, Yerevan. From there, I'd catch a *marshrutka* – a minibus in any condition from immaculate to totally shagged out – to my final destination, Stepanakert, the capital of Nagorno-Karabakh. This historically independent region is now claimed and fought over by both Azerbaijan and Karabakh's local Armenians. I'd end this mammoth trip there on September 2nd, Nagorno-Karabakh's Independence Day!

And yet.

I dunno.

Mmm.

I still felt I hadn't completed this journey properly. A bike ride should finish on a bike, not on a minibus. It was odd that cycling 5,500 miles could feel a failure.

I took out my one paper map, the one covering both Georgia and Armenia. With my finger I traced the route I'd originally planned, south-west from Tbilisi to Armenia, down through Yerevan and to the small town of Goris in the south, the gateway to the "safe corridor" from Armenia to Nagorno-Karabakh. I checked the distance again. No, it was out of the question. A long, *long* way out of the question.

But there was another possibility. Just like Abkhazia, government advice warned not to visit Nagorno-Karabakh under any circumstances and also to avoid those areas of Armenia close to Azerbaijan's border. I looked at Lake Sevan. At forty-six miles long and twenty wide it's the largest body of freshwater in the Caucasus. A quiet road ran along its northern shore and entered Nagorno-Karabakh on an alternative route to Stepanakert, one I hadn't considered before. I hadn't considered it because it ran *very* close to Azerbaijan's border, within three miles at its nearest point. Did this count as being too close? I didn't know. I did a little research to learn what to expect if I cycled this route. One website described it as the more "adventurous" way into Nagorno-Karabakh. Mmm, the more adventurous route into a region you're already warned off visiting at the best of times sounded...What was the word? Exciting? Reckless? Stupid?

More research was necessary.

Taking this approach was shorter than my original plan but no less mountainous. Reduced to a small subset of usable gears, my bike still wasn't capable of managing it, unless I was prepared to push it most of the way, and I wasn't. Maybe I should just forget it. Jump on the train instead. Yep, that would be the wisest, easiest, safest option.

*

"And you're using the wrong oil," said the owner of Bike House, looking at my gears.

"It's vegetable oil."

He laughed.

Within seconds of arriving, he'd diagnosed that my gears were kaput and had agreed to have them fixed by tomorrow. I turned to leave.

"Do you need a bike to get around the city?" he said.

I wasn't expecting that.

"Yeah. That'd be great."

"You can use mine."

This generous offer was actually a double-edged sword. It was of course very handy to be able to move around this sprawling city without relying on public transport, but after riding his bike for only a few minutes it made me realise just how awful my own frightcycle was, even before bits had started to fall off it. His was a sleek beast of rare beauty. I still can't believe he leant it to me, a complete stranger, without leaving any deposit. Obviously my bike didn't count.

It's easy to be misled into thinking Tbilisi is a uniformly gorgeous place if you go on the internet and look at all the photos of delightfully terraced and colourful wooden houses. These are only in one very small corner, which is indeed beautiful but hardly representative. Based on those internet photos, I'd built up an image of Tbilisi in my head before I'd arrived, one impossible to live up to. As a result it was crazier, grubbier and more decayed than I'd imagined it to be. I'm sure it must have a lot worthier things on offer than I discovered, but I left a little disappointed.

One thing I wasn't disappointed about, however, was that I was leaving by bicycle. I was going to finish this thing properly.

*

I was outside the hotel, loading my bike with panniers. The owner came outside too.

"Armenia?" he asked.

"Yes," I replied.

He laughed and gave me a massive whack of encouragement on my back.

The road out of Tbilisi was unpleasantly busy, but eventually the traffic thinned and the landscapes changed from urban decay to weirdly-shaped treeless hills. As I passed through villages, I received several waves, reassuring shouts and thumbs up as well as a high five from an excitable teen. Still, the quieter roads had their own danger. Trucks came worryingly close and loads of cars headed straight for me as they overtook others. Apparently, I had less right to be here than the cows.

I arrived in Bolnisi, a town of 14,000, for my final night in Georgia. In the early 1800s, a German colony was established here, but all its members who weren't married to Georgians were deported to Siberia by Stalin in the 1940s. Evidence of the Germans' presence could be found in the name of tonight's resting place – the only one I could find in town – the rather grand Hotel Deutsche Mühle, an old, pale stone building sitting on the Mashavera river, water destined for the Caspian Sea. And it wasn't just the name that stuck to its roots. It felt odd being in Georgia and sorting out the entire transaction in German.

The town itself was a single untidy main road and a

collection of scruffy lanes surrounded by an area of natural beauty. This place summed up Georgia as a whole. Its towns, especially its smaller ones, were rarely anything to get excited about, still tainted by all those years of Soviet building programmes, but the bits in between made a visit something that should probably be on everyone's wish list. And if you're a fan of *Fast & Furious*, you'll love the roads.

Tomorrow was going to be the first of a series of long days in the saddle. I decided to get an early night. I lay in bed, drifting off, when I was handed one final example of the Georgian memory that would stick with me most closely. A long squeal of brakes was followed by the satisfying punch of car-on-car action.

Chapter 16: Vodka for Breakfast

The route out of Bolnisi stayed flat for about fifteen miles, a rare treat in the lumpy Caucasus, and under a cool, overcast sky too. There were attractive if unusual landscapes to admire. It couldn't last.

First, the trees closed in, and then a mile into today's 1,600-metre climb the road surface gave way, a surprise as this was the only link between Georgia and Armenia around these parts. What looked on paper like a busy route was in reality a single car every twenty minutes, picking its way carefully around the potholes.

Even with my repaired gearing I had a lot of thirsty pushing to do. Water was running low. I hadn't passed a village all day, at least not one with the facilities to restock. I was pinning my hopes on Guguti, a place my map suggested was a proper town. Unfortunately, it wasn't, home to just 178 people and absolutely zero shops. Luckily for me, it had a fountain, but this was Guguti's sole positive. Creepy, dark wood shacks lined one side of the dirt track, dense forest on the other. If the Hostel filmmakers want to shift their horror to a hamlet, Guguti would make a great location.

I finally crawled to the top of the hill and the Armenian border post, and it was the most courteous one ever.

"Hello, mister," said the sweetly grinning guard, taking my passport.

He looked at it for a second and then gave it back. In the meantime, another official has moseyed on up.

"Welcome to Armenia," he said, smiling. Then he shook my hand. This had never happened at a border before.

Armenia is not a place high on many wish lists. Of the countries I'd seen on this journey, only similarly-sized

Moldova has fewer annual visitors. One reason may be its official slogan: "The Land of Stones". Maybe the tourist board could have another look at that.

I cycled into the 8,000-strong town of Tashir, a ropey hole with dozens of disintegrating tower blocks on its edge. I'd only seen a few miles of Armenia, but it had and would continue to have that oh-shit-everything's-falling-down feel of Moldova and Ukraine. Armenia had a better excuse than its former Soviet colleagues though. In 1988, a truly devastating earthquake left the country in bits. Up to 50,000 people lost their lives with another 130,000 injured. As a result of that seismic catastrophe, it wasn't possible to blame all its shoddy architecture on its Soviet past. The locals' attitudes certainly weren't modelled on their former masters either. Even on a day as grey as today, smiles came easily to Armenians.

Not so long ago, Tashir had been home to a number of Azerbaijanis, but when the war over Nagorno-Karabakh flared up they scarpered. This was probably a good decision. Communities of Armenians in Azerbaijan and vice versa took turns at butchering each other. The inter-country hatred hasn't reduced in the intervening years.

After stopping at a currency exchange and swapping what was left of my Georgian *lari* for Armenian *dram*, I reached today's destination, Stepanavan, a town twice the size of Tashir. It suffered the same physical flaws but was an improvement as its centre sat high above a narrow river, surrounded by craggy hills.

I found a little hotel as well as a pizzeria for dinner. The Armenian alphabet is yet another squiggly one, unique to itself and, at least on the face of it, totally unrelated to Georgia's. Luckily, the menu came in Russian and, more surprisingly, English. I can't imagine they get many tourists around here.

The only customer, I sat at an outdoor table near the statue of Stepan Shaumian, "the Caucasian Lenin" and the man after whom the town is named. He stands between two red stone pillars in the centre of a roundabout, his long jacket last seen on Peter Capaldi's Doctor and his angular fists clenched. He looks freezing, or angry, or both. Cars, mostly boxy, eighties-style Ladas, whizzed around him, almost all with tinted windows, like they had something to hide.

Speaking of tinted windows, the country set a tint limit in 2015 after a number of accidents involving pedestrians.

You're allowed to block out 25% of the light coming through your windscreen. But why would you want to? It's not like Armenia's future is particularly bright.

*

Another day, another 1,600 metres of hills, and another one of those horrendous tunnels. There was too much traffic to attempt cycling through. This one had all the loveable features of the others, a high, broken walkway and the illumination of a brothel during a power cut, but it added some new ones too. For the benefit of the drivers, tiny metal reflectors were fixed into the concrete every metre or two, offering me a great opportunity to trip over them. And somehow, cows had recently been inside, leaving ample slippery evidence. Wherever the roof leaked, the grime acquired from decades of filthy vehicles had turned into a sticky mud. It was a right bundle of laughs and yet it still wouldn't be the worst tunnel on this trip. That one lay ahead.

Down a steep hill, I entered the mess that is Vanadzor. During its Soviet era, Armenia's third largest city was a centre of chemical production. Locals joked – at least I hope it was a joke – that the air was so toxic it could dissolve nylon. There was also the suspicion the factories here were involved in the development of chemical weapons. It looks like the only people they managed to poison were themselves.

Bicycles were a rarity around these parts, and this was hardly surprising. Cycling through town was like playing the eighties arcade game Paperboy, cars pulling out on me from every junction and driveway. It's not as much fun when the cars are real.

On the other side of the Vanadzor horror show, the scenery improved. The bare hills stacked one behind the other, fading as the distance grew until it wasn't possible to tell where hillside ended and sky began. Unlike the natural beauty, the villages, or scattered collection of houses as they usually were, never grew more handsome. They looked painfully poor.

Still the people kept on smiling. And waving, and beep-beeping, and thumbs-upping. A young girl and her mum walked along the road. Their reaction to me suggested grown-ups don't ride bicycles in Armenia. I certainly didn't see any others. If the locals could derive some pleasure from how ridiculous they thought I looked, my purpose here was worthwhile.

"Hey, it's that dick on a bike your mum saw yesterday. Give him a wave!"

As I delved deeper into Armenia, the mountains grew around me, their tops obscured by lowering cloud. The air was peacefully still, and other road users all but disappeared. Here was serenity and I loved it.

Today's destination appeared, the spa town of Dilijan. Given its surroundings, it's sometimes been called "Armenian Switzerland". Yes, it was a vast improvement on the other places I'd seen here, but come on. The scenery might be comparable to the Land of Toblerone, but the town wasn't nearly fussy enough. And where was all the Nazi gold?

*

Ladies and gentlemen, may I now present the worst experience of the ride so far, the trip's most horrendous tunnel.

All the terrors I've mentioned so far in previous tunnels were here, but this was also the longest yet. The walkway, narrow at the best of times, supported a thick water pipe, not bolted to the wall or anything but meandering backwards and forwards across my path. When the walkway narrowed to the thickness of the pipe, I was stuck. I had to climb into the road, lowering my bike and its heavy panniers the one metre or so on to the tarmac below, gently but quickly and without damaging anything. But down there, amongst the

300

vehicles, was terrifying. It was too dark to cycle – my headlight was useless in this gloom – and so I still had to push. Whenever a speeding car or massive screaming truck approached, I turned around and held my flashing torch in its direction, just hoping they could see me in time. This was probably as effective as holding up a lit match and yelling, "Please don't hit me!"

I'd push my bike along the road and then notice the walkway had widened enough to allow me to escape the pit. Heaving the combo of bicycle and heavy bags a metre or more into the sky took all the strength I had, but once again the path would narrow and I'd have to descend to the tarmac. I didn't know the tunnel was over two miles long and that I'd climb in and out of harm's way at least four or five times, straining muscles at each exchange. On each occasion that the shattered pathway narrowed, or was dissolved completely by leaking rainwater, my heart sank, knowing I had to descend into the traffic again. And every time that I climbed out, I stopped for a sweaty breather, relieved I still hadn't been turned into road pâté. Ultimately, there was light at the end of the tunnel, literally, but it took forever to reach it. I don't ever want to do that again.

I emerged into bright sunshine, but it was too high an altitude to be hot. I rolled down a slope amidst surroundings that could easily have been Scotland's finest and saw beautiful Lake Sevan for the first time, sitting in its nest of hills. It lies at over 1,900 metres above sea level and is one of the largest freshwater lakes in Eurasia, eighty-four times the size of Lake Windermere.

At the bottom of the hill, I turned towards the lake. Weather conditions were perfect. This was some of the finest cycling of the entire ride. Taking a breather by the water's edge, a group of lads aged about twelve approached me. One of them asked me something in Armenian.

"English?" I asked.

"Thank you," he replied.

There was a second's silence.

"Hamburger," another one chipped in.

"New York," added a third.

This wasn't in my Top Five conversations of all time. I pedalled off to a chorus of "Ciao!"

I was now very near the Azerbaijan border, the region I'd been warned not to visit. Tourism had taken a kicking around here. There were many brand new but abandoned lakeside hotel complexes and others where the property developers had quit before reaching the project's end. It didn't help that Azerbaijan claimed Lake Sevan as its own, and with the weakest of arguments. The lake was supposedly within Azerbaijan's "historic lands", a complete joke when you realise Azerbaijan was only founded in 1918. Even its history isn't historic. Whatever the validity of their claims, never has a blue-sky holiday resort felt so eerie.

The smooth tarmac around the north of the lake eventually descended into rough surfaces, and I was glad to call it a day in Shorzha, one of the few places to offer accommodation on this remote side of the water. I found a couple of chalets in a walled field with a larger house at its far end. The tired-looking owner, Veleko, was standing nearby, talking on his phone. I waited for him to finish as he waved over Tigram, his English-speaking fifteen-year-old lad.

"I love England," Tigram said, although he'd never been there. I wonder what he loved about it. Maybe he was a big fan of terrible weather. Or perhaps it was just a long, long way from here.

If I'm being honest, the chalet was fairly grotty, with two huge cracks in its terrace. Had the effects of that earthquake reached as far as here? It didn't matter in any case, as I hadn't seen any other sleeping options. It would do, and besides the family was lovely. I was invited to meet the rest of them.

On the terrace of Veleko's house at the end of the field, extended family members were visiting and I was introduced to about fifteen people at once. One of them, Ahmed, spoke excellent English.

"Would you like a coffee, my English friend?" he asked.

Cake appeared too, and watermelon, and an apricot from the garden.

"I support Liverpool," Tigram said. "And you?"

"Blackburn Rovers."

He smiled and nodded as though perhaps he'd heard of them.

"I hope Armenia joins the EU," he then added.

That wasn't going to happen any time soon. They'd first have to sort out their differences with Azerbaijan, and peace didn't look any closer than when hostilities kicked off over Nagorno-Karabakh back in the late eighties. It wasn't just the independence-grabbing bits of countries that suffered. As with Georgia and Moldova, it was also the parts left behind.

Tigram was a great one for coming out with simple, powerful, stand-alone statements.

"I think Russia is enemy of Armenia," was his next one. Russia is certainly an enemy of a lot of places, but if any European nations might have Russia to thank for something, Armenia was one of them. As was Azerbaijan. Russia helped broker the most recent ceasefire between them. But maybe that's why they were the enemy in Tigram's eyes. Perhaps he preferred both countries to grind each other down until there was no one left to fight. This deal, by the way, wasn't altruism on Russia's part. Victory for one side didn't help Putin. With both countries mired in a frozen conflict, neither would be able to join NATO.

On the table was a box of chocolates with wrappers displaying various Armenian landmarks. Veleko handed one to me but only after careful consideration of the options. He chose the country's Government Building. Tikram told me he'd selected it to honour the recent revolution that ousted the government only a couple of months earlier. And maybe a drink was needed to celebrate.

"Vodka?" Veleko asked.

There was a grumble of disapproval from some of the women around the table. They weren't going to let the old fella get away with a piss-up. He poured me a large tumbler but only half-filled his own. This restraint wasn't the behaviour I'd been led to expect in the Caucasus. We clinked glasses and together knocked them back in one. I felt I carried the reputation of Western Europe on my shoulders and was glad I downed it all without collapsing in a coughing fit.

The party broke up. Ahmed and his missus were leaving the lake. We said our goodbyes and I returned to my cracked terrace. There was no Wi-Fi and the television didn't work. Instead, I did what I would've done a hundred years earlier and read a book.

Before the sun set, I looked to the bare, rounded hills behind the chalets. Azerbaijan was just six miles from here, on the other side. It was unsettling to imagine the Azeri army pouring over the top. Do the people around here ever think about it? Do they ever think about anything else? On this warm, windless evening, with a full moon reflecting in the lake, it felt like such a peaceful spot, but if Azerbaijan ever wanted to reclaim its imaginary "historic lands", it'd all be shattered in a heartbeat.

The night darkened and I continued to read my book by the terrace light. The only other chalet was taken by Ahmed's teenage kids. I could hear them singing. One of the girls came over later and gave me a bowl of popcorn. Later still, Veleko dropped off some watermelon and nectarines. These were kind people.

It was time for bed. Despite 1,500 metres of ascent today I'd stopped feeling tired, running once again on adrenaline and the excitement of getting to the end without cheating. I just hoped I could keep it up. The hardest, longest day was yet to come.

*

Between the big day that lay ahead and the long climbs of the previous three, I had one day of physical respite. Today I'd hug the shoreline of this pretty lake until it ran out near Vardenis, refuel as best I could and get as much sleep as possible before making my assault of Nagorno-Karabakh the next morning.

"Breakfast?" said Veleko.

I'd planned to get away by ten and then cycle today's fifty miles as slowly as I could, but it was a shame to pass up such a kind offer. On their terrace I sat down with him and Soya, who I'd assumed was his wife but who turned out to be his sister.

Breakfast consisted of cold barbecued vegetables – peppers, tomatoes and aubergine – an exceptionally tasty dish given the simplicity of its ingredients, and a panful of scrambled eggs and tomatoes that included lots of herbs and a hint of chilli. It was an unusual meal with which to start the day, but it was only going to get weirder.

"Beer?" Veleko asked, opening a litre bottle.

There was a small, gnarly piece of cold meat on the table in front of me. It looked older than Veleko. He kept telling me to eat it. I'd accept a beer if only to help wash it down.

"Yes, please," I replied, but he'd already poured one for me.

I tried the meat and took a gulp of beer. Nope, the beer wasn't going to help. I suspect I was eating a family heirloom, that one piece of animal cooked back in the nineties that only came out as a withered showpiece if guests arrived.

"Vodka?" asked Veleko.

Still masticating, my glass was full before I could answer.

While we knocked the vodka back, Soya disappeared for a moment and returned with a photograph of a young man standing by a monument, a complex wooden carving.

"Who's that?" I asked.

It was Veleko, taken a decade or three earlier, beside his own handiwork here in the centre of Shorzha. He was a sculptor, and a good one. Then a painting appeared. This sad-eyed old man was an artist of rare skill. It was cruel his work couldn't reach a wider audience. How many Michelangelos have died unknown in a distant corner of an unconnected land?

*

The dusty road was hot today, unprotected by cloud cover, no wind to speak of. On this wild, forgotten gravel track, the lake on my right, bare mountains to my left, I didn't see more than a single car every half an hour. Occasionally I'd pass a village set back from the road. There was never any sign of activity. Perhaps they were merely deserted ghost towns. Undisturbed by humans, eagles cried out and swooped joyously overhead. At some undefined location, I passed the closest point to the Azerbaijan border. The Azeri soldiers were still invisible, somewhere over those hills.

As the border receded, I hit Geghamasar, the largest settlement of the day but still home to just a thousand people. Armenian soldiers, several dozen of them, milled about the road, unfocussed. They didn't look very fit. Some of them would have struggled to make it into a Sunday League football team. Most of these poor sods were conscripts, forced to fight for twenty-four months because all those years ago they happened to exit a vagina within the wrong arbitrary line. Given how unlikely it is any of us are born at all, it seemed a cruelly efficient way to extinguish the opportunity.

But the rich need to keep reinforcing the notion of nationalism, dressed up as patriotism, in order to safeguard their property and privilege, getting the poor to kill "the enemy" on their behalf, and gladly.

An hour or so later, with the lake behind me, I cycled on to a vast plain and into the town of Vardenis. With a population of 12,000, it was a metropolis around these parts. It also had the feel of a Wild West frontier town, a place where if you had trouble with a fellow townsman you took the law into your own hands. The streets were wide and flat, the pavements rubble, and from just about everywhere you could see the dusty, desert-like hills beyond. To complete the illusion, just up the road was a large gold mine. The only things missing were a couple of tumbleweeds and a gunfight.

I wandered the dilapidated roads, sharing a laugh with a bunch of taxi drivers hanging around a street corner. I had no idea the source of the humour, probably something about my appearance. It didn't matter. A smile's a smile. Another source of levity came from the broken roads. Every car that scraped past looked like it'd been written off a decade earlier.

I popped into a supermarket and was followed around the aisles by one of the staff, a young woman. Was she there to help or ensure I didn't steal anything? Her attentions continued to the checkout where, entirely needlessly, she loaded my purchases on to the counter. Throughout the whole interaction, she'd stayed silent. I paid and walked out of the shop.

"Bye bye," she croaked in English in a tiny voice as I left, to a fit of giggles from the girl on the checkout. Maybe she just wanted to talk.

Armenian fast food was the only sustenance I could find. I selected a couple of local surprises, a fried thing stuffed with mashed potato and herbs, and a variation on a sausage roll. They were both very tasty. A bloke eating at another table came over and handed me a rolled flatbread covered in *smetana*, or sour cream. That was kind of him, but I was still hungry and I needed more calories for tomorrow's monster ride. I bought two more potato whatjamacallits and demolished them quickly. And then two more.

Tomorrow would be the hardest cycling day of my life, around a hundred miles long but also close to 3,000 metres of climbing – that's over two Ben Nevises, or two-thirds of a Mont Blanc – and on a terrible, terrible bike into a country still at war.

Sometimes these ideas look better on paper.

Chapter 17: An Unholy War in the Garden of Eden

Nagorno-Karabakh (Artsakh)

I was still wary of where I was about to go today. After all, it was only in 2016 the ceasefire collapsed completely and the war between Azerbaijan and Nagorno-Karabakh, or in reality between Azerbaijan and Armenia, flared up again. That time around, the conflict lasted just four days, but many died. The official figure, the combined total confirmed by both sides, was around two hundred dead, including fifteen civilians, and a similar number wounded. However, if you believe what each country *claimed* they'd inflicted upon the other, the total killed was ten times this amount. Maybe each side inflated figures for propaganda purposes, or perhaps they'd both employed Diane Abbott to do the counting.

I checked the news for anything reassuring about Nagorno-Karabakh, or Artsakh as it's known locally. Germany's Angela Merkel was currently in Azerbaijan and promising to find a resolution to the troubles. Surely, if hot heads were going to explode, it wouldn't be on the day Europe's most influential statesperson was offering to lend a hand. That was reassuring. Or maybe the Armenians would kick off, rightly believing that a solution announced in Azerbaijan would obviously involve returning Artsakh to the Azeris. Mmm, not so reassuring.

The alarm had gone off at half six and I was on my bike by quarter to seven. I decided to leave my stupid helmet behind. I'd only worn it because the travel insurers wouldn't pay out without it. Given their fondness for wiggling out of a contract, I had an inkling that cycling into a war zone would nullify my policy too. Therefore, assuming I now had no insurance, I could lose the pink lid. I'd ride as I wanted, with the sun on my head and the wind in what was left of my hair.

Starting on this vast plain, the first few miles were easy, riding eastwards, directly into a low and blinding morning sun. As the hills reappeared, I passed what looked like a checkpoint. No one came out to see what I was doing and I continued warily. This road had recently been resurfaced to facilitate the supply of the frontline troops as quickly as possible. It was easily the best tarmac in Armenia and probably the entire Caucasus. It was smoother than George Clooney wrapped in ermine playing a saxophone.

And then came the switchbacks, the ones that'd take me swiftly up to 2,419 metres and the Sotk Pass, the gateway to NK, as it likes to be known in its cooler moments. I laboured ever upwards. In the young chill air of what promised to be a scorcher, it was just a case of grinding out all those metres of ascent. Sooner than I thought I was entitled to, I reached the pass. This was it. A cloud of excitabugs flittered through my stomach.

Officially, once I crossed this line, I'd become *persona non grata* in the part of Azerbaijan its government actually has control over, and I could be arrested if I ever tried to enter. I wasn't sure how they'd actually know I'd been here, especially as the Artsakh authorities don't stick or stamp anything into your passport, although rumours of spies are rife. Whatever, I reckon I could live with it.

I stopped and waited, thinking. On the other side of this flat, fifty-metre-long notch cut through these grey hilltops lay Nagorno-Karabakh, a land at war but also a place with a legendary beauty. There was no border fence here. Artsakh was independent but also an extension of Armenia. Any formalities would be dealt with at the first town.

I rolled forward, slowly, wanting to savour this moment. Inch by inch, the virgin vista of a brand new country expanded before my eyes. I stopped again. Ahead of me I could see nothing but mountains, bald green hills in the foreground fading to pale cyan peaks torn from the horizon. This spectacular land was supposedly one of the contenders for the location of the mythical Garden of Eden. My gaze was averted by a snake slithering past me.

"Hello, mate," it said with a hiss. "Fancy an apple?"

Of course, it didn't. That'd be mental. Regardless of the country's bogus Biblical connections, the scene before me was truly awesome. The grey ribbon of my route wended downward through the slopes, disappearing out of sight, miles in the distance. The next half an hour was going to be heavenly, a warm descent with the breeze on my noggin and no helmet to empty my brains out of at the bottom. I pushed off and smiled.

About ten miles later I entered a small village as the land flattened. Cars were parked around a hut. Inside were a couple of uniformed men. There was no barrier across the road, but all who passed in either direction had to present themselves here.

I leant my bike against a wall and approached the hut, handing my passport to one of the men. He slowly wrote my details into an oversized ledger. His pen hovered over the column requiring a vehicle registration plate number.

"Which is your car?" he asked.

I smiled.

"No car. I'm on a bicycle."

He guffawed, either out of disbelief or a mocking pity. Into my passport he inserted a piece of paper that I needed to present to the Ministry of Foreign Affairs in the capital, Stepanakert, later today. There was no way I'd get that far before it got dark. It would have to wait until tomorrow. I didn't mention this.

I left the relative excitement of the checkpoint and returned to the solitude of the hills, tumbling down a sensational gorge beside a blue-green river. This was perfect cycling, mostly because I didn't even have to turn the pedals.

Almost no one lived out here. Most of the land that was being fought over was empty bar its mountains. I travelled for miles without seeing a dwelling of any kind, or even a car. No kindly shop owner stood at the roadside to help the stranded wayfarer. The place felt beautifully raw and rawly beautiful.

Among the wilderness my back tyre became suddenly bouncy. I stopped and gave it a squeeze. Damn it! It had lost air, too much to continue. As I attempted to refill it, my pump fell apart in my hands. This wasn't good, not at all, not out here. I screwed it back together and tried again. If this didn't work I'd be dumping the bike here and thumbing a lift from a non-existent driver. This time it held firm and I got enough air inside to carry on.

I continued on my mostly downward roll and came to a tiny collection of houses around a small grave commemorating the war dead. I stopped for breakfast. From the supermarket yesterday I'd bought some everlasting, laboratory-manufactured croissants. It was only now I realised they were six weeks past their best, exceeding an already generous use-by date. Maybe that woman was following me around to make sure I only bought up the old crap their real customers wouldn't touch.

As I ate my arid buns, an old woman came out of her house and argued loudly and angrily with her neighbour. It can't be much fun in these twenty-people hamlets if you don't get along. Being desperately poor is one thing. Being friendless here might tip you over the edge. And in Artsakh there were a *lot* of edges.

This land felt very poor, poorer than rural Moldova as well as the rest of Armenia. It was the same story as Abkhazia. Another war, another claim for independence, another empty plate.

I kept moving. The closer to the front line I got, the more evidence of war appeared. A rusting burnt-out tank lay at the roadside beside another war grave, and in the little town of Getavan – was that just a name or an instruction from the Weather Gods? – a walled garden contained yet more graves, this time less than tastefully fronted by heavy artillery. Is a massive gun really what a grieving partner or parent wants to see when it's that sort of thing that ended their loved one's existence?

A nearby building showcased Artsakh's flag. How does a brand new country come up with what is essentially its national logo? In this case they'd simply nicked Armenia's and then, realising they had to differentiate themselves somehow, handed the project over to a graphic designer whose artistic skills only stretched as far as Microsoft Paint. He opened the JPEG of their neighbour's flag, hacked a few pixels out of it and clicked Save. Google it and see what I mean.

The next evidence of war came in the form of land mines, or at least signs warning about them. I was still only a hill or two from Azerbaijan. An alluringly blue lake lay in front of me, and yet all around its shore was studded with explosives. This was dangerous. The spot could have been an ideal location for wild-camping. Without seeing those signs and wandering blindly to the water's edge, the rest of this bike ride might have been, er, problematic.

I reached an important point in today's journey. At vowel-deprived Drmbon, my route to Stepanakert turned south-east. I could have stayed on the road I was currently on, but I wasn't going to do that. For one, it'd take me many miles out of my way but, more seriously, directly to the front line. I'd read a blog by a couple of cyclists who'd wandered blindly into Nagorno-Karabakh with no knowledge of the area nor its conflict. They'd taken this road right to the action without knowing where it led. When faced with distant tanks and artillery pointing at their heads, they became rightfully terrified and hotfooted it out of there. As I've said before, I'm not reckless. I was here to see the country, not the war.

I was about two-thirds of the way through today's distance, but I hadn't even scratched its hills yet. From here on in, on a sweatily hot afternoon, I was given a beating. Five hundred metre uphill followed five hundred metre downhill followed five hundred metre uphill, over and over again. I pushed when I had to and stopped to take in the gorgeous views frequently but mostly to grab some breath. Again, I hardly passed a house. This was as wild as Europe got, and I suspect I was probably looking fairly wild myself too.

Between the earlier mine-filled turn-off and Stepanakert, the internet assured me just one bed was to be had, in a place about twenty miles short of the capital. I hoped this was true. By now the sky was darkening. There was only another half an hour of cyclable light – certainly not enough to reach Stepanakert – when my hotel appeared like a mirage.

I hadn't booked a room. I wasn't sure I was capable of getting this far. I'd surprised myself, but I was also utterly shagged out. I can't tell you how much I was hoping this establishment was open. Yes, to wild-camp was possible, but a stray mine could be anywhere. Please, please, please be open. Of course it would be. I rolled down the driveway of the ironically named Paradise Hotel, walked up to its main doors and pushed. They were locked.

Bugger.

But what was that noise? Out here, miles from civilisation, I could hear voices. I wandered around the back of the hotel to its murky green swimming pool, the colour of an Everglades swamp. Five or six men sat around a table, chatting and drinking. They seemed surprised to see me.

With a handful of words in Russian we understood each other. Yes, the hotel was open, and yes, I could have a room. One of them showed me to it but never gave me a key. It had a leaking sink with a missing hot water tap and the handle to the tiny terrace's door fell off in my hand, but I'd stayed in worse. He told me it'd take ten minutes for the shower's hot water to come on. I waited twenty and it was still freezing. It really didn't matter. There was a more pressing need.

I'd done thirteen hours of high intensity cycling today with only a ten minute break for that late breakfast. I was understandably ravenous. Surely a hotel literally in the middle of nowhere would have a restaurant or at least a snack bar. I returned to the party of blokes. I did a non-specific I-need-calories sort of mime and the main man led me to the kitchen.

"Do you have any food?" I somehow asked.

He looked blank.

"No."

Ah.

Plan B: Drink myself full.

"Beer?"

He nodded, opening a large, surprisingly fancy refrigerator. I noticed six bottles inside.

"How many?" he asked.

"Six," I replied.

His eyes went wide. He took out two beers and handed them to me. He managed to explain that I should come and help myself to the rest when I wanted them, to prevent them getting warm.

He was about to close the fridge door when he held up a finger, instructing me to wait and then rummaged around the back of the cooler. He produced a mysterious package wrapped in white paper. Perhaps this quantity of alcohol required a food-based accompaniment by law. He carefully unwrapped it and presented me with a huge dried fish. It was mine for free. It was all the food there was.

Back outside my room, carrying two bottles and a plateful of smelly fish, I realised I couldn't get in. The door had jammed. Back again I went to the gang of boys outside. The owner/manager/lackey stood up wearily. I think he was getting a bit sick of me. Nevertheless, he tried various strategies to get inside my room. The winning one involved entering the bedroom next to mine, climbing from one balcony to the other and then breaking in through my terrace door.

I could finally start to cool down, relax and get a bit triumphantly drunk. The ride wasn't over yet, but I'd broken its back. I'd also nearly crippled myself in the process – a hundred miles with 3,000 metres of ascent will do that to a man like me – but from here it was mostly flat or downhill.

I hungrily tore off a piece of dried fish and popped it into my mouth. I would've preferred it if the fishmonger had descaled the thing before smoking it but, y'know, those plasticky bits were extra calories. It tasted alright, like a cold kipper, although it was tough and chewy at times, and it took a serious amount of hand-washing to remove its stench afterwards.

I lay back, tipsy, thinking about today. Over the years I'd cycled pretty much everywhere in Europe, and while there were highlights scattered across the continent I couldn't think of many places to rival what I'd seen here. Perhaps mountainous Montenegro under a blue sky came close, or maybe the far north-west of Scotland under a more brooding one. But no, this had been nearly a hundred miles of glory, totally empty bar its geological bumps and crevices. This was something else.

More people should come here and experience this, many, many more people, but that isn't going to happen while opposing troops face each other down and our governments warn us away.

*

"Bliss was it in that dawn to be alive, but to be, er, middle-aged was very heaven!" as William Wordsworth nearly said. Besides, I wouldn't have appreciated this as much if I were a young whippersnapper. Those youthful limbs would have hopped gleefully over such mountains with nary a beadlet of sweat. I'd toiled for this, and on the sort of bike Sisyphus would've been lumbered with in Hades. Today really, finally, was it!

On this, the first of September, the sun shone, warming the morning air. It wasn't all downhill to the capital, Stepanakert, but compared to the humongous climbs of yesterday it might as well have been. After the empty roads of the previous twenty-four hours, the traffic approaching this city of 55,000 independence-seeking souls came as something of a shock, but a short-lived one.

On the edge of town was its symbol, or in reality the symbol for the whole of Artsakh. The monument is carved from volcanic rock and goes by the name "We Are Our Mountains". It depicts stylised heads of *tatik* and *papik*. That's grandma and grandad to you. It's a pleasingly iconic image, although I imagine it might annoy feminists since granny appears to have had her mouth bricked shut.

In the shadow of the monument, a few stalls were set up to sell tourist trinkets and t-shirts. The only thing missing was the tourists. I decided to get a shirt, my one frivolous splurge of the trip. I hadn't seen Stepanakert yet but I'd already fallen for this wannabe country's rugged wilderness. If I was going to buy one piece of tourist crap, it'd be here, somewhere sublime and right at the end of my journey so I didn't have to lug it about for thousands of miles.

To honour all those Romanians and Ukrainians I'd seen walking around in garments sporting English phrases that they almost certainly didn't understand, I decided to copy them. I went for a white shirt depicting the monument towering above me, the country's plazzy-looking flag and a few words in Armenian. What did they say? No idea! That was the point. I'd walk around in blissful sartorial ignorance, just like everyone else in eastern Europe.

"Everything's going to be alright," said the stallholder, after taking my money and handing me the t-shirt.

"What?"

"Your t-shirt," he continued, pointing to an identical one hanging from a railing. "That's what it says. Everything's going to be alright."

"Thanks," I replied with undetectable sarcasm.

As far as motivating slogans go, there was something nervously unsure about this one, and with good reason. Was it really going to be alright? Since 1988, the war has claimed over 40,000 lives. Peace looked optimistic.

I took my purchase and walked up the steps towards this finishing-line monument. I sat beside it, taking in what I'd done.

This was it. I'd made it! Over a period of five months I'd cycled through eighteen UN countries. More importantly, I'd seen thirty-nine wannabes and come very close to several others. In total, I'd travelled just short of a nice round 10,000 kilometres, or a very unround 6,199 miles, and climbed 94,523 metres or 10.68 Everests in the process. Christ, I needed a rest.

First, however, I needed a bed, and I wasn't sure how easy it was going to be to find one. Tomorrow was the country's big Independence Day party.

I didn't need to worry. The first place I tried, an interestingly ramshackle sort of B&B, had space. Fifteen pounds bought me a comfy bed, a decent breakfast and a room with an out-of-tune piano. I gave it a tinkle, but even Chopin would've sounded like Les Dawson.

"Get settled in," said the friendly owner, "and then come into the yard and I will hospitalate you."

Eh? I was hoping her creative use of English meant "provide hospitality" rather than "hospitalise".

She turned out to be an expert in hospitalation. After a lovely lunch I headed to the city's tourist office, and the size of the place gave some indication of Artsakh's current ambitions in this department. It had the dimensions of the TARDIS, if the Doctor's flying police box were no bigger on the inside. Sitting within was a lonely, cramped but smilingly helpful young woman. She asked me to sign the visitors' book. Although it was late afternoon I was her first caller today. Yesterday had been slow too, with just a solitary Czech face to smile at, the poor lass.

Weird Armenian script aside, Stepanakert's main street could have been found in any semi-affluent medium-sized European town, except for the number of soldiers milling about. It seemed every male from sixteen to twenty-five was in battle fatigues. They looked smarter and fitter than the motley crew I'd seen in Armenia a few days earlier. There was also a sprinkling of older blokes dressed in more formal, senior military attire. In contrast to the younger guys, their uniforms came as standard with a large paunch.

Stepanakert was curious when you considered its recent history. Judging by its main street, the town seemed to be doing better than anywhere else I'd seen in Armenia. Its tarmac was smooth and its pavements unbroken. Once you reached the top of the road, you could turn right on to Renaissance Square and things got even better architecturally speaking. Here sat the National Assembly and the Presidential Palace.

Confused by what I was experiencing, I went to get a beer to celebrate the end of my adventure. I sat at a terrace overlooking the main street. On other tables were young soldiers drinking milkshakes. That's not an image you see every day. During my hour there, two wedding parties tore down the road, one that included a professional cameraman protruding from the lead car's sunroof. Someone had money in this damaged land.

I strolled to the market. On the way there, three or four kids stopped to say hello to me. The Artsakh flag hung everywhere I went. A banner across the road said, "Independence is the only option!" Angela Merkel and every single Azerbaijani would beg to differ.

The market was only one block from the main street, but already the superficial gloss was gone. The glitzy front the main street and Renaissance Square had put on didn't extend any further into Stepanakert or Artsakh.

I knew the country had suffered. Both sides had bombed each other mercilessly. Only twenty miles from here was an Azeri town called Agdam. It had once been home to 40,000 people. Now it was wiped from the map. In comparison, Stepanakert looked like it had got off relatively lightly, but not scot-free.

As I entered the market, the old women behind the numerous stalls smelled fresh blood. They called out to me en masse like Sirens, but not in any way sexually alluring. Their products didn't tempt me either. Big drums of pickled vegetables had generated an unpleasant froth on top. There was, however, one thing I was seeking and that was *jengyalov hats*, not something to stick on your head, but rather Artsakh street food.

"If I had to eat one food for the rest of my life, that would be it," said Michael, an Australian lad, over lunch today at the B&B.

He was setting expectations that would be hard to live up to. So what is it? Imagine rolling out a round of pizza dough, piling a mountain of fresh but oiled herbs on top, folding the dough over to seal the thing and then rolling it flat again. This is then griddled and eaten warm. Personally I found it a little bland, but the Australian was vegan and therefore his taste buds had been recalibrated accordingly.

The herby bread hadn't done the trick. I popped into a supermarket and bought some local cheese to finish the job. It wasn't what I'd been expecting. It unravelled into long strands with both the thickness and texture of a power cable, tasting simultaneously smoked and fishy. I didn't know how much of this was intended and how much was due to its being over a month out of date.

I still had more of the city to see. The poverty away from the glossy main street was even clearer to appreciate on the way to the town's graveyard. Literally a hand grenade's throw from the spruce buildings of Renaissance Square, the roads were mere dirt tracks with shoddily put together houses. The graveyard itself was unusually unkempt for a proud nation dotted with tidy war graves. Weeds covered the broken, rubble-strewn pathways between the unfortunate occupants. Unsurprisingly, most of the deaths had come in the early nineties, at the height of the fighting.

Keeping the mood sombre I headed to the Museum of Fallen Soldiers. This place was put together by the relatives, usually the mothers, of local combatants killed in action. It was a collection of medals, old passports, a weapon or two and hundreds and hundreds of photos of young men. Where would they be today and what joys would they be sharing if only they'd walked away? Surely, even the Garden of Eden isn't worth such loss of life.

My spirits had been understandably lowered, but those of the locals hadn't. They were laughing, and I think it was at me, usually after a downward glance in my direction. Then the penny dropped. I was the only adult male in the whole of Stepanakert walking around in shorts. To them, I must have looked like Jimmy Krankie.

*

The next morning, sitting around the breakfast table, I spoke to Australian Michael again. We'd been chatting about the weather. I'd found the previous evening quite humid.

"I thought it was a bit chilly last night," he said.

"Spoken like a true Australian," I replied.

He smiled.

"And how did you like your jengyalov hats?" he asked.

"It was alright. I reckon it needed a bit of cheese and bacon in it."

"Spoken like a true Englishman," he said with another smile.

Touché.

The others around the table had come from far and wide. There was a second Australian, a Korean-American and a Russian woman travelling with her French boyfriend. They were all here for today's celebrations.

After what Polish Lucasz had said about the qualities, or lack thereof, of English women, I figured I'd gather some more evidence from this international community. Generally speaking, the group agreed wholeheartedly with Lucasz.

"Yeah, they're not great," said the Korean-American lad. "But Scottish women are freakin' beautiful."

Sorry about that, English women, but I'm sure you, dear reader, are simply stunning. As is your partner and most of your children.

The schedule today was determined by the authorities. There was some sort of ceremony down at the war memorial and then a concert on Renaissance Square tonight.

On another hot afternoon I strolled lazily to the memorial. Dance music blared from speakers hidden about the streets. Hundreds of people were walking in the opposite direction, waving little Artsakh flags. They were dressed smartly, contributing to a mood of respectful celebration.

I eased my way through the masses and reached a tall stone monolith, the Monument to the Fallen in the Great Patriotic War. A sizeable crowd hung around it and among the gravestones that tumbled down the nearby hill. Peaked-cap older soldiers stood stiffly, talking seriously to each other, keeping their conversations away from the ears of the civvies. Pretty girls in purple velvet gave out long-stemmed red and white carnations to lesser mortals, who then placed them solemnly on to war graves. A bunch of teenage kids were holding a twenty metre-long tricolour flag and looked confused as to what should happen next. What happened next was nothing. This was it. Respects had been given. It was time to go.

As I walked away, a bi-toothed old fella came up to me and shook my hand. He asked in Russian where I was from. I told him and he smiled widely. Then two children, a boy and girl both aged about twelve, stopped me.

"Hello," the girl said. "What is your name?"

These people were *so* friendly.

"Steven. And yours?" I asked.

"This is Harold and I am Sophie," she replied.

"I'm very pleased to meet you," I said and shook their hands.

They both smiled.

"Have a nice day," said Harold.

"You too."

Were these the politest kids in the world? Or merely using me for English practice? It didn't matter. I wonder how often that happens to Armenian visitors in Blackburn.

*

The evening was here. It was time for the show. If I'm being honest I wasn't expecting much. The acts would have to be local or seriously committed to drive the mountainous six hours from Yerevan, Armenia's capital. After all, Stepanakert's airport was rebuilt in 2009, but the Azeris promised to shoot down any plane that tried to use it. Roads were the only way in. Or a really, really exciting flight.

As I stood there with a Frenchmen called Eric in a rapidly growing crowd of several thousand, my fears were mostly realised. I didn't plan to stick around for long. If one event in Artsakh lent itself to terroristic opportunism, this was it. I'd watch the first couple of acts and then wander back.

First on to the stage was a gang of twenty or so children.

"They sing well," said Eric.

"They're miming," I replied sourly. "Only three of them have microphones."

He looked more closely.

"Ah yes, I thought they sounded too good."

They threw themselves about until out of breath but with undiminished vocals.

More acts appeared. Next came a miming crooner, then more miming kids followed by a group of miming drummers. The party's music was as fake as the country's independence. Superficially everything looked alright, but examined more closely it fell apart.

I found myself being drawn in. I'd expected it to be bad, but it had become funny-bad. Next up were three nineteen-year-olds who didn't even nearly fill the generals' uniforms they wore. Ten regulars danced behind them with torn-off sleeves displaying arms the girth of mine, ones that had clearly never been near a battlefield. They jumped around camply to a naff but catchy tune. There was something of the Village People about them.

And from there it only descended.

"One more rubbish act and I'm leaving," I announced. None of this was worth being suicide-bombed for. An old man climbed on to the stage. "I've a bad feeling about this." What followed was pop-opera, for pity's sake. "See you later, Erik!"

I wriggled my way through the dense crowd as a drone buzzed overhead. It wouldn't take a criminal genius to seriously mess up this party. I was glad to be getting out of there.

The disco-opera faded as I walked the dark, deserted lanes. The main street had been closed to traffic to complete the sense of isolation. With peace returning to my brain, I thought about the last few days.

Whatever happens now, the future looks bleak for Artsakh. Stay pseudo-independent and in a state of perpetual war that ravages your economy, or let Azerbaijan back in and submit to the inevitable ethnic slaughter, or run away and leave this remarkable place behind forever. Neither option seemed great.

Then the music stopped for good. The new-found peace

was shattered with an explosion that ripped through the city, echoing among Stepanakert's embattled alleyways. I spun around to see red and white lights illuminating the sky.

At least that answered one question I'd always had. How do people in war zones celebrate at festivals? Surely not with fireworks? Wouldn't the locals be nervous of repeated loud bangs and blinding flashes? Apparently not here, and definitely not on Independence Day. And maybe if they celebrated it hard enough, it might just all come true.

*

My alternative route through Europe's wannabe countries was over. We were done.

Through Facebook I found a woman in Yerevan, who knew a woman in Stepanakert, who had a connection to the university here. She was more than happy to take my bike, for use by students when they visited the city, and I was more than happy to let her have it. It was probably more suited to zipping around town than the long-distance nonsense I'd put it through. Everyone was happy, the students, the bicycle and me.

If I should die, think only this of me: That there's some corner of a foreign field, that is for ever my shit old bike.

THE END

Also from Steven Primrose-Smith

The No. 1 Amazon International Bestseller
NO PLACE LIKE HOME, THANK GOD
A 22,000 Mile Bicycle Ride around Europe

After a near fatal illness, Steven Primrose-Smith decides that life is too short to hang around. Inspired, he jumps on his bicycle to travel a road that stretches 22,000 miles across the whole of Europe.

During his ride through 53 countries, climbing the equivalent of 20 Everests, he dodges forest fires, packs of wild dogs and stray bulls, is twice mistaken for a tramp, meets a man in Bulgaria who lives under a table, discovers if ambassadors really do dish out pyramids of Ferrero Rocher at parties, transforms into a superhero after being savaged by radioactive mosquitoes near Chernobyl and comes close to death in France, Norway, Ukraine and Russia.

Such a massive challenge requires calories and Steven gets his from the more unsavoury elements of European savouries: brains, testicles, lung and spleen stew, intestine sandwiches, sausages famous for smelling of poo, a handful of maggots and even a marmot. Nobody eats marmots.

But the distance and his culinary adventures are only a part of the mission. His real objective is much more difficult. Will he be able to confirm something he has long suspected or will he, after all his searching, eventually find somewhere in Europe worse than his home town of Blackburn?

"There are many books about cycle touring but few are as entertaining, informative and engaging as this one...The result is a funny and informative account of his travels to some of the Continent's well-known and more undiscovered corners. The writing is excellent..." – CYCLE Magazine

HUNGRY FOR MILES

Cycling across Europe on £1 a Day

After blowing all his cash on his previous long-distance bike ride (*No Place Like Home, Thank God*), Steven Primrose-Smith wants to go cycling again. Without the necessary funds, he decides to see if it's possible to travel thousands of miles on a budget of just £1 a day.

Against advice, he puts together a team of complete strangers, including a fresh-faced student, a Hungarian chef, and a man with the world's worst bike, the beard of a goblin and a fetish for goats.

While cycling from Liverpool to Gibraltar through England, Wales, France, Spain and Portugal, they plan to supplement their cash-strapped diet by fishing and foraging. It's just a pity no one knows anything about either.

People quit, nerves are strained, and faces and bikes are both smashed. Will anyone make it to Gibraltar?

Amazon reviews for *Hungry for Miles*:

"A very humorous and frank account of an extremely difficult challenge and I really enjoyed reading it."

"Another great book from this author, easily as good as No Place Like Home. You know you are reading a good book when you can't put it down and are sad when it comes to an end...good fun and highly entertaining."

"He's obviously one of life's top blokes. He can strike the balance between fact, fiction, humour, sadness and in this case famine...Thank you for sharing your intelligent wit and passion for all things good..."

ROUTE BRITANNIA

A Spontaneous Bicycle Ride through
Every County in Britain

Part 1, The Journey South and **Part 2, The Journey North**

Tired of seeing Britain continually attacked by the media, politicians and the British themselves, Steven Primrose-Smith wants to see it for himself. All 97 counties of it! Surely it can't be as bad as everyone tells him.

After twenty years living abroad, he thinks the time is right to search his homeland for the best of British using new eyes, those of a foreign tourist, and in the only way he knows how – by bicycle. Armed with a list of recommendations gathered from friends and strangers alike and the most spontaneous of routes, he pedals 5,000 miles through damp English country lanes, soggy Welsh moorland and windswept Scottish mountains. He gets wet quite often.

Following on from the success and irreverent style of both *No Place Like Home, Thank God* and *Hungry for Miles*, Steven seeks out the quirky in the people he meets, the places he visits and the food he eats.

Can his initial store of positivity survive the journey, or will it be ground down by the traffic, the weather and his British, vegetable-free diet of beer, pies and pork scratchings?

Amazon reviews for *Route Britannia*:

"Steve's done it again; he's written another enjoyable cycle tour book. It was another page turner."

"Have really enjoyed Steven's other two cycling books...This was no exception."

GEORGE PEARLY IS A MISERABLE OLD SOD

Seventy-year-old British ex-pat miserymonger George Pearly lives on the Costa del Sol, all alone except for his ancient, three-legged dog, Ambrose. George hates his life and everybody in it. These feelings are mutual. Everyone hates George too.

From this unhappy equilibrium the situation quickly deteriorates. First, George discovers he is dying of a mystery illness. Then his 35-year-old ape-child nephew, Kevin, moves into George's tiny and once tranquil home with a passion for Vimto, Coco Pops and slobbing around in his greying underpants. Worst of all, George's neighbours start to disappear and all accusing fingers point towards George.

Pull up a sun lounger, grab yourself a piña colada and enjoy a murder-mystery romp on Spain's sunny southern coast.

Amazon reviews for *George Pearly Is A Miserable Old Sod*:

"A bit like Tom Sharpe on speed – ridiculous plot, outlandish characters, unbelievable situations – great. Whizzes along and is great escapist stuff and light reading."

"Loved this – George Pearly is indeed a Miserable Old Sod and very funny with it – couldn't put it down."

"This book made me laugh out loud, much to the embarrassment of my son. Original and quirky."

LOVE AND OTHER COMPLETE WASTES OF TIME

It's 1986 and Adam is Evie's mysterious high school crush. On the night that she's determined to take it to the next level, Adam suddenly disappears, presumed murdered.

After pining over his memory for twenty-nine years, Evie accidentally stumbles upon Adam in a supermarket, now inexplicably disguised as a pineapple and claiming to have just been released from prison. But something doesn't appear to be quite right about him. In fact, nothing seems quite right. He's stuck in the 1980s in more ways than one.

Evie is torn. Despite being the doting mother of her eight-year-old son and happily married to a successful lawyer, she finds herself unable to resist this blast from the past. But when she eventually learns Adam's amazing secret, Evie makes a rash decision that threatens to destroy everything she holds dear and leave her little son howling motherless throughout eternity.

36931808R00188

Printed in Poland
by Amazon Fulfillment
Poland Sp. z o.o., Wrocław